# MAPS
of Narrative Practice

# MAPS
## of Narrative Practice

## Michael White

W. W. Norton & Company
New York • London

All cases presented in this book are composite case studies.

For information about permission to reproduce selections from this book, write to Permissions, W. W. Norton & Company, Inc., 500 Fifth Avenue, New York, NY 10110

Manufacturing by R. R. Donnelley, Harrisonburg
Book design by Anna Oler
Production Manger: Leeann Graham

Library of Congress Cataloging-in-Publication Data

White, Michael (Michael Kingsley)
  Maps of narrative practice / Michael White. — 1st ed.
     p. ; cm.
  "A Norton professional book."
  Includes bibliographical references and index.
  ISBN-13: 978-0-393-70516-4 (hardcover)
  ISBN-10: 0-393-70516-1 (hardcover)
  1. Narrative therapy. I. Title.
  [DNLM: 1. Psychotherapy—methods. 2. Narration. WM 420 W586m 2007]

RC489.S74W45 2007
616.89'165—dc22
                                        2006038468
ISBN 13: 978-0-393-70516-4
ISBN 10: 0-393-70516-1

W. W. Norton & Company, Inc.
500 Fifth Avenue, New York, N.Y. 10110
www.wwnorton.com

W. W. Norton & Company Ltd.
Castle House, 75/76 Wells St., London W1T 3QT

  5 6 7 8 9 0

*I dedicate this book to my mother, Joan, ever-loving and generous, and indefatigable in her intention for her children to have opportunities in life that were not available to her.*

# Contents

# Acknowledgments

Some time ago I was approached by W. W. Norton to write a book that would be an introductory text on narrative practice, and that would also be informative for readers with a strong familiarity with this subject. I was excited about this idea, and responded to this invitation in the affirmative. Now, three years later, it's complete! I would like to acknowledge some of the people whose support enabled the completion of this project.

First and foremost, thanks to Cheryl White, who believed in the existence of this book long before I had written a word of it, and who provided encouragement throughout this writing project. Second, thanks to David Denborough for his unflagging interest in the development of this writing project, and for his enthusiastic response to, and feedback on, early versions of the chapters. Without these contributions from Cheryl and David, this book would not be.

Thanks also to Susan Munro who originally proposed this book project when she was an editor with W. W. Norton, and to Deborah Malmud, for her general support and for her endorsement of early drafts of these chapters. Susan's confidence about this proposal, and Deborah's endorsement of it, confirmed and sustained my efforts.

And thanks to Casey Ruble for her copyediting efforts. I so appreciated Casey's vital interest in the manuscript, and her suggestions and thoughtful proposals for the restructuring of sections have made it a better book that it would have otherwise been.

# MAPS
of Narrative Practice

# Introduction

This book is principally about maps of narrative practice. Why maps? Well, on a personal level, I have always had a fascination with other worlds. I grew up in a working-class family in a mostly working-class community, and although access to other worlds of life was limited, I was always deeply curious about those worlds. When I was a young boy it was maps that made it possible for me to dream those other worlds up and imaginatively transport myself to other places.

Then, on my 10th birthday, I received the gift of a bicycle. To this day I have never received another gift that meant as much to me as this bicycle (and to this day I cannot live without access to a bicycle). I now had means of visiting other worlds. Guided by maps, and in the company of my younger brother, our friends, and our dog, Prince, I would ride for whole days into the worlds that neighbored on my community—worlds that I became fascinated with but was barely able to touch the surface of. I can still recall my wonder on the occasion of first riding into a middle-class world that looked like the "American dream" of the 1950s, one that had become familiar to me through radio and billboard advertising and through the few magazines I had managed to get my hands on.

The most significant venture out of my world of origin occurred when I was 13. My father had purchased a "good" car, and we packed up and went on a holiday of a lifetime—a camping trip through southern South Australia, into Victoria, a neighboring state to the east, and all the way to Melbourne, via the Great Ocean Road. I was totally unprepared for the immensity of the world that I experienced on this trip. I encountered geographical landscapes and territories of life that I couldn't have imagined and had adventures that to this day are vivid in my mind.

Each evening, in the light of a kerosene lamp, I poured over maps. This contributed significantly to my anticipation of the adventures ahead and to my acute wakefulness throughout this holiday. I do not recall our having any specific travel goal at the outset of each day, just a number of possible destinations. And the routes to these possible destinations were not predetermined. The principal agenda was to find the most scenic byways.

These expeditions into the worlds that neighbored on the community I grew up in, and the memorable journey from Adelaide to Melbourne via the south coast, are in my distant past. But even now I relish the opportunity to pour over maps, both in the course of traveling for my work and during my preparation for the occasional cross-country journeys I take while piloting Cessna and Piper aircraft. My lifelong fascination for maps has led me to look at them as a metaphor for my work with people who consult me about a range of concerns, dilemmas, and problems. When we sit down together I know that we are embarking on a journey to a destination that cannot be precisely specified, and via routes that cannot be predetermined. I know that we will probably take some extraordinarily scenic routes to these unknown destinations. I know that as we approach these destinations we will be stepping into other worlds of experience.

And I know that the adventures to be had on these journeys are not about the confirmation of what is already known, but about expeditions into what is possible for people to know about their lives. This is evident in so many ways. For example, in the context of therapeutic conversations, people invariably modify their goals or embrace objectives that suddenly become important to them making changes that they could not have foreseen at the outset. At the outset of a therapeutic conversation a person may table an agenda to become more independent, but over the course of the conversation discard this in favor of a goal to more openly embrace an ethic of partnership in acts of living. Or a couple might initially present a desire to resolve differences in their relationship, but then, midstream in the therapeutic conversation, substitute this with the objective of acknowledging and celebrating difference in their relationship.

The maps that I review in this book are, like any maps, constructions that can be referred to for guidance on our journeys—in this case, on our journeys with the people who consult us about the predicaments and problems of their lives. Like other maps, they can be employed to assist us in finding our way to destinations that could not have been specified ahead of the journey, via routes that could not have been predetermined. And, like other maps, the maps that I present in this book contribute to an awareness of the diversity of avenues that are available to preferred destinations, avenues that can be charted and rendered familiar. I have formulated these maps over the years principally in response to requests from others to render more transparent the therapeutic processes that I have developed. I will emphasize here that the maps of this book are not *the* maps of narrative practice or a "true" and "correct" guide to narrative practice, whatever narrative practice is taken to be.

As the author of these maps, it is important for me to emphasize that I do not use them to police my conversations with the people who consult me. Therapeutic conversations are not ordered, and I make no effort to determine my response to people's expressions ahead of these expressions. I am aware, however, that maps like those presented in this book help me to respond to people in ways that open opportunities for them to explore neglected aspects of the territories of their own lives. This provides people with avenues of possibility for addressing the predicaments and problems of their lives in ways that they wouldn't have imagined.

Maps like these shape a therapeutic inquiry in which people suddenly find themselves interested in novel understandings of the events of their lives, curious about aspects of their lives that have been forsaken, fascinated with neglected territories of their identities, and, at times, awed by their own responses to the predicaments of their existence. And I believe that maps like these shape a therapeutic inquiry that contributes to the rich development of therapists' stories about their work and about their lives generally, which can be a source of inspiration. This has certainly been true for me.

On occasion, in teaching contexts, I have been asked why it is necessary to have maps for therapeutic practice. My response: "It is not at all necessary." However, I believe that we all refer to guiding ideas of some sort in the development of therapeutic conversations, although very often these guiding ideas have become so taken for granted and accepted that they are rendered invisible and unavailable to critical reflection. I believe that this is a hazardous development, for it has the potential to restrict us to the unquestioned reproduction of what is familiar in terms of therapeutic practice, regardless of the consequences on the lives of the people who consult us. Having said this, I do appreciate the fact that not everyone will relate to the "map" and "journey" metaphors, and that there is a whole world of metaphors that can be used to characterize therapeutic practices. I welcome efforts to translate the practices described in this book into terms associated with alternative metaphors.

I should also note that therapists who are unfamiliar with the maps described in this book may initially find them awkward, unnatural, or unspontaneous to use. This is to be expected: When new territories of therapeutic conversation are being entered into, it can take considerable time to become familiar with such territories and to become proficient in the skills associated with these explorations. The key is practice, practice, and more practice.

Interestingly, it is this rigorous practice that enables spontaneity—the expressions of life that seem most spontaneous to us are those that we have had the most practice in. As is the case for musicians who perform skillful improvisation, good improvisation in the context of therapeutic conversations is founded on meticulous attention to the development of therapeutic skills. And the possibility for the further development of our skills is never-ending.

I view my own practice as an apprenticeship without end, knowing that I will never arrive at a place where I will be wholly satisfied with my contribution to effective therapeutic conversations. To date, there has not been one occasion on which I could say that I wouldn't change some aspect of my contribution to a therapeutic conversation if I had the opportunity to start all over again. This acknowledgement is not to negatively judge or devalue my part in these conversations, and it does not subtract from the enjoyment that I experience in them. Rather, it is about maintaining a reflective perspective on what I do as a therapist.

For me, taking a journey into the unknown with a map in hand always fills me with anticipation. I hope that in the writing of this book I have managed to convey a sense of the delight and fascination that I routinely experience in journeys undertaken in therapeutic conversations. And I hope that the maps that I have presented in this book will be useful to you, the reader, in your own explorations of therapeutic practice.

# 1
# Externalizing Conversations

**M**any people who seek therapy believe that the problems of their lives are a reflection of their own identity, or the identity of others, or a reflection of the identity of their relationships. This sort of understanding shapes their efforts to resolve problems, and unfortunately these efforts invariably have the effect of exacerbating the problems. In turn, this leads people to even more solidly believe that the problems of their lives are a reflection of certain "truths" about their nature and their character, about the nature and character of others, or about the nature and character of their relationships. In short, people come to believe that their problems are internal to their self or the selves of others—that they or others are in fact, the problem. And this belief only sinks them further into the problems they are attempting to resolve.

Externalizing conversations can provide an antidote to these internal understandings by objectifying the problem. They employ practices of objectification of the problem against cultural practices of objectification of people. This makes it possible for people to experience an identity that is separate from the problem; the problem becomes the problem, not the person. In the context of externalizing conversations, the problem ceases to represent the "truth" about people's identities, and options for successful problem resolution suddenly become visible and accessible.

## Jeffrey

As I walked down the stairs with a couple I'd been meeting with, I became aware of a commotion in the waiting room. In the midst of this, I heard the reassuring voice of our receptionist. The commotion subsided, and I assumed that whatever this had been about, it was now being taken care of. The couple booked another appointment, and I consulted my datebook about my next consultation. This was to be a meeting with a family, Beth, Andrew, and their son Jeffrey. It was their first visit. I entered the waiting room but found no one present.

I was then aware of the sound of raised voices coming from the street, and I decided to investigate. As I was about to step out into the street, I was nearly flattened by a woman rushing in the opposite direction. "Oh, I'm sorry. I'm sorry!" she blurted out. "Are you Michael White?" I hesitated for a moment, a fraction concerned about the potential consequences of acknowledging this, and then answered that yes, I was. The woman quickly explained that her son, Jeffrey had taken off down the street with the rocking horse from our waiting room. Somehow Jeffrey had known that there was a horse-racing track at the end of this street, and he had obviously wanted to try it out. Beth, Andrew, and eventually our receptionist had taken off after him, attempting to convince him that this wasn't a good time to embark on an adventure like this. The situation had then deteriorated into a wrestling match, but Beth assured me that everything was now under control, and that the rest of the party would be along soon.

Sure enough, we were soon all seated in my interviewing room— Beth and Andrew on chairs, and Jeffrey on the rocking horse which had grown an extra pair of legs and that had apparently become short sighted, for it was crashing into virtually everything there was to crash into. I found this curious, but managed to turn my attention to Andrew and Beth to inquire about the purposes of their visit. In response to my question, Andrew suddenly launched himself out of his chair and leapt at me—at first I though he'd leapt at me and missed, assuming that he was perhaps also a bit short-sighted. Fortunately, it turned out that this maneuver was not one of malice but rather an attempt to save the whiteboard behind my chair from crashing onto me. Although feeling a fraction unsettled by this event, I was grateful for his efforts. After a few minutes Andrew and Beth's attempts to establish some order in the room were moderately successful, and I took this as an opportunity to again inquire as to the purposes of their visit.

**Andrew:** I thought that you would quickly figure that out.

**M:** Not shortsightedness?

**Andrew:** What?

**M:** Nothing really. I think it would be best if I had your words on this.

**Andrew:** Okay. As I'm sure you've guessed, we've been having a really hard time with Jeffrey. He's got ADHD. This has now been confirmed by two pediatricians and an educational psychologist.

**Beth:** Yeah, it has been pretty full-on for most of Jeffrey's life, and we haven't really known what we were dealing with until recently. We're only just learning about ADHD.

**M:** So the diagnosis is pretty recent?

**Beth:** We've known for sure since the start of this year— that's about 8 or 9 months. But we have suspected it for a long while.

**M:** What's it been like to have this diagnosis?

**Beth:** It's been quite a relief, hasn't it Andrew?

**Andrew:** Yeah, we are both relieved to at least have a name for it.

**M:** So, where do I fit in?

**Andrew:** We've just seen another pediatrician about some concerns we've had about the medication, and he suggested we make an appointment with you. He said that you'd seen lots of kids like Jeffrey, and that you could have some things to offer.

**M:** What are your concerns about the medication?

**Beth:** It's certainly much easier for us and lots of other people when he's on this medication, but there are changes to his personality that we are both worried about, aren't we Andrew?

**Andrew:** Yeah. We were worried that we were losing something, so we've backed off a bit on this. And the other thing is that we just felt that we hadn't exhausted all of the avenues. So that's why we're here.

**M:** Does Jeffrey know he has ADHD?

**Beth:** Yeah. We've told him as much a we know. We think it's important for him to know because it's about his life.

**M**: You said that you feel that you haven't exhausted all of the avenues?

**Andrew:** We have tried lots of things, including what's called "behavioral methods." We've come to see you because we hoped there'd be something more.

**Beth:** Or that maybe you could get through to Jeffrey somehow.

**M:** Okay.

Jeffrey was now under my chair, bumping the underside of it with his back, pretending to be a rodeo horse. I was concerned about the possibility of his injuring his back, and also about my precarious position in this scenario. So I took some time out of my conversation with his parents to encourage Jeffrey to be a camel, which I hoped would have a more desirable outcome. While I was doing this, I asked Jeffrey if it was true that he had ADHD. He didn't answer this question, but he did seem to want to know more about what he would be doing if he were a camel. Then Andrew asked, "So what are we going to do?"

**M:** (*turning back to Beth and Andrew*) Right now, I don't really know what can be done.

**Andrew:** What else can we tell you that would be of help? What else do you want to know? We just have to find a way forward here, and we heard that you see lots of kids like Jeffrey.

**M:** Well, for a start, it would be helpful for me to know what sort of ADHD he has.

**Beth:** What sort of ADHD he's got? Do you mean that there a different sorts of . . . .

**M:** Yeah. There are lots of them, and until we figure out what sort of ADHD Jeffrey has, we won't be able to do much. We'll just be barking up the wrong tree.

**Beth:** (*turning to Andrew, looking quite indignant*) They never told us this! Not once did anyone say anything about this!

**Andrew:** Well, maybe Michael can tell us . . .

**M:** Making diagnoses is not my specialty.

**Andrew:** But surely you have seen a lot of this, and you'd be able to . . .

**M:** Yes, I have seen a lot of children who have been diagnosed with ADHD. But my work with them has not involved me making this diagnosis.

**Andrew:** Are you serious? Are you really serious? (*turning to Beth*) So just what are we going to do next?

**M:** I do have an idea about how we might find out what sort of ADHD is giving you all such a difficult time.

**Beth:** (*with a "this looks promising" expression on her face*) Okay, let's hear it.

**M:** (*turning to Jeffrey, who has just upended a box of crayons*) Jeffrey, what sort of ADHD have you got?

*Jeffrey shrugs his shoulders.*

**M:** All right then Jeffrey, tell me this. Just tell me this one thing. What color is your ADHD?

**Jeffrey:** (*momentarily bewildered and turning to his parents, who both shrug; then turning back to me*) Dunno.

**M:** Ah-hah! I knew it! Now I know why Jeffrey's ADHD is just free to run around upsetting everything. How could Jeffrey do anything to stop this if he doesn't even know what his ADHD looks like? Jeffrey, how could you do anything about what your ADHD is up to?

*Jeffrey gives me a puzzled look, and Andrew and Beth exchange glances that register silent questions about whether they have come to the right place for consultation. Then Beth shrugs as if to say, "Oh well, we are here now, and we might as well play along to see where this goes."*

**M:** Actually, I do think that I recognize something. It's looking more familiar to me. Yes, I think I do know what sort of ADHD Jeffrey's got! I am sure I have seen it before.

**Andrew:** Good, good. This is encouraging. What is it?

*Jeffrey looks expectant.*

**M:** Jeffrey, you have a younger brother, don't you?

*Jeffrey nods.*

**M:** What's his name?

**Jeffrey:** Christian.

**M:** I haven't met your brother Christian. But just like you have a brother, I think your ADHD has a brother, and I have met him. Do you want to know who he is?

**Jeffrey:** Tell me, tell me.

**M:** Do you know about twins?

**Jeffrey:** Yup.

**M:** Well, I think that your ADHD has a twin too, and I've met him. Yes, I met him right here in this room just a few weeks ago. This twin was doing just what your ADHD's been doing. Up to exactly the same tricks, crashing into everything, knocking the whiteboard over, pretending to be a horse and tipping things all over the place. That's how I recognized your ADHD. I've seen it before!

*Jeffrey is now clearly engaged. Beth and Andrew are both smiling, looking relieved, and nodding for me to continue.*

**M:** Do you want to see a picture of your ADHD's twin brother?

*Jeffrey, at a loss for words, nods.*

**M:** Okay. I met a boy who had a name a bit like yours. His name was Jerry. And Jerry had this ADHD in his life that was upsetting everyone and making a mess of everything. Jerry didn't know what his ADHD looked like either. So he was really stuck with his ADHD doing whatever it liked. Anyway, one night Jerry decided to get a picture of his ADHD. Do you know what he did?

**Jeffrey:** What?

**M:** Jerry had this great idea. He woke himself up in the middle of the night and got a good look at this ADHD. His ADHD was just lazing around with his feet up smoking a cigarette, figuring out new tricks to play on Jerry and waiting for Jerry to wake up so he could get going with them. Anyway, before this ADHD could jump back inside him, Jerry took a picture of it with his mind. And the next morning he painted it. I can show you what Jerry's ADHD looks like because he also painted a copy for me. Wait here and I'll go and get it.

**Jeffrey:** (*eyes now open very wide*) Show me! Show me! Show me!

**Beth:** Wait, wait. Michael will have to go and get it.

**M:** (*exits the interviewing room for his office and returns with a large painting of Jerry' ADHD, which looks awesome*) Look at this, will you!

*Jeffrey seizes the painting.*

**M:** Careful! Be careful! Hold onto it tight! Who knows what would happen if this ADHD got free. If your ADHD and Jerry's ADHD were on the loose together and teamed up with each other, who knows what would happen to this whole building, or to this whole neighborhood!

**Andrew:** We'd all have to run away.

**Beth:** So hold onto it tight, Jeffrey. Here, I'll help.

*Jeffrey firmly holds the painting while studying it wide-eyed.*

**M:** But Jeffrey, I am not exactly sure that this is your ADHD's twin brother. And we have to know for sure if we are going to do anything about it.

**Beth:** How could we find out?

**Jeffrey:** (*with enthusiasm*) Yeah, yeah! How can we find out?

**M:** I don't know. I was going to ask you and your mum and dad about this.

Andrew and Beth took the lead in speculating about what might be done to confirm this twinship. Although Jeffrey flatly rejected all of their proposals, I was quite drawn to several of them and asked permission to make a note of them for later reference in my work with other families. Then, suddenly, Jeffrey had an idea of his own:

**Jeffrey:** I know! I know!

**M:** What?

**Jeffrey:** I will wake myself up in the middle of the night and take a picture of my AHD before it jumps back into me! I will. I'll do it. (*At this point I discovered that Jeffrey always dropped a D out of this description. He didn't have ADHD after all, but AHD.*)

**Beth:** That's a great idea, Jeffrey! And then you could paint a picture of it in the morning and bring it back here for Michael to see.

**Andrew:** Yeah. That's a great idea. When will you do it?

**Jeffrey:** I'll do it tonight. Wake up all of a sudden and get a picture of AHD. It doesn't matter how fast AHD is, I'm going to be faster.

**M:** Sounds like a good plan.

**Andrew:** What can we do to help out? Should we remind Jeffrey about this plan before he goes to sleep tonight?

**M:** I'd recommend that you say nothing. Don't mention it. AHD could get wind of this and try to outsmart Jeffrey. We don't want to give AHD any warning about Jeffrey's plans. AHDs can be pretty tricky, can't they Jeffrey?

**Jeffrey:** Sure can!

**Andrew:** Well, that's a relief, really. Do you mean we can just sit back and . . .

**M:** What you could do is this. At breakfast you and Beth could simply say to Jeffrey, "Did you do it?" If Jeffrey says yes, you could then celebrate this in some way, and help him to paint his AHD. If he says, "Did I do what?" you could say, "Never mind. It's nothing." And you could do this each morning until Jeffrey has followed through with his plan.

**Andrew:** That's easy.

**M:** Not entirely, because it would be good if you and Beth could harmonize on this. You could even practice before you leave this room.

*Beth and Andrew both laugh.*

Three weeks later we met again, this time under very different circumstances. All was quiet in the waiting room, and I wondered if this family was late for the appointment. But no, Jeffrey, Andrew, and Beth were present, all looking rather expectant. Jeffrey was holding something behind his back that was making a crinkling sound. We walked up to my interviewing room, Jeffrey holding back slightly. Beth, Andrew, and I were seated before Jeffrey's entrance. I was facing the door, and to my horror suddenly there appeared an incredibly gruesome AHD that at first appeared to be on the loose.

**M:** (*leaping off my chair in surprise*) Oh no, what's this?! Help! Help! Everybody help! There's an AHD loose in my room!

**Beth:** Oh no! Jeffrey! Help us!

**Jeffrey:** (*suddenly appearing from behind his painting, a large grin on his face*) Tricked you!

**M:** Oh, what a relief! It's you, Jeffrey! You sure did trick me. But hold onto that thing. Don't let it go.

**Jeffrey:** I've got it. It's okay, I've got it.

Together we studied Jeffrey's AHD, and carefully compared it to Jerry's ADHD. We all agreed that it was a twin to Jerry's ADHD, but that Jeffrey's was a mutated version of Jerry's—a "mutant ninja" version, and therefore even more difficult to deal with. Jeffrey was quite animated during this time, telling stories about some of the tricky things that his AHD had got up to, and about how he had managed to intercede in order to save the day. This provided an opportunity for me to ask questions about some of the consequences of AHD's activities:

**M:** Now we know who your AHD is, let's figure out what he's been doing to your life. Where should we start with this?

**Beth:** Well, where do we start is a good question. There's so much to say about it. In lots of ways AHD has ruled our lives.

**Andrew:** AHD has been getting in the way of Jeffrey at school. It's got Jeffrey into all sorts of trouble. AHD has been making trouble for you at school, hasn't it Jeffrey?

**Jeffrey:** (occupied in painting yet another picture of his AHD) Sure has.

**Andrew:** It's also been giving some of his teachers a bit of a headache, hasn't it Jeffrey?

**Jeffrey:** Sure has.

**Beth:** AHD has also been messing things up a bit with other kids, and getting Jeffrey into some fights, hasn't it Jeffrey?

**Jeffrey:** Sure has.

**M:** Messing things up with other kids in what sort of way, Jeffrey?

**Jeffrey:** They just want me to go away by myself.

**M:** What about your mum and dad, Jeffrey? Has AHD been getting in between you and your mum and dad? Has it been giving you and them problems?

**Jeffrey:** Sure has.

**M:** What sort of problems?

**Jeffrey:** It gives you headaches, too, doesn't it mum?

**Beth:** Yeah, that's right. And it tires me out.

**M:** What about your dad?

**Jeffrey:** Ah . . . well, it gets him all grouchy, doesn't it Dad?

**Andrew:** That's true. And I don't feel very happy with myself about this.

**M:** AHD is messing things up between Jeffrey and his teachers, and between him and other kids, and between him and the two of you. What does this tell you about AHD? What does this say about AHD?

**Andrew:** Maybe that it's a bit mean.

**M:** Jeffrey, do you think that your dad is right, that AHD is mean?

**Jeffrey:** Yeah, it's mean. And it's naughty too.

**M:** You said that AHD was tricky. Tell me more about its tricks.

In the ensuing discussion, the tactics and strategies employed by AHD were described in terms that were relevant to Jeffrey, and some of the consequences of these tactics and strategies were drawn out in more detail. This provided a foundation for a closer examination of the plans that AHD had for Jeffrey's life. I then consulted Jeffrey and his parents about their position on the consequences of AHD's actions and on the plans that AHD had for his life.

> **M:** I am getting a clearer picture about what AHD's been up to. It's been messing things up between Jeffrey and his mum and dad, between Jeffrey and other kids, and between Jeffrey and his teachers. And about how it's been making Jeffrey feel funny in his tummy. And it has also been upsetting Jeffrey's mum and dad. I've also got a clearer picture of the plans that AHD has for Jeffrey' future. AHD wants to be Jeffrey's only play friend, to keep Jeffrey to himself.

**Andrew:** This is the first time that we've taken stock of all of the trouble that AHD has been causing us. Jeffrey, isn't this the first time that we've got a good picture of what AHD has been up to?

**Jeffrey:** Sure is.

**M:** So what's this like for all of you? I mean, is what AHD's up to okay with everyone?

**Beth:** No way. I am not at all happy with this.

**Andrew:** Me neither. We want to get our family back from AHD, don't we Jeffrey?

**Jeffrey:** Yeah. We want our family back, don't we dad?

**M:** And what about the plans that AHD has for Jeffrey's life? The plans that AHD has to be Jeffrey's only play-friend. Jeffrey, are you happy to go along with these plans?

**Jeffrey:** No way.

**Beth:** These plans would give Jeffrey a miserable life, and he wouldn't want that, would you Jeffrey?

**Jeffrey:** No way. No way.

**M:** Okay, so there's no one in this room who's happy about what AHD has been up to?

**Jeffrey:** Yes, there is.

**M:** Who?

**Jeffrey:** AHD's happy about it. (*Jeffrey, Beth, Andrew, and I all laugh.*)

**M:** All right. I understand that apart from AHD, there's no one in this room who's happy about what AHD's been up to, and there is no one who's happy to go along with AHD's plans.

**Beth:** That's right.

**Jeffrey:** No way.

**M:** Okay, that's established. Now I'd like to know anything that you can tell me that would help me understand why what AHD's been up to isn't okay for you. And about why AHD's plans are not okay for you.

As our discussion continued, I learned about the relationships that Jeffrey and his parents wanted with each other but that AHD was interfering with; the connections that Jeffrey wanted with other children and teachers that AHD was inhibiting; and some of the plans that Jeffrey had for his own life that didn't fit with what AHD had dreamed up for his future. In the course of this conversation, Andrew and Beth remarked that this was the first time they'd heard Jeffrey put into words some of the ideas that he had for his own life.

At the end of this second meeting we were engaged in a conversation about the sort of initiatives that might be available to Jeffrey and his parents for subverting AHD's activities. These were initiatives that would fit with some of the intentions they'd defined in this review of their dissatisfaction with AHD's influence. Jeffrey contributed seven proposals for such initiatives, and he was quite clear about his intention to put AHD in its proper place—he wanted to keep AHD as a special friend, but he didn't want to just stand back and let AHD rule his life.

At the third meeting I learned that Jeffrey had experienced some success in following through on a couple of the initiatives he had proposed. I interviewed the family about these initiatives, and some of the knowledges and skills Jeffrey had demonstrated became more visible to everyone. Jeffrey clearly experienced pride in the identification of these knowledge and these skills, as well as in how he'd put these to work in following up on his plans for his own life. Beth and Andrew had contributed to these initiatives by arranging circumstances that were favorable to them. They also had experienced some success in following up on their own proposals for the further development of the sort of relationships they wanted with each other and with Jeffrey.

I met with this family for another six meetings over a 3-month period, and during this time Jeffrey and his parents further developed the ability to curtail AHD's activities. They also became more adept in shaping their own actions according to what was important to them. Beth and Andrew had met with Jeffrey's primary school teacher to explain their new approach to AHD's activities, and she played a significant role in establishing conditions favorable to the success of this approach within the school context.

At follow-up I learned that everything was going according to plan. Although at times AHD could still be a handful, there was good progress in Jeffrey's ability to respond to his parents' efforts to assist him through these crises, and Jeffrey was better able to foresee the consequences of his own actions. He was getting along much better with other children, and his teacher was reporting positive developments in his capacity to concentrate on educational tasks and in his cooperation in the class room.

## Looking Back: The Genesis of My Research on Externalizing Conversations

It has now been more than 20 years since I wrote my first piece on externalising conversations (White, 1984). In the period leading up to the writing of this piece I had been exploring the relevance of externalizing conversations in my work with many families of young children. These were children who had been referred to me for a range of problems that were considered chronic and intractable. I had found these explorations of externalizing conversations enthralling and the responses of these children and families highly reinforcing and rewarding. In deciding to commit these explorations to print, I chose encopresis (soiling) as my first subject, as it routinely sponsors a sense of failure, shame, hopelessness, and defeat, and because significant conflict, frustration, and exhaustion invariably surround it. I wanted to illustrate the potential of externalizing conversations to provide a context in which family members who had been cut off from each other could come together to undertake shared and collaborative initiatives to address their problems. I wanted to illustrate the potential of externalizing conversations to contribute to the development of an interactional definition of and solution to these problems. And I wanted to illustrate how problems that were not only considered intractable and chronic but also unpleasant and serious in their social consequences could be approached in playful, lighthearted, and joyful ways.

I could not have predicted the high level of interest that this article on encopresis aroused in the professional community. This encouraged me to further my explorations of externalizing conversations with different problems and in a range of contexts, and to commit more of these explorations to print. At this time, many other therapists also began to explore externalizing practices in their work with children, young people, and adults, in individual, couple, family, and group therapy settings. Before long, numerous practitioners were contributing to a burgeoning literature on this subject, providing accounts of wonderful innovations.

In this chapter I have four main purposes. First, I will provide a summary of some of the ideas that have informed the development of externalizing conversations. Second, I will discuss the therapist posture that is usually associated with externalising conversations. Third, I will review the metaphors that are sponsored in supporting people's efforts to address the problems of their lives. And fourth, I will provide a map that represents externalizing conversations in terms of four categories of inquiry.

## Ideas Informing the Development of Externalizing Conversations

As noted earlier, many of the people who seek therapy believe that the problems in their lives are a reflection of their own identity or the identity of others. When this is the case, their efforts to resolve problems usually have the effect of exacerbating them instead. This leads people to even more solidly believe that the problems of their lives are a reflection of certain "truths" about their nature and their character, or about the nature and character of others—that these problems are internal to their self or the selves of others.

There is an irony to this, for it is often the case that these very internalizing understandings (and the actions that are shaped by these understandings) are principally implicated in the development of these problems in the first place. Because the habit of thought that constructs these internal understandings of people's lives is significantly a cultural phenomenon, many of the problems that people consult therapists about are cultural in nature. The history of this cultural phenomenon has been traced by a number of historians of thought, including Michel Foucault (1965, 1973). It is not my intention in this chapter to provide an extended account of Foucault's contribution to an understanding of the development of this phenomenon, which I have done elsewhere. Here, just a few comments about his contribution will have to suffice.

Foucault traced the origin of these internal understandings of life and identity back to the mid-17th century in Western culture. He proposed that this was, in part, the outcome of developments in:

- "Dividing practices" that separated, through the *ascription* or *assignment* of a spoiled identity, the homeless, poor, mad, and infirm from the general population
- The objectification of people's bodies through the location of, and classification of, disorders within these bodies
- "Normalizing judgment" as a mechanism of social control that incites people to measure their own and each other's actions and thoughts against norms about life and development that are constructed within the professional disciplines

The development of these dividing practices, of this scientific classification, and of this mechanism of normalizing judgment fostered the objectification of people's identity. In this objectification of identity, many of the problems that people encounter in life come to represent the "truth" of their identity. For example, in the context of the professional disciplines, it is not uncommon for therapists to refer to a person as "disordered" or "dysfunctional," and in wider culture it is not uncommon for people to consider themselves or others "incompetent" or "inadequate" by nature.

Externalizing conversations in which the problem becomes the problem, not the person, can be considered counter-practices to those that objectify people's identities. Externalizing conversations employ practices of objectification of the problem against cultural practices of objectification of people.

When the problem becomes an entity that is separate from the person, and when people are not tied to restricting "truths" about their identity and negative "certainties" about their lives, new options for taking action to address the predicaments of their lives become available. This separation of the person's identity from the identity of the problem does not relinquish people from a responsibility to address the problems that they are encountering. Rather, it makes it more possible for people to assume this responsibility. If the person is the problem there is very little that can be done outside of taking action that is self-destructive. But if a person's relationship with the problem becomes more clearly defined, as it does in externalizing conversations, a range of possibilities become available to revise this relationship.

## Unravelling Negative Identity Conclusions

Externalizing conversations also make it possible for people to unravel some of the negative conclusions they have usually reached about their identity under the influence of the problem. For example, I was consulted by a young woman named Sarah, who had a history of cutting and depression who strongly believed that she was "hateful," and who hated herself on account of this. This "self-hate" was a dominant feature of her experience. We were soon engaged in an inquiry into what self-hate had persuaded Sarah to believe about her identity ("I am worthless and useless and I deserve my lot in life"), about what it required her to do to her body ("treat my body in rejecting and punitive ways"), about its agenda for her relationship with others ("to isolate me from others"), and so on.

This opened an opportunity for the further characterization of self-hate: I solicited an account of what self-hate's activities reflected about the sort of attitudes it had toward Sarah's life and an account of the way in which self-hate would speak if it were a voice that was actually out there in the world. This stronger characterization of self-hate provided the foundation for an inquiry that traced the echoes of these attitudes and this voice into Sarah's history. This allowed Sarah to, for the first time, link her experience of self-hate with the attitudes and voices of people who had perpetrated tyranny on her during childhood. The externalizing conversation that facilitated the unravelling of these conclusions about hatefulness also created space for the development of a re-authoring conversation (see Chapter 2). The development of these conversations was associated with a rapid diminution of the cutting and of the depression that had maintained such a strong presence in Sarah's life.

It is quite common for this unravelling process to reveal the history of the "politics" of the problems that bring people to therapy. This is a history of the power relations that people have been subject to and that have shaped their negative conclusions about their life and their identity. This unravelling deprives these conclusions of a "truth" status and calls them into question. As an outcome, people find that their lives are no longer tied to these negative conclusions and this puts them in a position to explore other territories of their lives. In these explorations they invariably arrive at more positive conclusions about their identity. I have found this sort of unravelling or deconstruction of people's negative conclusions about life to be a very helpful aspect of externalizing conversations.

## Therapist Posture

The form of inquiry that is employed during externalizing conversations can be likened to investigative reporting. The primary goal of investigative reporting is to develop an exposé on the corruption associated with abuses of power and privilege. Although investigative reporters are not politically neutral, the activities of their inquiry do not take them into the domains of problem-solving, of enacting reform, or of engaging in direct power struggles with those who might be perpetrating abuses of power and privilege. Investigative reporters are not usually "hotly" engaged with the subjects of their investigations. Rather, their actions usually reflect a relatively "cool" engagement.

In response to the investigative questions posed by the therapist, the people in therapy also assume an investigative-reporter-like position. In this way they contribute to building an exposé of the character of the problem, its operations and activities, and the purposes that inform these operations and activities. At this time, people are not encouraged to focus on efforts to resolve the problem, reform the problem, or engage in a direct struggle with the problem.

*Exposing the dynamics of the pt*

For example, a therapist might be consulted by a person who has a diagnosis of schizophrenia and is considered to be chronically ill. At the outset of the first meeting, an account of what is of greatest concern to the person is elicited. Such concerns are usually voiced in terms of the more pressing experiences of daily life; they are very rarely stated in terms like "schizophrenia." These concerns may be expressed as particular quality of life issues, as a sense of personal failure and inadequacy, or as experiences of tyranny that are perpetrated by the "hostile voices" (auditory hallucinations). For example, I met with Harold, who expressed a primary concern about the harassment that the hostile voices were subjecting him to. The externalizing conversation that developed in relationship to this did not encourage a hot engagement with these voices. It did not encourage Harold to confront the voices, discipline them, or wrestle with them in any way. Rather, Harold was encouraged to characterize these voices by typifying the way that they spoke, by describing the tactics of power they used to establish dominance, by identifying the strategies that they employed to establish themselves as an authority on the motives of others, and by determining the agendas and the purposes that were expressed in all of this.

Many aspects of this sort of exposé will contribute to the reduction of the felt influence of such voices. For example, the development of an account of the tactics and strategies of power employed by the voices has the effect of reducing their power. And as the highly partisan nature of their pronouncements becomes more visible, these pronouncements are dispossessed of the previously unquestioned "truth" status given to them. This exposé also paves the way for people to identify the other purposes they have for their lives and the things they hold precious that contradict the agenda of the hostile voices.

There is then space for these other purposes and values to become more richly known, for the history of the purposes and values to be drawn out, and for the development of action plans that are in harmony with these purposes and values. At times this development also provides the opportunity for people to identify voices that might be supportive of these other purposes and values, or voices that have been nonpartisan and can be recruited as "invisible friends." It is my experience that the successful revision of a person's relationship to auditory hallucinations invariably has a significantly positive effect on the person's quality of life and reduces the vulnerability to psychotic experience. This was certainly the case for Harold, who considered the revision of his relationship to the voices of schizophrenia a turning point in his life.

In emphasizing the importance of a "cool" engagement with the problems and concerns that people bring to therapy, I am not suggesting that therapeutic conversations should be unemotional or should disengage people from their experience of these problems and concerns. To the contrary, I find that externalizing conversations routinely assist people to give expression to a range of experiences of life that they previously have not had the opportunity to express.

In the "cool" engagement characteristic of the early phases of externalizing conversations, the person has the opportunity to transcend the "playing field" of the problem—that is, address the problem in a territory that is not the home territory of the problem. In so doing, people usually experience a reduction in their sense of vulnerability to the problems of their lives and begin to feel less stressed by their circumstances. This outcome is nowhere more important than in situations where there is a significant stress element to the problems that people consult therapists about. For example, with regard to schizophrenia, there is a clearly established correlation between stress and psychotic episodes. It stands to reason that any therapeutic conversation that encourages a "hot" engagement with the voices of schizo-phrenia—that promotes a direct confrontation with these voices—will render people with this diagnosis more vulnerable to psychotic experience.

At a certain point in the development of these externalizing investigative-reporter conversations—when people are experiencing a degree of separation from the problem definitions of their identity, and when they are beginning to give voice to intentions and values that contradict those associated with the problems—a second posture in relation to the problem is usually taken up, often in alternation or conjunction with the investigative-reporter posture. This is a posture in which people initiate action to diminish the influence of the problem and to pursue what they have identified as important to them.

This second-phase posture, and the actions that follow from it, are significantly shaped by the metaphors that are employed to characterize the influence of these problems. For example, if people characterize this influence as oppressive, the posture assumed will be oppositional and people will take action to "liberate" their lives from the problem. If people characterize this influence as unjust, the posture assumed will be a moral one, and the action taken will provide redress to this injustice. If people characterize this influence to be uninformed, a teaching posture will be assumed, and action will be taken to educate the problem about what is in the best interest of the people's lives.

Despite the diversity of metaphors that people employ to represent the problem's influence in their lives, at times in the literature it is assumed that these metaphors are principally those that encourage people to engage in "contests" or "battles" with their problems in order to "defeat" or "vanquish" them. Critiques of externalizing conversations are often based on the perception that this is what is proposed for externalizing conversations; that is the routine employment of adversarial metaphors. These critiques argue that such metaphors reproduce patriarchal discourses of life and identity, prompt highly individual and autonomous accounts of identity to the detriment of relational understandings of life, foster the development of dualistic, either/or conceptions of human action, and obscure the context of people's experiences. Although the concerns raised in critiques like these are grounded in a misperception of what I have proposed for externalizing conversation, I believe it is still important to consider them. As therapists, we are responsible for the consequences of what we do, say, and think. We have a special responsibility to consider the ways in which we may have unwittingly reproduced assumptions about life and identity that are disqualifying of diversity in people's acts of living, and the ways in which we may have inadvertently colluded with the power relations of local culture. Continually questioning the metaphors we support in therapeutic conversations is part of this special responsibility.

Introducing or prioritizing these "contest" or "battle" metaphors can also be hazardous for reasons other than those just cited. If metaphors within externalizing conversations constrict success in terms of vanquishing or defeating the problem, and then later the person finds themself experiencing a reemergence of the problem, he or she may view this reemergence as tantamount to personal failure. This will be highly discouraging of renewed initiatives to revise one's relationship to the problem. Because of the significance of the metaphors selected in externalizing conversations, I will now explore this subject in more detail.

## Metaphors

The matter of metaphor is highly significant. All metaphors that are taken up in the development of externalizing conversations are borrowed from particular discourses that invoke specific understandings of life and identity. These discourses influence the actions people take to solve their problems, and they are shaping of life in a general sense as well. In response to a perception that externalising practices routinely encourage people to engage in a contest or battle with their problems in order to defeat and vanquish them, I recently reviewed all of the articles that I'd written over the past twenty or so years on this subject. In this review I discovered that in just one of these articles I had presented battle and contest metaphors. This was in the first piece I published on externalising conversations, and it presented these "contest" and "battle" metaphors along with others that constructed the task quite differently. In undertaking this review I listed an array of metaphors that people had taken up in defining the actions they had taken in revising their relationships with the problems of their lives, and also listed the apparent source of these metaphors. This list included:

- Walking out on the problem (from the concept of agency)
- Eclipsing the problem (from astronomical conceptions of life)
- Dispelling the problem (from magical conceptions of life)
- Going on strike against the problem (from the idea of civil action)
- Becoming deacclimated to the problem (from the concept of climate)
- Setting themselves apart from the problem (from the concepts of separation and individuation)
- Defying the problem's requirements (from the idea of resistance)
- Disempowering the problem (from the idea of empowerment)
- Dissenting the problem's influence (from the idea of protest)
- Educating the problem (from the concept teaching)
- Escaping the problem or freeing their life of the problem (from the idea of liberation)
- Recovering or reclaiming the territory of their life from the problem (from geographical conceptions of life)
- Undermining the problem (from geological conceptions of life)
- Reducing the influence of the problem (from the concept of personal agency)
- Declining or refusing invitations to cooperate with the problem (from the concept of a civil society)
- Departing the problem's sphere (from the journey idea)

- Engaging in acts of redress against the problem (from the concept of justice)
- Coming out of the shadow cast by the problem (from the idea of light)
- Disproving the problem's claims about their identity (from the concept of objectivity)
- Reducing the problem's grip on their lives (from physiological conceptions of life)
- Repossessing their lives from the problem (from commercial understandings of life)
- Taking their lives out of the hands of the problem (from puppetry)
- Resigning from the problem's service (from the concept of employment)
- Salvaging their lives from the problem (from the maritime world)
- Commencing comebacks from problems (from the world of sports)
- Stealing their lives from the problem (from the idea of theft)
- Taming the problem (from the concept of training)
- Harnessing the problem (from the equine world)

The diversity in these metaphors is very much due to the fact that most of them were coined by people who have sought therapy. However, having said this, it is also true that I routinely play a significant role in the selection of the metaphor that is most comprehensively taken up in therapeutic conversations. It is my experience that when people are characterizing the action they aim to take or have taken in revising their relationship to the problem of their lives, only very rarely do they use just a single metaphor. It is seldom possible to pursue all of the metaphors people bring up in the context of therapeutic conversations, so some are inevitably favored over others. The favoring of some metaphors over others is based upon what seems most viable to me and upon the ethical considerations that have already been covered in this chapter. For example, a child attempting to resolve his encopresis might invoke the metaphor of "beating Mr. Mischief" (competition metaphor) with the intention of "getting my life back from Mr. Mischief" (reclamation metaphor). In such circumstances I would usually give priority to the reclamation metaphor when inviting the child to draw out and build upon these initiatives. This is because the reclamation metaphor does not represent the task as an adversarial one. Another child, attempting to resolve her fears, might speak in terms of "vanquishing" these fears, and "giving them an education." In this circumstance, I would be more likely to focus the therapeutic inquiry on the program that the child had developed to educate the fears rather than on her acts of vanquishing the fears. This selection would be based on my concern about the consequences of routinely reproducing battle and contest metaphors in the context of therapeutic conversations.

In my conversations with Jeffrey, Beth, and Andrew, when the focus turned to the sort of action that this family might initiate to revise their relationship with AHD, several metaphors were employed. One of these was about "killing off" AHD. I focused instead, however, on a "reclaiming" metaphor that was also proposed, and this guided the further development of proposals for action and reflections on the consequences of these actions. It was in this context that Jeffrey became quite clear about his intention to put AHD in its proper place as a wanted and special friend but not one who would rule his life.

On the few occasions when only a single metaphor for action is apparent at the outset of the conversation, and when I have ethical concerns about the extensive employment of this metaphor, my participation with it is usually strictly provisional. As the conversation develops other metaphors for action inevitably surface. I cannot recall a therapeutic conversation in which the prioritizing of these other metaphors wasn't possible and in which this wasn't highly effective.

## Totalizing

It is important for therapists to be wary of contributing to the totalizing problems—that is, defining problems in terms that are totally negative. This totalizing of the problem is founded upon the dualistic, either/or habits of thought that have become quite pervasive in Western culture, and it can require special effort on behalf of therapists to remain conscious of such thinking, and its associated hazards. This consciousness is important because totalizing can obscure the broader context of the problems that people bring to therapy and can invalidate what people give value to and what might be sustaining. The following two examples of therapeutic encounter illustrate the importance of avoiding totalizing problems.

Jeanine, a single-parent mother with a child who was physically and intellectually challenged, sought consultation over what had been determined to be unrealistic hopes that rendered her vulnerable to considerable frustration and episodes of acute disheartenment. Jeanine had been advised to seek therapy with the goal of letting go of these hopes and for the purpose of grieving their loss. However, an externalizing conversation about these hopes provided her with an opportunity to fully express her experience of both the positive and the negative consequences of these hopes. Among other things, these hopes had sustained Jeanine's efforts to ameliorate some of the hardships that her son would have otherwise faced. But these hopes had also been very hard taskmasters for Jeanine to shoulder. As the externalizing conversation proceeded, Jeanine began to develop a new clarity about the purposes to which she wished to continue to apply these hopes, including the diversion of some of them to help her develop neglected aspects of her own life.

At follow-up it was ascertained that this conversation had provided Jeanine with an opportunity to revise her relationship with these hopes. In the context of this revision, her hopes were honored but no longer tied to a singular commitment. Jeanine had become more able to monitor the allocation of hope to a range of purposes that she highly valued, and she became less vulnerable to frustration and disheartenment. If, in the context of therapy, these hopes had been totalized as a hurdle to overcome, the possibility of such an outcome would have been lost.

Martin, age 8, and his parents consulted me about his fearfulness. This fearfulness had been a feature of Martins life since he was 4, and it was becoming increasingly pervasive in its effects. It was associated with negative physical phenomena, including headaches and stomachaches, with profound insecurity in social contexts, with insomnia, and with a range of highly preoccupying worries. Martin's parents hadn't left a stone unturned in their effort to get to the bottom of this. However, all of their investigations had been to no avail, and they now risked concluding that he was simply a fearful boy.

We were quickly underway with an externalizing conversation, and for the first time Martin openly characterized his worries. I encouraged him to name each of these worries and to clearly distinguish them from one another, to graphically describe them, to develop an exposé of their activities and operations, to provide an account of the consequences of those activities and operations, and to reach some conclusions about what this all said about what these worries had planned for his life. In this way the externalizing conversations rendered the intangible tangible; boundaries or borders were assigned to a problem that had previously had an all-encompassing presence in Martin's life. As we were all becoming more familiar with the nature of these worries, I found the opportunity to inquire about the forces that might be supportive of these worries. As the worries were now richly characterized, Martin had little difficulty in relating them to the context of his life. I learned from him that these worries were powerfully supported by global events, including the 2004 tsunami, the AIDS epidemic in Africa, the war in Iraq and Afghanistan, and suicide bombings in the Middle East. How had he come to be so well informed about these events? Unbeknownst to his parents, he regularly watched news of world events on television.

Martin now found himself in a conversation with his parents that validated his worries. These worries were no longer considered irrational. Not only did Martin now feel joined in his worries, but he also experienced an honoring of what he attributed value to in life, and felt his parents' pride in him over this. He was now not simply a fearful boy in their eyes, and their joining with him in conversations about these concerns and in making plans for addressing them was deeply relieving to Martin. The negative physical consequences of these worries quickly resolved, as did his insomnia and much of his insecurity, and although he remained highly concerned about world events, this concern was no longer in the category of preoccupation that made it impossible for him to proceed with his life. If, in the context of therapy, these worries had been construed in totally negative terms, Martin and his family might never have addressed his concerns in this way.

## A Final Note About the Metaphors of Action and the Hazards of Totalizing

Although I have raised questions about the employment of adversarial metaphors and metaphors that construct totalizing descriptions of problems, I do not mean to suggest that these metaphors and totalizing descriptions are never preferred. At times I am consulted by people who have a strong sense that they are fighting for their survival. For these individuals, metaphors of battle and contest and a totalizing of the problem best fit their experience of the problem, at least at the outset of therapy. These people have often been subject to various forms of abuse and exploitation, and I am always cognizant of the fact that the development of a fight mindset, and actions that are informed by this, may have been critical to their survival.

In these circumstances I acknowledge the importance of this mindset, honor their understanding about the nature of the actions that have ensured survival, and join in explorations of further possibilities for action that are shaped by these metaphors. However, I do not *introduce* battle metaphors and do not *initiate* a totalizing of the problem. When people embrace a singular fight metaphor, I remain alert to other metaphors that might be employed in describing action or proposals for action in the revision of the person's relationship to the problem. Remaining alert to the emergence of other metaphors allows for the possibility of gradually focusing on something other than "the fight." A sole focus on fight metaphors has hazards that I have already touched on, and it can contribute to an entrenched "fortress mentality" with regard to life, as well as to an increased experience of vulnerability and, over the longer term, a sense of fatigue and reduced personal agency.

## Other Externalising Conversations

The primary subject of this chapter has been the use of externalizing conversations to address the problems for which people seek therapy. However, externalizing conversations can also be used more broadly in revisioning and redeveloping what is often defined as people's "strengths" and "resources." For example, in a piece I recently wrote on narrative approaches to working with children and their families, I included an example of a double externalization (White, 2006). Gerry and his family had consulted me about Gerry's eating problem. In therapy, I first supported the externalization of the eating problem as a "naughty little phobia." I then encouraged an externalization of the strength it would take to engage in valued activities that he'd been excluded from on account of his frailty. This strength was characterized as "tiger strength," and, in the context of the externalizing conversation, a description of this "tiger strength" was developed in ways that would not have been possible had this phenomenon retained the status of an internal quality. The externalization of this strength provided Gerry and his parents with a foundation to free his life from the "naughty little phobia."

## The Statement of Position Map: Four Categories of Inquiry

Ten years or so ago, in response to requests to provide a map for the development of externalizing conversations, I undertook a videotape review of a series of externalizing conversations with the intention of drawing out the specific categories of inquiry that gave shape to these. As an outcome of this, I developed a "statement of position" map that I incorporated into workshop notes and began to introduce in teaching contexts. This map provides an account of externalizing conversations as four principal categories of inquiry. (Examples of this map are included at the end of this chapter.)

I have been presenting and illustrating this map in teaching contexts for many years now, and the participants of these events have found this representation helpful in the development of their own externalizing practices. Drawing out the four categories of inquiry in this way has served to unpack externalizing practices, rendering them more transparent and more available to replication, to unique applications, and to further development.

As with all of the maps described in this book, the statement of position map can be of assistance in the guiding of therapeutic inquiry, and it is particularly relevant in situations in which people present problem-saturated accounts of their lives or have formed highly negative conclusions about their identities or the identity of their relationships. The map does not speak for all aspects of externalizing conversations, and is not essential to the development of therapeutic conversations informed by a narrative perspective.

I refer to these four categories of inquiry as a "statement of position" map because it establishes a context in which people, including young children, can be radically consulted about what is important to their lives. It is in the context of such consultation that people find opportunity to define a position on the problems of their lives and to have a stronger voice about the foundation of their concerns. This is frequently a novel experience for people, as they often have found themselves subject to the position that *others* have taken on their problems and predicaments.

This is also a statement of position map in that it is through this inquiry that the therapist's position is clearly defined. This is a decentered position in that the therapist is not the author of people's positions on the problems and predicaments of their lives. But it is also an influential position, as it is through the introduction of these categories of inquiry that the therapist provides people with an opportunity to define their own position in relation to their problems and to give voice to what underpins this position.

This decentered but influential role can be difficult to achieve, for we are often meeting with people who are expressing considerable degrees of frustration and hopelessness, who have exhausted all other known avenues, and who are desperate to achieve some relief from pressing concerns. Under these circumstances, therapists are quite susceptible to taking a position on the people's problems and to acting on this position unilaterally through recourse to "expert knowledge" and a range of interventions. This privileges the therapist's voice in attributing meaning to people's problems, imposes the therapist's own understanding about the consequences of the problems, prompts the therapist to take a position on these consequences on behalf of the people seeking consultation, and justifies the therapist's position in terms of what he or she assumes is important to these people: "I can see that this (*problem as defined by the therapist*) is having these (*consequences as drawn out by the therapist*) in your life. This is a (*position authored by the therapist*), and we will have to do something about this because (*justification founded upon therapist's normative ideas about life*). When the therapist takes authorship in this way, the door closes on collaboration, and therapist is set up to feel burdened and exhausted while the people who are seeking consultation feel impotent.

### Inquiry Category 1. Negotiating a Particular, Experience-Near Definition of the Problem

In this first stage, the therapist supports people in the negotiation of the definition of the predicaments and problems for which they are seeking therapy. In this negotiation, these predicaments and problems are richly characterized. It is through this characterization that "experience-distant" and "global" definitions are rendered "experience-near" and "particular."

An "experience-near" description of the problem is one that uses the parlance of the people seeking therapy and that is based on their understanding of life (developed in the culture of their family or community and influenced by their immediate history). In using the word *particular*, I am acknowledging the fact that no problem or predicament is perceived or received in identical ways by different people, or in identical ways at different times in a person's life. No predicament or problem is a direct replica of any other predicament or problem, and no predicament or problem of the present is a carbon copy of the predicament or problem it was in the past. In my work with Jeffrey, Beth, and Andrew, this experience-near, particular definition of ADHD was generated in various ways, including through painting. The distinctive shape of this problem became highly visible—it was uniquely characterized to the extent that it was even differentiated from its identical twin, Jerry's ADHD. Jeffrey's ADHD was like no other ADHD, and what he knew about it was presented in the terms in which he experienced life.

Quite often, and particularly in work with children, this rich char acterization is achieved through the personification of the problem. Spencer, age 7, was brought to see me by his parents, Sue and Rod, who defined his problem as "encopresis." This was a longstanding problem that had defied many efforts to resolve it. Sue and Rod spoke of their acute frustration over Spencer's total lack of enthusiasm for any initiative that might have the potential to alleviate this problem. From Spencer's general demeanour I gained the sense that he felt resigned to the fact that he was the problem and that there was nothing that he could do to change this. In response to my questions about his comprehension of encopresis, Spencer confirmed that he understood this term, but it was clearly apparent that this global definition of his soiling was one that was experience-distant to him. I then initiated an inquiry that I hoped would assist the family in characterizing this phenomenon in ways that were particular and experience-near:

**M:** Okay, so tell me, what's it like for all of you to be living under the reign of this encopresis?

**Sue:** (*smiling in recognition of the pun*) It comes down in torrents at times, and it sure is messy.

**Rod:** (*also amused*) Sometimes we are up to our knees in it. It gets very slippery. We wind up going in all sorts of weird directions, scooting all over the place. That's a pretty fair summary, isn't it?

**Sue:** Yeah. Things sure do get out of control, and it makes it hard to get things done, doesn't it Spencer?

**Spencer:** (*looking a little less uptight*) Yep.

**M:** What would you say about the nature or the character

of an encopresis that went around messing up people's lives when it wasn't invited to do so? What would you say about an encopresis that caused these sort of slip-ups and made it difficult to get things done?

**Sue:** Well, I'd say it was an encopresis who was up to mischief.

**Rod:** I'd say that too.

**M:** What would you say, Spencer?

**Spencer:** Let's see. Yep, I'd say that.

**M:** What would you say, Spencer?

**Spencer:** It's Mr. Mischief.

**M:** Okay, so it is Mr. Mischief! It is really good to know this!

**Spencer:** Sure is!

I proceeded to interview Spencer and his parents about their experience of Mr. Mischief, and this helped them more richly characterize the problem. For example, the operations and activities that Mr. Mischief engaged in when messing up people's lives, including the tactics and strategies that he employed, were defined, and what this said about the plans that Mr. Mischief had for Spencer's life were drawn out. The more that this problem was defined in particular and experience-near terms, the more animated and knowledgeable Spencer became. It turned out that he didn't know how to treat encopresis, but he did know how to out-trick Mr. Mischief. With his parent's assistance, Spencer went on to use this knowledge to "get his life back" from Mr. Mischief.

In this example, the "professional" description of the problem as encopresis was displaced by one that was more local to Spencer's life— Mr. Mischief. In presenting this example I am not proposing that we convert all professional diagnoses into descriptions drawn from popular culture, but I do believe that through rich characterization, any description can be rendered experience-near and particular. For example, in my externalizing conversation with Jeffrey, Beth, and Andrew, a version of the professional term *ADHD* was richly characterized.

It is in the rich characterization of problems that people's unique knowledges and skills become relevant and central to taking action to address their concerns. During this process, people become aware of the fact that they do possess a certain know-how that can be further developed and used to guide them in their effort to address their problems and predicaments.

### Inquiry Category 2. Mapping the Effects of the Problem

This second stage in the development of externalizing conversations features an inquiry into the effects/influence of the problem in the various domains of living in which complications are identified. This can include:

- Home, workplace, school, peer contexts
- Familial relationships, one's relationship with oneself, friendships
- Identity, including the effects of the problem on one's purposes, hopes, dreams, aspirations, and values
- One's future possibilities and life horizons

This inquiry does not have to be exhaustive, but it should include some account of the principal consequences of the problem's activities and operations. For example, in my conversations with Jeffrey, Beth, and Andrew, considerable attention was paid to the consequences of AHD's activities with regard to familial relationships and Jeffrey's relationship with his teacher and peers. Attention was also given to the consequences of the problem in terms of Beth's physical experience and Andrew's moods. With Sarah, the young woman who had a long history of cutting and depression, my conversations focused on the consequences of self-hate's activities with regard to her relationship with her own body and her connections with others.

This inquiry into the effects or influence of the problem places the externalizing conversation on a firm footing, and at this point the transition from the more commonplace internalizing conversations is highly evident. For example, at the outset of my meetings with Sarah, she informed me that she was, among other things, "worthless" and "useless" and that she "deserved her lot in life." She also informed me that others had tried to talk her out of these conclusions, and that she took this as a sign of either their insincerity or a lack of understanding. This had an alienating effect in her relationships with others, and Sarah was open about the fact that she predicted that I would "try the same stunt." This I managed to avoid. However, before long, Sarah was responding to my questions about what the self-hate had been persuading her to think about herself—that she was "worthless," "useless," and "deserved her lot in life." These are the terms that were strongly featured in Sarah's internal dialogue and in her internalizing conversations with others, but now they were being expressed in an externalizing conversation that was opening a space between Sarah's identity and her negative conclusions about her identity. I did not attempt to challenge these negative conclusions when they were presented as the "truths" of Sarah's identity. Rather, the externalizing conversation had the effect of dispossessing these conclusions of a truth status and provided an opportunity for them to be unravelled.

### Inquiry Category 3. Evaluating the Effects of the Problem's Activities

In this third stage, the therapist supports people in evaluating the operations and activities of the problem, as well as its principal effects on their lives. This evaluation is usually initiated with questions like: Are these activities okay with you? How do you feel about these developments? How are these developments for you? Where do you stand on these outcomes? What is your position on what is unfolding here? Is this development positive or negative—or both, or neither, or something in between? If this were served up to you as a fate in life, would you have any questions about it?

These questions and others like them invite people to pause and reflect on specific developments of their lives. For many this is a novel experience, for it is very often the case that this sort of evaluation has been mostly undertaken by others. For example, I couldn't count the number of young people I've met who have not had a voice in the evaluation of the consequences of the predicaments of their lives. Instead, this evaluation has been voiced by their parents, schoolteachers, therapists, social service workers, the police, and so on.

Because being consulted about this subject can be such a novel experience, it is usually important for the therapist to preface these evaluation questions with a brief summary of some of the principal effects of the problem that were drawn out in the second stage of the externalizing conversation. I often refer to these summaries as editorials, and they provide people with a surface upon which to reflect when responding to the evaluation questions. For example, in my conversation with Virginia, age 16, and her parents, Russell and Verity, it was clear that she had been more or less a passenger in the process of evaluating some significant complications in her life. In seeking her position, I first gave a brief summary of what I understood as one of the principal consequences of these complications:

> **M:** Virginia, I understand that, apart from other things, your parents' concerns about these complications lead them to be somewhat preoccupied with what is happening in your life. And that this preoccupation means that they are attending much more closely to aspects of your life. You said that this has the effect of closing things down for you.
>
> **Virginia:** Yes. That's exactly it.
>
> **M:** Okay. Well, what is this like for you?
>
> **Virginia:** What's this like for me?
>
> **M:** Yes. How is this for you? What's your position on this?
>
> **Virginia:** I don't like it. It feels like I am always being supervised. I don't like it and it doesn't help. It's incredibly frustrating.
>
> **M:** You don't like it? You don't like this supervision?
>
> **Virginia:** No, I don't like it and it doesn't help. It makes things worse, and it's incredibly frustrating.
>
> **M:** Say a bit more about your experience of this. What

other words would you use to describe this discomfort and frustration?

**Virginia:** Well, its like this . . .

After Virginia had given a fuller account of her experience of this consequence, I interviewed both Russell and Verity about their experience of this preoccupation with what was happening in Virginia's life. Until now, it hadn't been possible for the family to be open to one another's perceptions about the predicament they'd been struggling with. This inquiry made it possible for them to develop some mutual understandings about their experiences of the consequences of the predicament.

In my conversation with Jeffrey, Beth, and Andrew, I also prefaced my evaluation questions with an editorial: "I am getting a clearer picture about what AHD's been up to. It's been messing things up between Jeffrey and his mum and dad, between Jeffrey and other kids, and between Jeffrey and his teachers. And about how it's been making Jeffrey feel funny in his tummy. And it has also been upsetting Jeffrey's mum and dad. I've also got a clearer picture of the plans that AHD has for Jeffrey's future. AHD wants to be Jeffrey's only play friend, to keep Jeffrey to himself." This editorial provided a reflecting surface that assisted all the family members in speaking about their experiences of AHD's activities and about their position on the consequences of these activities.

At this time care is also taken to ensure that people have the opportunity to articulate all the complexities of their position on the effects of the problem. Therapists often fall into the trap of assuming that people would evaluate the consequences as wholly negative. They then prematurely bring closure to this inquiry and proceed to develop the therapeutic conversation on this assumption. However, people's positions on the problem and its consequences are often complex and mixed. For example, one of the principal consequences of the operations of self-hate in Sarah's life was cutting, and I was aware of how important it was for me not to make assumptions about her experience of this:

**M:** Sarah, I'm just wondering whether it would be okay to change tack for a bit. I've been getting a pretty good idea of what self-hate demands of you, and I'd like to ask some questions about how this is for you.

**Sarah:** That's fine. Go ahead.

**M:** Okay. Would it be okay to start with the cutting?

**Sarah:** Sure, sure. It's no secret.

**M:** When we were talking about how the self-hate had your treating your own body, you said that it required you to cut. I wanted to know what this was about, and you said that it was partly about disciplining your body. So my question is, what's this like for you?

**Sarah:** Well, it's . . . I don't know how to answer your question, because it is just how it is. Cutting is just how it is.

**M:** So it is something that is okay by you?

**Sarah:** Michael, I am really surprised that you are asking this question.

**M:** Why?

**Sarah:** Because most people just try to talk me out of it.

**M:** That's not on my agenda.

**Sarah:** Good! Because the truth is that when I see my blood running, it's about the only time that I feel relief. It's probably about the only time that I feel anything at all.

**M:** So you don't have any questions about it?

**Sarah:** What? No, I don't think so.

**M:** I'm not trying to talk you out of cutting. But if cutting were a fate that was served up to you at birth—if cutting were a destiny that was allocated to you, when other destinies were allocated to other infants—you wouldn't have any questions about it?

**Sarah:** I didn't say that.

**M:** Sorry . . .

**Sarah:** I guess if my life started all over again, I suppose I'd have a question or two about the cutting.

**M:** Okay. I'm just wanting to get some idea of where you stand on this cutting. Am I right in understanding that this is something that you are mostly for, something that brings relief, but also something that you have a small question about?

**Sarah:** That's a pretty good summary of the situation.

The complexity of people's position on these consequences is also evident in variations in their evaluations. For example, a person might be favorably disposed toward some of the consequences but not others.

### Inquiry Category 4. Justifying the Evaluation

This fourth stage features an inquiry into the "why" of people's evaluations. This inquiry is usually initiated with questions like: Why is/isn't this okay for you? Why do you feel this way about this development? Why are you taking this stand/position on this development?

However, this inquiry can be initiated in other ways, too. At times it is more appropriate to call for a story that will provide an account of the "why": Would you tell me a story about your life that would help me to understand why you would take this position on this development? What stories about your history might your father share to throw some light on why you are so unhappy about this development? It was this version of the "why" question that I pursued in my conversation with Jeffrey, Beth, and Andrew: "Okay . . . now I'd like to know anything that you can tell me that would help me understand why what AHD's been up to isn't okay for you. And about why AHD's plans are not okay for you." As with the evaluation questions, these justification questions are usually prefaced by editorials.

Justification ("why") questions have had a history of bad press in the counseling and psychotherapy fields. I can recall attending training events in the early 1970s where we were counseled never to ask why questions, but to restrict our inquiries to "how" and "what" questions. This seemed unacceptable to me. When I asked the leaders of these events, "Why this discrimination against the mind?" they responded by throwing up their hands in exasperation. This prejudice against "why" questions may be partly due to the way in which the word has been employed in the wider culture. In this context, "why" questions have often served as a form of moral interrogation, which is diminishing and demeaning of others: Why did you do this? Why are you such a problem? Why would you think such a thing?

The class of "why" questions that I am promoting, however, is not associated with moral judgment of this sort. These "why" questions play a profoundly significant role in helping people to give voice to and further develop important conceptions of living, including their intentional understanding about life (for example, understanding their purposes, aspirations, goals, quests, and commitments), their understanding about what they value in life, their knowledge about life and life skills, and their prized learnings and realizations. Over the years I have continued to ask "why" questions, even in my work with young children. People's responses to these questions have powerfully reinforced this practice.

Another benefit of "why" questions is that they help people develop more positive identity conclusions that displace those associated with the problem definitions of their lives. For example, upon encouraging Sarah to evaluate her cutting as a requirement of self-hate, I learned that she would have a question about this if her life were beginning anew and if cutting was a fate that was assigned to her future:

> **M:** I am interested in the fact that you would have a small question about this. I'd like to know what the question would be. And I would also like to understand why you would have a question about cutting as a destiny that was served up to you.
>
> **Sarah:** About why I would have a question about this?
>
> **M:** Yeah.

**Sarah:** I can't believe that you are asking me this.

**M:** Why?

**Sarah:** Well, everybody else questions the cutting. But you're asking me why I would question it?

**M:** Yes, that's what I am asking.

**Sarah:** Surely you'd know. Of all people, surely you'd know. Aren't you supposed to be doing something about this cutting? Isn't that your job?

**M:** I know the inside of my life, not the inside of your life. I know what questions I might have, but not the questions that you might have. So, what's this question about cutting all about?

**Sarah:** Surely you'd think that I was entitled to a little something in life!

**M:** Entitled to a little something! So this question has something to do with what you might be entitled to, even in some small way?

**Sarah:** I'm a bit surprised to hear myself saying this, but I guess so.

**M:** These are important words. These words about a sense or an idea of being "entitled to a little something in life." Would it be okay if I ask some more questions about this, as I'm curious about the history of this idea? About the history of this sense in your life?

**Sarah:** Yeah, that'd be fine.

**M:** Okay. Is there any story about your history that you could tell me that would give me some understanding of why you can relate to this idea of being entitled to a little something?

During this conversation, Sarah gave voice to a conclusion about her life that contradicted all of the negative conclusions about her identity that were associated with self-hate—that she was "useless," "worthless," and "deserved what she got." I did not point out this contradiction, as it is not my intention to directly challenge these negative conclusions. To some extent, these negative conclusions had already been unpacked in the context of the exposé that was developed in the early part of the externalizing conversation. At this point, as Sarah gave voice to the conclusion about being entitled to something in life, I initiated the first of a series of conversations that developed a relational and historical account of this conclusion. These conversations were structured according to the re-authoring conversations map that is presented in Chapter 2. Among other things, these re-authoring conversations gave rise to a range of understandings about what Sarah intended for her life and about what she held precious.

It is in this way that externalizing conversations open gateways to rich story development. As in my work with Sarah, it is usually the case that the intentional understandings—understandings that life is shaped by specific intentions that people actively and willfully engage and embrace in their acts of living—and the understandings about what people give value to, are defined at this point in the development of externalizing conversations, and provide an excellent point of entry to re-authoring conversations. This was also clearly illustrated in my work with Virginia and her parents:

**M:** Virginia, you said that you didn't like this supervision. That it doesn't help. And that it is frustrating.

**Virginia:** Yeah.

**M:** Would you say a little about why you don't like it?

**Virginia:** Why I don't like it?! It's not just that I don't like it. I don't need it!

**M:** Why don't you need it?

**Virginia:** I'm perfectly capable of looking after my own life.

**M:** Has this always been true?

**Virginia:** No, of course not! Not when I was just a kid.

**M:** Okay. What is it about your life that you are looking after now that you wouldn't have been so capable of looking after when you were younger?

**Virginia:** Well, for a start, I know how to look after my own safety now.

**M:** All right. This suggests two things to me. First that there are aspects of your life that you are valuing. Second, that you have developed some skills in maintaining your safety. Does this fit?

**Virginia:** Yeah, that's it. Of course.

**M:** Could I ask you some questions that would help me to understand these developments?

**Virginia:** Sure, go ahead.

As the conversation evolved, with the assistance of further questions from me, Virginia provided an account of what she was now valuing about her life and of the skills she had developed in looking out for her own safety. Her parents, Verity and Russell, were surprised and reassured to hear this. This account of what Virginia was valuing about her life, and of her skills in maintaining her own safety, provided a point of entry to a re-authoring conversation in which these developments were more richly described. In this re-authoring conversation some of the themes of Virginia's life became linked to some of the significant themes of Verity and Russell's life. This provided a foundation for Virginia to take further initiatives in caring for her life and to refine these initiatives in the maintenance of personal safety. This was an antidote to the preoccupation that had been shaping of Verity and Russell's responses to their daughter.

In making a strong case for the resurrection of the "why" question, I want to acknowledge that I do not expect an immediate response to these questions. The internal understandings of human action that are the vogue of contemporary Western culture have displaced the intentional understandings that are so important in challenging negative conclusions people have formed about their lives, in redefining people's identity, and in rich story development. When human action is assumed to be a manifestation of some element or essence of a self that is determined by human nature, or by a distortion of human nature, it is rare for people to be invited to reflect on their lives in a way that allows them to determine what certain events might say about what is important to them. Because of this, "why" questions can be very unfamiliar to people, and an "I don't know" response to them can often be expected. When faced with these responses, therapists can provide more support to people in their effort to answer so that they have an experience of being knowledged about these matters.

This support can be given in many ways. I have already mentioned the importance of prefacing "why" questions with an editorial account of the principal effects of the predicaments and problems of people's lives, and of the evaluations that have been made about them. Another option in responding to an "I don't know" is to invite people to extend the review of the principal effects of their problems and predicaments, and of their evaluation of these effects, so that there is a more solid foundation for reflection in relation to the "why" questions that have been introduced.

Yet another option is for the therapist to provide an account of how others have responded to similar "why" questions: "A couple of weeks ago I was meeting with a guy who was facing a similar situation, and who was also very dissatisfied with similar developments in his life. When I asked why he was so dissatisfied, he said that _____. Would this fit with any conclusions that you might have, or would your response be entirely different?" These accounts of the responses of others usually contribute to a foundation for people to be knowledged about the "why" of their own position on developments in their lives; another person's "why" account often makes it possible for people to distinguish their own position.

When young children give an "I don't know" response to "why" questions, the introduction of a guessing game can be helpful. A child's parents and siblings can be invited to make guesses about why the child is concerned about certain developments. The therapist can also contribute to this stock of guesses. The child can then be interviewed about whether any of these guesses came close to the mark, and if so, about what words the child would use to develop this "why." If the child determines that these guesses have not come close, he or she can be interviewed about how he or she knows this. This usually helps the child put words to his or her own "why."

The "statement of position map" provides a foundation for the charting of externalizing conversations. This map was implicit in my early work with externalizing conversations, and others have found it helpful in the development of their own work. I recommend using the map to chart externalizing conversations as a skills-development exercise, and I have provided examples of this on the following pages. Figures 1.1 and 1.2 represent the charting of my first two meetings with Jeffrey and his parents; Figure 1.3 represents the charting of my first meeting with Sarah; and Figure 1.4 represents the charting of my initial consultation with Virginia and her parents.

Although the map presents a linear account of the progression of these conversations, in actual practice, a strictly linear progression is rarely seen and clarifications of people's responses at one level of inquiry can bring about revisions in, or the embroidering of, responses at another level of inquiry. For example, at the outset of my conversation with Spencer and his parents, encopresis was characterized in terms that were particular and experience-near. Then the effects of this problem on the lives and relationships of family members were briefly explored, and this provided a foundation for the further characterization of the problem in terms of what this might say about Mr. Mischief's intentions for Spencer's life and future. This back-and-forth development is usually evident at all levels of inquiry.

Figure 1.1 Charting Externalizing Conversations (Jeffrey, First Session)

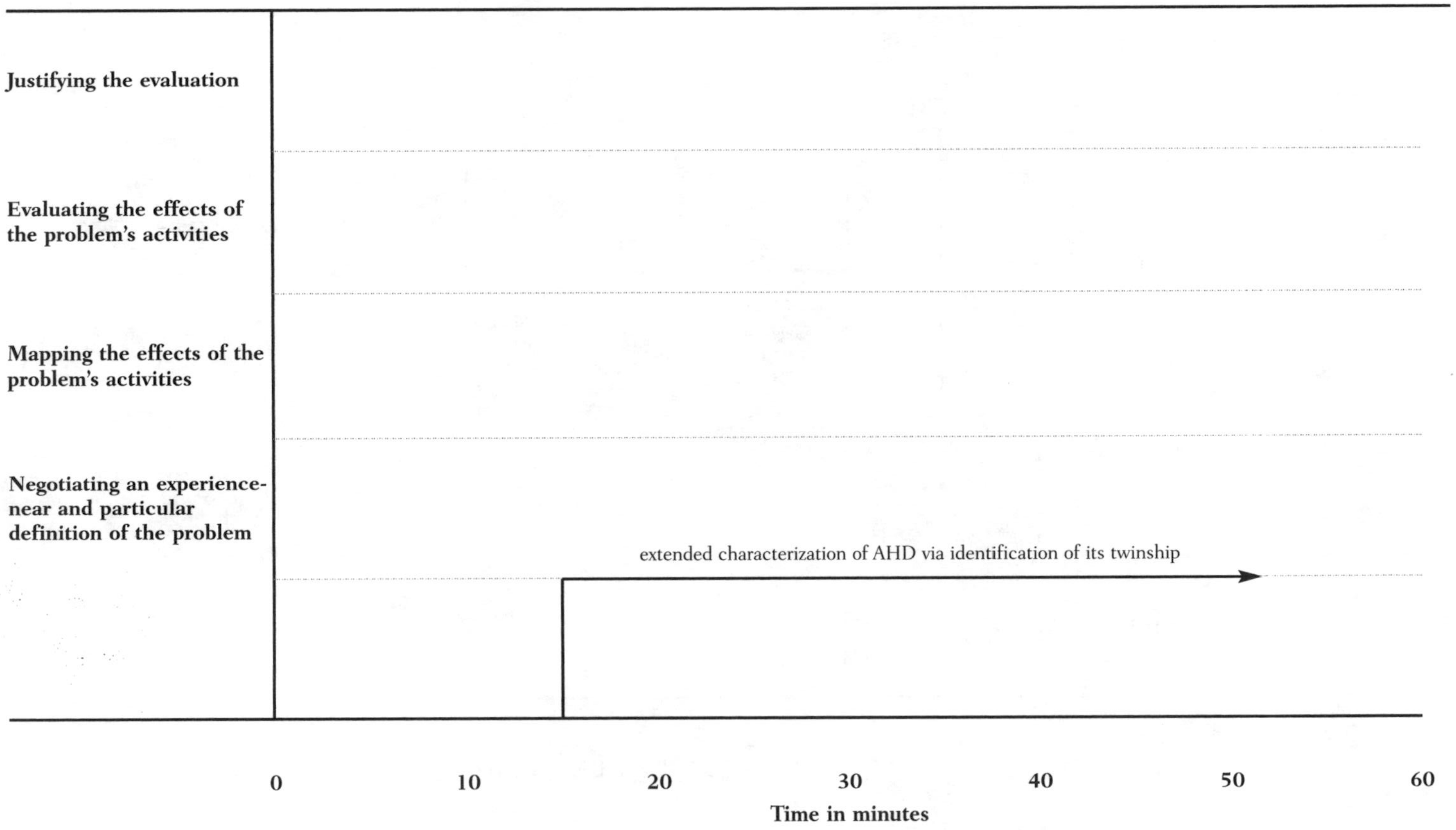

Justifying the evaluation

Evaluating the effects of
the problem's activities

Mapping the effects of the
problem's activities

Negotiating an experience-
near and particular
definition of the problem

extended characterization of AHD via identification of its twinship

0        10        20        30        40        50        60

Time in minutes

Figure 1.2 Charting Externalizing Conversations (Jeffrey, Second Session)

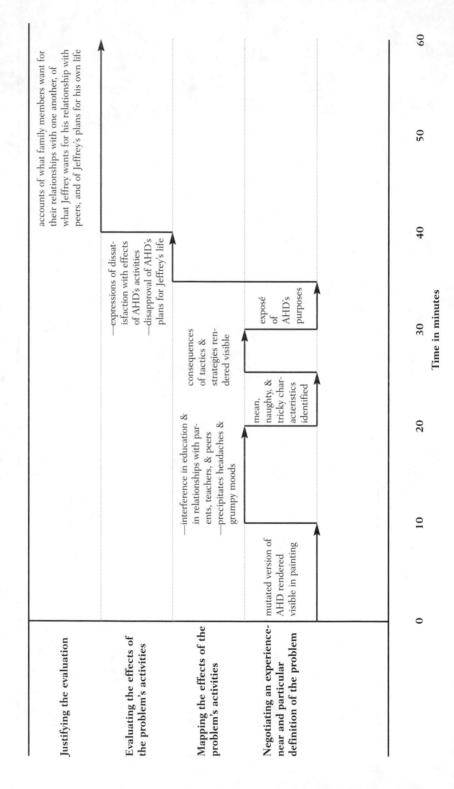

Figure 1.3 Charting Externalizing Conversations (Sarah)

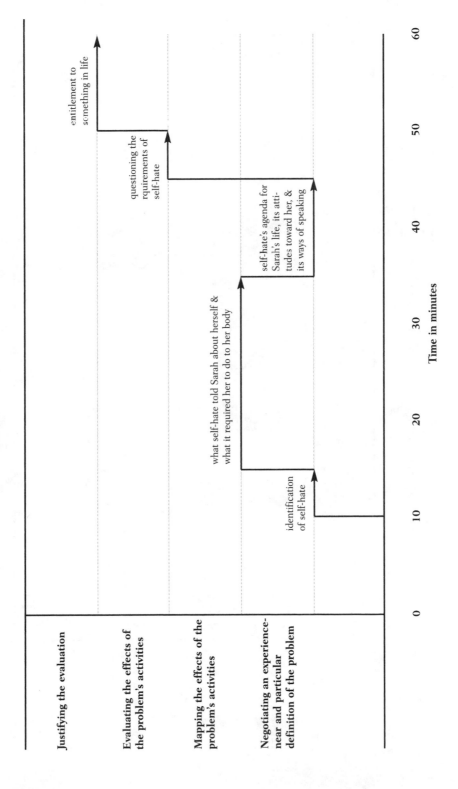

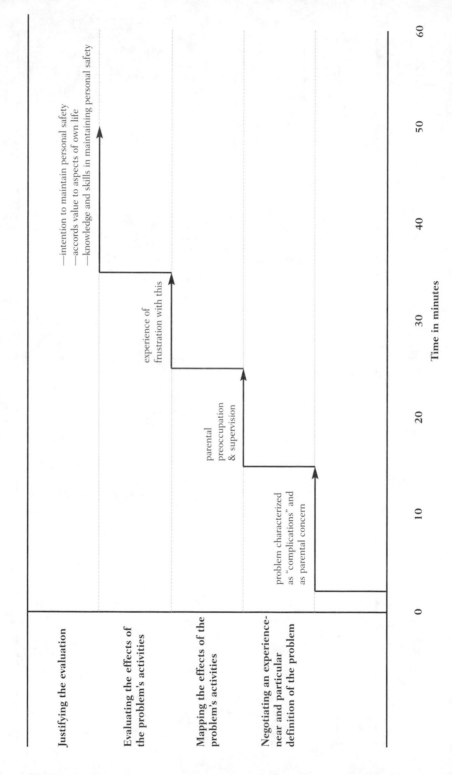

Figure 1.4  Charting Externalizing Conversations (Virginia)

## Conclusion

This chapter provided an overview of externalizing conversations. It was not my intention to include all that might be said about externalizing conversations, for this would take more than a book. Rather, I wanted to provide a "living" account of some of the possibilities associated with these conversations by illustrating all of the ideas discussed with examples of actual practice.

It has at times been assumed that externalizing conversations are complicit with a trend toward constructing people as autonomous units of thought and action. It is my hope that I have given sufficient illustration of the practices of externalizing conversations to dispel this assumption. These practices make it possible for people not only to redefine their relationship with the problems of their lives, but also to redefine their relationships with each other in ways that acknowledge each other's voices in the development of their sense of identity. This type of redefinition fosters a more relational sense of identity.

I do not introduce externalizing conversations in all of my consultations. There are many occasions upon which I meet with people whose identities are not defined by the problems that they are seeking consultation over, and upon which a point of entry to rich story development is immediately apparent. However, the option for externalizing conversations is one that I am ever conscious of and one that I will continue to develop.

There is a sense in which I regard the practice of externalizing to be a faithful friend. Over many years, this practice has assisted me to find ways forward with people who are in situations that were considered hopeless. In these situations, externalizing conversations have opened many possibilities for people to redefine their identities, to experience their lives anew, and to pursue what is precious to them.

# 2
# Re-Authoring
# Conversations

**W**hen people consult therapists they tell stories; they speak about the history of the problems, predicaments, or dilemmas that have brought them to therapy, and they provide an account of what led to their decision to seek help. In doing this, people link the events of their lives in sequences that unfold through time according to a theme or plot. These themes often reflect loss, failure, incompetence, hopelessness, or futility. Along with this, people routinely refer to the figures or protagonists that feature in the story, and they share with therapists their conclusions both about the identity of these figures or protagonists and about their motives, intentions, and personal characteristics. Re-authoring conversations invite people to continue to develop and tell stories about their lives, but they also help people to include some of the more neglected but potentially significant events and experiences that are "out of phase" with their dominant storylines. These events and experiences can be considered "unique outcomes" or "exceptions."

It is these unique outcomes or exceptions that provide a starting point for re-authoring conversations. They provide a point of entry to the alternative storylines of people's lives that, at the outset of these conversations, are barely visible. The therapist facilitates the development of these alternative storylines by introducing questions that encourage people to recruit their lived experience, to stretch their minds, to exercise their imagination, and to employ their meaning-making resources. People become curious about, and fascinated with, previously neglected aspects of their lives and relationships, and as these conversations proceed, these alternative storylines thicken, become more significantly rooted in history, and provide people with a foundation for new initiatives in addressing the problems, predicaments, and dilemmas of their lives.

## Liam and Penny

Penny called for an appointment for her son, Liam, age 15, whom she was very concerned about. She'd had these concerns for many years, but they had been significantly exacerbated by events of the last several months. Liam had dropped out of school 4 months ago, had become more withdrawn and rarely emerged from his bedroom, and was now quite noncommunicative and morose. On the day prior to calling for an appointment, Penny had happened across his diary. She initially experienced a dilemma about whether or not to read it, but the magnitude of her concern for him resolved this dilemma for her. Upon reading some recent entries, Penny found her worst fears confirmed. The diary entries were saturated with the theme of suicide—in fact, they suggested that Liam had already made two suicide gestures. She also learned that Liam considered himself to be messed-up and damaged, and that he felt socially and emotionally paralyzed.

Penny was now desperate and had called me on the advice of her general practitioner. She said that she was losing hope for Liam's life. She had hoped that Liam would improve following their escape from his father, a highly abusive man, some 2 years ago. Liam's father had subjected both Liam and Penny to regular assault, and he had been very skilled at controlling both of them and at cutting off any escape routes. Penny explained that she'd tried many times to free herself and her son from this situation, but Liam's father had always managed to circumvent these efforts through acts of intimidation and threats of retribution. These threats of retribution were principally against Liam's life.

Penny described a little of the nightmare that she and Liam had endured, and she talked of the guilt that she harbored over what Liam had gone through during this time. She also spoke of the rising hopes and expectations that she had experienced upon finally escaping the violence of this man. However, to her dismay, things did not improve for Liam as she had expected they would. Liam remained disinterested in life. He had become increasingly isolated and increasingly convinced that the future held nothing for him. He could now see no horizons of possibility in his life.

I said that I would clear a space in my schedule to meet with Liam, and I wondered aloud how Penny might succeed in getting him to see me. Penny said that this would not be easily achieved, as Liam was likely to be resentful about her taking this initiative without consulting him and would be furious with her if he sensed that she had read his diary. When I asked Penny about what she thought the consequences of this fury would be, she predicted that Liam would not surface from his room for a few days, and that even when he did he would only speak to her grudgingly for several more days. She was worried that making this appointment without consulting him would contribute to his negative frame of mind and lessen the chances that he would agree to talk with me. But she was also sure that if she did consult Liam about making an appointment, he would veto the idea.

Penny wanted my thoughts about how she might encourage Liam to attend this appointment. I suggested that she ask him to join her in this meeting with me for her sake. Penny could honestly tell him that she had become increasingly preoccupied with worry about recent developments in his life, and that this preoccupation was now quite pervasive. She could let him know that it was making it virtually impossible for her to concentrate on the tasks that were required of her in her workplace, to engage in any semblance of a social life, and to feel emotionally present in her connections with others. She could also explain that it was interfering with her sleep and her appetite, and that she was now at a crisis point and in desperate need of help.

Penny thought that there was a good chance that Liam would respond to this request by agreeing to come with her to the appointment. By the end of our telephone conversation she had decided to tell him about reading his diary, explaining that she'd felt driven to do so by these preoccupying concerns. Penny thought that she'd be able to weather the storm provoked by this admission, and she requested an appointment in 4 or 5 days time.

Five days later I met with Penny and Liam. Liam made it clear that he was attending this meeting for his mother's sake, and that he would not have come on his own account. For the present, he'd "agreed to come along for the ride" and would reserve his judgement about the value of this exercise. However, he did confirm that he'd concluded that his life was pointless, that it wasn't worth trying anything, that he was messed up, and that he had no future. Following is a transcript of our conversation, taken from a point about 15 minutes into our first meeting.

**Liam:** So my mum's told you about what we went through. But it was worse for her than it was for me.

**M:** It was worse for her than it was for you. In what way?

**Liam:** He gave me a pretty hard time, but it was more painful for my mother.

**M:** Were you concerned about what she was being put through?

**Liam:** What do you think?!

**M:** Sometimes people get a bit desensitised to violence, and even though it still has a devastating impact on their lives and on the lives of others they become a bit oblivious to this.

**Liam:** Well, I wasn't oblivious to this. Of course I was concerned about what he was doing to her. It was terrible.

**M:** Tell me, were you more concerned for yourself or your mother? Or were you concerned about yourself and your mother equally?

**Liam:** Mum, of course.

**M:** Penny, does it surprise you to hear this?

**Penny:** Which part?

**M:** That through all this time Liam was more concerned for you than he was for himself.

**Penny:** Well, no. It doesn't surprise me at all.

**M:** Liam was more concerned for you than he was for himself. What did this suggest to you about what was important to Liam? Or about what was precious to him?

**Penny:** Well . . . I know we've had our ups and downs, and recently Liam hasn't seemed to want me in his life much. But I have still always known that I was precious to him.

**M:** How did you know this?

**Penny:** A mother just knows these things about her son. These are just the things that a mother knows.

**M:** Are there any stories that you can tell me about Liam's actions that would be a reflection of what was precious to him? Of what he held precious? Are there any stories you can tell me about him that would help me to understand how you knew this about him?

**Penny:** There's probably lots of things that I could tell you. But I don't really know where to start right now.

**M:** Any starting point would be fine. If you could think of some story that you could tell me about Liam's actions that reflect the extent to which he held your life precious, that would be helpful to me.

**Penny:** Okay. Maybe I could start by telling you about something that happened when he must have been, let's see, about 8 years old. It was on a Sunday morning. I distinctly remember that. And his father was hitting me for some reason or other. I always tried to protect Liam from seeing these things, but it wasn't always possible to do this. Anyway, suddenly I heard glass smashing. This interrupted his father, and we went into the living room and I saw that someone had thrown a rock through the front window. There was broken glass all over the carpet. I looked out the window, and guess who I saw running off down the street? It was Liam. His father took off after him and Liam copped a thrashing for this. I tried to stop it. It was one of those really terrible situations. I felt torn apart by it.

**M:** Liam distracted his father when he was hitting you?

**Penny:** Yes, he distracted his father. He did this even though he would have known that he was going to cop a belting for it.

**M:** Liam, do you remember this?

**Liam:** Nope.

**M:** Penny, what sort of step was it that Liam took on that Sunday all of those years ago? How would you name this action of Liam's?

**Penny:** I don't really know, I haven't thought much about it. I guess that I even tried to put it out of my mind because of what happened to Liam. And because I wasn't able to do anything. It was horrible. I wouldn't be talking about this if you hadn't asked about it.

**M:** Did Liam's action fit with that sense of pointlessness about life that he was just talking about? Was this an example of Liam just accepting what life was serving up to him?

**Penny:** No, no. Of course not. There's no way that it fits with that.

**M:** Okay, so what does it fit with? What might be a good way of naming this action that Liam took in throwing a rock through the window?

**Penny:** Well, like I said, I haven't really thought about this. But I suppose when I think about it, yes, the word that I would use is that he was "protesting." He was protesting what I was being put through.

**M:** So "protest" might be a good name for this step.

**Penny:** Yeah. For sure. This would fit.

**M:** Liam, can you relate to this way of describing what you did?

**Liam:** Nope. Not really.

**M:** Penny, you witnessed Liam protesting what you were being subject to when he was just 8 years old. What did this suggest to you about him? What's your guess about what this reflects in terms of what Liam values?

**Penny:** It told me that he was a very brave little boy. That he had lots of courage. Now when I think back, it just seems even more amazing to me that he did such a thing.

**M:** It told you that he was a brave little boy. And what did it say to you about what might be important to him? About what he values?

**Penny:** Well, I guess it says a lot to me about what was important to him about fairness. Which, when I think about it, is surprising, isn't it, because he'd seen so much that was unfair.

**M:** So it suggested courage and fairness. Can you relate to what you're hearing, Liam?

**Liam:** Nope. Not that bit about courage. And not really that stuff about fairness either.

**M:** Okay. You don't relate to this. Can you see how your mother might have arrived at those conclusions about courage and fairness?

**Liam:** Well, yeah. I guess so. I suppose I can see how she would get this idea about me.

**M:** Penny, were you surprised to see that it was Liam running off down the street? Did the action that Liam took on the basis of where he might have stood on fairness surprise you?

**Penny:** No, of course not. I think that I would have always known this about Liam.

**M:** How would you have known that?

**Penny:** It's just another one of the things that a mother knows, I guess!

**M:** Is there anything that you could tell me about Liam, when he was younger still, that would have confirmed what you knew about him? That would fit with what you understood about how important fairness was to him?

**Penny:** Okay. Let's see. Well, yes, there is something. Probably lots of things. Liam must have been about 6 and he was in his second semester in first grade at school. There was this development where he started to come home from school ravenous. He was just so hungry. He'd raid the pantry and the fridge. So I'd give him some extra treats for his lunch. This went on for nearly 2 weeks and by the end of this time he was taking a truckload of food to school! So I spoke to his teacher about this. She didn't know what was going on, but she said that she'd put him under observation. Guess what she discovered? You remember, Liam. I told you about this before.

**Liam:** I don't remember hearing this before.

**Penny:** What the teacher discovered was that Liam was sitting with three other kids at lunchtime. Two of these kids were very sad because they were missing their mothers. The other kid was being terribly teased and was also really sad and crying a lot. And what did Liam do? He was sharing his treats with them to make them all feel better.

**Liam:** I don't remember this.

**M:** What was it like for you as Liam's mother to hear this about him?

**Penny:** Mostly I just felt so proud of him for this. So proud of my son that he could do this for these other kids despite all of the heartache we were going through at home.

**M:** Penny, I'll ask you to paint the scene a bit more for Liam as you drive home after this meeting. Maybe you could describe the lunchroom, tell him what you know about these other kids, remind him about what this teacher looked like. Anything that might help him to remember this.

**Penny:** Okay, I'd be glad to.

**M:** What sort of step was this? You told me that you thought Liam felt paralyzed in life. It doesn't sound like this fits with paralysis, or with being messed up.

**Penny:** No, it's definitely not about that. I'm trying to think of a good word. Let's see. Perhaps rescuing. Yes, I think you could say that he was rescuing these boys.

**M:** Rescuing these other children. Can you relate to that, Liam?

**Liam:** I suppose so.

**M:** Can you think of another name for what you did?

**Liam:** No. Rescuing will do.

**M:** Penny, when I asked you about Liam throwing a rock through the window, about what this said about him, you said that it told you about his courage and about what was important to him in terms of fairness. Thinking back on these events when he was 6 years old, how did this act of rescuing other children shape your picture of him as a person?

**Penny:** Let's see. Well, I know it said a lot about where he stood on injustice, even as a little boy.

**M:** About where he stood on injustice. Anything else?

**Penny:** Like what?

**M:** Just about anything else that might have been important to him, or about what life was about for him.

**Penny:** Maybe about the sort of ideas that Liam had about what life should be about. Maybe about the dreams of a little boy. Yeah, that's it. And about how he wouldn't let those dreams go.

**M:** Liam, I keep asking you the same question. Can you relate to what your mum just said about justice and about the dreams of a little boy?

**Liam:** Yeah, I guess. I suppose I can. Yeah, I guess it fits.

**M:** Let me get this clear. Are you saying that you can relate to this bit about justice and about what you thought life should be about? About the dreams of this little boy?

**Liam:** Yeah. Yeah, I guess so.

**M:** Just a guess?

**Liam:** No, not just a guess. It adds up.

**M:** I'd like to understand how it is that you're able to relate to what you're hearing from your mum about these stories of your history, and about the conclusions that she has reached about who you are in light of these stories.

**Liam:** Okay.

**M:** So, the question is: How is it that you are able to relate to what you are hearing? Is there anything that's happened in your life in more recent years that would fit with what we are learning about you? With what I am hearing about where you stand on what is fair and just, with what your mother is telling me about what's important to you, about the dreams of this little boy?

**Liam:** I don't know. What do you think, Mum?

**Penny:** Maybe when you spoke to your cousin Vanessa.

**Liam:** Yeah. That's probably it.

**M:** What?

**Liam:** Well, just before we got away from my dad I told my cousin what I was going through because I thought it was a bit like the same for her. Like, Vanessa's dad is my dad's brother, and he's pretty rough, and I thought that she was probably having a hard time. Anyway, she did tell me about some of the bad things that were happening to her, and it was appalling. She'd never told anybody else.

**M:** What happened then?

**Penny:** About 8 months after Liam reached out to her the child-protection people got involved. And this was all because of what Liam did.

**M:** Your mum's words were that you "reached out" to your cousin. Would this be a good name for this step, or would some other name fit better?

**Penny:** No, that works. "Reaching out" works.

**M:** I've learned about actions in rescuing. I've learned about actions that have to do with protest. And I've learned about actions that have to do with reaching out. All of these are part of your history. Putting these actions together, what's this all about?

**Liam:** What do you mean?

**M:** If these were all part of a direction in life, or part of a project in life, or a particular pathway that you have been taking in life, what might be a good name for this?

**Liam:** Well, I suppose . . . Do you mean, well, something like . . . well, like salvaging something. Maybe "salvaging life" or something?

**M:** Yeah, yeah. Salvaging life.

**Liam:** Maybe it's more like . . . No, that will do.

**M:** Okay. It's about salvaging life. Okay, this says a lot to me. Penny, what's your guess about what this suggests to me about what Liam is aspiring to?

**Penny:** Well, it might be saying something to you about a young man who's had strong beliefs about what's okay and what's not. Maybe it would be saying something to you about a young man who knows something about what makes life worthwhile.

**M:** Yeah, that fits with my image. Liam?

**Liam:** I don't know. It's a bit hard for me to . . . Maybe you'd be thinking about that stuff about what Mum said about my dreams and things. You know, what she said.

**M:** About your dreams about what life should be about?

**Liam:** Yeah.

**M:** And about how you held onto those dreams despite everything?

**Liam:** Yeah, I guess so. I guess that would be it.

**M:** That fits too. I have a question. The things that we've been learning about you, about what's important to you, about what you've held onto despite what you've been through, about dreams about what life should all be about, about how this is all about salvaging life. If you were able to keep this knowledge about your life close to you, to draw support from this, what's your guess about what this would make possible for you? What is your guess about what this would make possible for you to do? What steps could you take that would fit with this?

**Liam:** Phew! That's a big one.

**M:** Sure it is. But we've got lots of time.

**Penny:** Maybe you could try contacting that guy Daniel who used to be your friend. You haven't seen him for ages. Daniel's also had some pretty hard times, didn't he?

**Liam:** Yeah. He's been through a lot.

**M:** What do you think of Penny's idea about contacting him?

**Liam:** I reckon I could do this. I could give him a buzz and maybe catch up with him.

**M:** What sort of step would this be if you took it? Would you say it was a step in rescuing, protesting, or reaching out? Or something else?

**Liam:** I dunno. Probably reaching out.

**Penny:** Yeah, it would be an example of that. I know that this boy Daniel is still having a pretty hard time.

**M:** Penny, if you witnessed Liam taking this step to contact Daniel, what would this suggest to you about his purposes in doing this?

**Penny:** Maybe something about him wanting to get more connected to his hopes. Yeah, something about picking these hopes up again.

**M:** How would that be for you, to witness Liam picking up these hopes again?

**Penny:** Brilliant. Just brilliant.

**M:** Liam?

**Liam:** Yeah. She's right. It would have to be about picking up the hopes again.

**M:** Okay. It would be to pick up the hopes again. I'd like to ask a few questions about what you've been learning about yourself as we've been piecing together the steps that you've been taking in salvaging your life. What do you think this reflects about your plans for your future?

**Liam:** Well, I guess . . .

Liam did contact Daniel. This was the first of many steps that he subsequently took that were in harmony with the conclusions about his life and his identity that were developed and redeveloped in my conversations with him and his mother. Liam became increasingly engaged in these conversations, and in our fourth meeting he announced that he'd realized that the depression he'd been struggling with for so long was "fake depression." In stating this, he was not implying that he had been "faking it" or that he still didn't have a significant struggle with this depression. Rather, he had reached this understanding on the basis of a realization that he wasn't messed up: "How could you have real depression if you weren't messed up?" Liam went on to say that "even fake depression is pretty bad, but at least you know that you are going to recover from it, and that makes a big difference."

In the course of our meetings there were many other dimensions to the development of this storyline of Liam's life. In one of these, he experienced his life linked to the stories of his great uncle's life around shared themes, intentions, and values. This great uncle was a man who had played a vitally important role in rescuing Penny from the abuses that she was subject to in her family of birth.

At the eighth and final meeting, I'd been reviewing with Liam many of the initiatives he'd been taking in recent months. Not all of these

had been well received by others. For example, some of Liam's initiatives in reaching out had been rejected by others. Upon inquiring
about how he had responded to these rejections and about why this
hadn't discouraged further initiatives, Liam said that he was a veteran
of rejection, and that, on account of this, there wasn't much new for
him to experience in terms of rejection. Further, he said that he was
"probably much better equipped to cope with rejection than other
kids who were from more normal families and who might not have
experienced the rejections that I've been through."

When I asked him about the implications of this for his future,
Liam concluded that future rejections were less likely to be a hurdle
to him than they might be for many others. This constituted a new
realization for Liam that was particularly important to him—that he
was uniquely abled on account of all that he had been through, rather
than disabled. Although we would continue to lament the abuses that
he'd been subject to for a good part of his life, we were all able to celebrate these conclusions about Liam's uniquely abled status.

## The Structure of Re-authoring Conversations

This chapter is about a map for narrative practice that I refer to as a
"re-authoring conversations map." It has been a mainstay of my therapeutic practice for many years. In the original development of this
map I drew significantly from Jerome Bruner's (1986) explorations of
the narrative metaphor, specifically from his analysis of literary texts.
In this analysis it was his goal to develop further understandings of the
meaning-making activities that people engage with in everyday life.

I was drawn to this because I perceived parallels between the activity of writing literary stories and therapeutic practice. It was my perception that just as "great storytelling . . . is about compelling plights
that . . . must be set forth with sufficient subjunctivity to allow them
to be rewritten by the reader, rewritten so as to allow play for the
reader's imagination" (Bruner, 1986, p. 35), effective therapy is about
engaging people in the re-authoring of the compelling plights of their

lives in ways that arouse curiosity about human possibility and in ways
that invoke the play of imagination.

In describing the participation of readers in the construction of the
storyline of the text, Bruner referred to the "journey" metaphor and to
the "mapmaking" analogy. This resonated for me strongly. This
metaphor and this analogy seemed clearly pertinent to therapeutic
practice. Bruner (1986) made the following observation about the
reader's engagement with texts:

> . . . as they begin to construct a virtual text of their own, it
> is as if they were embarking on a journey without maps—
> and yet, they posses a stock of maps that might give hints,
> and besides, they know a lot about mapmaking. First
> impressions of the new terrain are, of course, based on
> older journeys already taken. In time, the new journey
> becomes a thing in itself, however much its initial shape
> was borrowed from the past. (p. 36)

Similarly, when people first engage in therapeutic conversations in
which they reconstruct the stories of their lives, it often seems that
they are departing from the familiar and embarking on journeys to
new destinations without maps. And yet, as this reconstruction gath-
ers pace, it quickly becomes clear that these people are drawing from
a stock of maps relevant to journeys already taken, and that they know
a lot about mapmaking. In the course of these conversations, the "new
journey" becomes a "thing in itself, however much its initial shape was
borrowed from the past."

With literary texts, the narrative mode "leads to conclusions not
about certainties in an aboriginal (original and objective) world, but
about the varying perspectives that can be constructed to make experience comprehensible" (Bruner, 1986, p. 37). Bruner proposed that
this contribution to increasing the options available to the reader to
render experience comprehensible is the great writer's gift: "The great
writer's gift to a reader is to make him a better writer" (Bruner, 1986,
p. 5). In a similar vein, in therapeutic contexts the narrative mode can

open space for "varying perspectives that can be constructed to make experience comprehensible," and skillful practice can assist people to have a fuller participation and stronger voice of authorship in the construction of the stories of their lives.

## Texts and Dramatic Engagement

According to Bruner (1986):

> Stories of literary merit, to be sure, are about events in the real world, but they render that world newly strange, rescue it from obviousness, fill it with gaps that call upon the reader, in Barthes's sense, to become a writer, a composer of a virtual text in response to the actual. In the end it is the reader who must write for himself what he intends to do with the actual text. (p. 24)

Well-structured novels are highly absorbing of the reader. This is because the authors of these novels exercise an array of options in fostering dramatic engagement in the reading of the text. This provides readers with many invitations to contribute to the development of the storyline and to live out the drama of it. For example, well-structured novels have many gaps in the storyline that must be filled in by the reader. Good writers do not spell everything out, and the reader is required to participate in putting two and two together to make four, in bringing together specific events into sequences unfolding across time in the revealing of the plot, and in reconciling this with the underlying theme of the story. Thus, the reader is given the task of developing and reconciling what Frank Kermode (1981) referred to as *sjuzet* (the linear events that make up the plot) and *fabula* (the timeless underlying theme) in the "fusion of scandal and miracle."

But it is not just the *sjuzet* and the *fabula* that are further developed and reconciled in the reading of literary texts. Bruner, borrowing significantly from the literary theorists Griemas and Courtes (1976), proposed that stories are principally composed of two landscapes—a

"landscape of action" and a "landscape of consciousness." The landscape of action is the "material" of the story and is composed of the
sequence of events that make up the plot (*sjuzet*) and the underlying
theme (*fabula*). The landscape of consciousness is composed of "what
those involved in the action know, think, or feel, or do not know, think
or feel" (Bruner, 1986, p. 14). This landscape features the consciousness of the protagonists of the story and is significantly composed of
their reflections on the events of the landscape of action—of their
attribution of meaning to these events, of their deductions about the
intentions and purposes that are shaping of these events, and of their
conclusions about the character and identity of the other protagonists
in light of these events. Like the development of the plot of the landscape of action, the development of the landscape of consciousness
must be reconciled with the *fabula*, the timeless underlying theme of
the story:

> In any case the fabula of a story—its timeless underlying
> theme—seems to be a unity that incorporates at least three
> constituents. It contains a plight into which characters
> have fallen as a result of intentions that have gone awry
> either because of circumstances, of the "character of char-
> acters," or most likely of the interaction between the two . . .
> What gives the story its unity is the manner in which
> plight, characters, and consciousness interact to yield a
> structure that has a start, development, and a "sense of
> ending." (Bruner, 1986, p. 21)

Just as there are gaps in the landscape of action to be filled in by
the reader, there are gaps to be filled in the landscape of consciousness. Although this landscape of consciousness is partially developed
through the author's representation of the consciousness of the protagonists, and at times through a representation of the author's own
consciousness, the reader's contribution to the landscape of consciousness is a significant factor in the unification of the text, and in
its thick or rich development.

In entering this landscape of consciousness, the reader attributes a range of intentions and purposes to the actions of the protagonists and reaches conclusions about their character and identity. The term *landscape of consciousness* is apt, for it not only represents the consciousness of the protagonists and of the author of the story, but also is significantly filled out by the reader's consciousness.

Numerous mechanisms are employed by good writers to draw the attention of readers to these gaps in the landscapes of action and consciousness, and to encourage them to step into these gaps with their imagination and lived experience. For example, authors rely significantly on the triggering of presupposition to achieve this. They also take care in the arrangement of these gaps: For instance, good writers ensure the provision of adequate clues and structure the text to invoke the curiosity and fascination of the reader. Good writers arrange these gaps to ensure that they are not so large as to exhaust the reader's meaning-making resources in their efforts to fill them, and not so insignificant as to lose the interest of the reader. It is mechanisms like these that provide the reader with a foundation for dramatic engagement with the text, that give readers "a good workout" in the development of a virtual text that invariably exceeds the actual in significant aspects. Bruner quoted Iser (1978), who employed the term *indeterminacy* to describe this characteristic of the literary text:

> . . . it is the element of indeterminacy that evokes the text to communicate with the reader, in the sense that they induce him to participate both in the production and the comprehension of the work's intention. (p. 61)

In summarizing Iser's understanding of the function of this indeterminacy, Bruner (1986) observed that:

> It is this "relative indeterminacy of a text" that "allows for a spectrum of actualizations." And so, "literary texts initiate performances of meaning rather than actually formulating meanings themselves." (p. 24)

## Texts and Life

I was quite drawn to this dual landscape conception of story structure on account of my interest in the narrative metaphor and in the activity of meaning-making. My interest in the narrative metaphor is founded on the assumption that people give meaning to their experiences of the events of life by taking them into frames of intelligibility, and on the conclusion that it is the structure of narrative that provides the principle frame of intelligibility for acts of meaning-making in everyday life. This assumption is associated with a premise that it is in the trafficking of stories about our own and each others' lives that identity is constructed. The concepts of landscape of action and landscape of consciousness bring specificity to the understanding of people's participation in meaning-making within the context of narrative frames.

*Landscape of action = behaviours + events*

*Landscape of consciousness = what is known, not known, thought & felt*

In borrowing this dual-landscape conception from literary theory, it is not my intention to propose that life is simply a text. But I do believe, as do many others, parallels can be drawn between the structure of literary texts and the structure of meaning-making in everyday life. The concepts of landscape of action and landscape of consciousness seem relevant to an understanding of people's meaning-making activities in life, of the construction of personal narratives, and of the constitution of people's identity through everyday acts of life. Further, these concepts seem particularly relevant to the therapeutic task, which I believe to be principally about the redevelopment of personal narratives and the reconstruction of identity.

## Implications for Practice          *central therapeutic task*

Further parallels can be drawn between the structure of literary texts and the structure of therapeutic practice. The authors of texts call the attention of the reader to gaps in the storyline and encourage readers to fill in these gaps by stretching their minds, by exercising their imagination, and by recruiting their lived experience. Rich story development is the outcome. Therapists who prioritize rich story development in their consultations with people do the same. These therapists draw people's attention to gaps in the storylines of their lives—usually these are gaps in what might be called the "subordinate" storylines of people's lives—and encourage them to fill in these gaps by stretching their minds, exercising their imagination, and recruiting their lived experience. And just as good writers give considerable thought to the arrangement of these gaps, so too do therapists who have a focus on rich story development. These therapists take care in constructing the scaffolding of these gaps, ensuring that they are not so large as to exhaust people's meaning-making resources in their effort to fill in the gaps and not so insignificant as to lose people's interest. The outcome of this is that people experience a good workout in the context of therapeutic conversations and become dramatically engaged with many of the neglected events of their own lives.

I have found these concepts of landscape of action and landscape of consciousness to be invaluable in the development of my practice. They have provided me with a foundation for the refinement and further development of therapeutic conversations that contribute to rich story development, and they have offered a map for the shaping of, and for the charting of, these therapeutic conversations. These are conversations that invariably contribute to the rich development of some of the alternative storylines of people's lives, the traces of which are ever-present in people's expressions of living. In these conversations, people's lives become more evidently multistoried as these traces are identified and thickened. In this chapter I give illustrations of these conversations and reflect on the significance of the concepts of landscape of action and landscape of consciousness in the shaping of them.

In describing the relevance of these concepts to therapeutic practice, I have substituted the term *identity* for *consciousness*. I made this substitution because of the confusion that arose around my use of this term. At times, the mention of consciousness was taken to denote an awareness of injustices. At other times this term was taken to denote the mechanism of the mind that is engaged when making choices. At yet other times it was taken to denote actions in life that were conscious in contrast to actions that were products of "the unconscious." Because of this confusion, I will substitute "landscape of identity" for "landscape of consciousness" in this chapter, while acknowledging that the term *identity* represents only part of what is intended in the term *consciousness* as it is applied to the analysis of literary texts and as it might be applied to the understanding of rich story development in therapeutic contexts.

Apart from dispelling this confusion, the term *landscape of identity* does have benefit in the emphasis that it gives to the significance of the therapeutic endeavour—it emphasizes the irreducible fact that any renegotiation of the stories of people's lives is also a renegotiation of identity. Awareness of this encourages a fuller engagement on behalf of therapists with the sort of professional ethics that are associated with an acknowledgment of the life-shaping aspects of therapeutic practice and a greater awareness of the responsibility that we have for what we say and do in the name of therapy.

In drawing parallels between the structure of literary texts and the structure of therapeutic practice, I am not proposing that the activity of the author of a literary text and the therapist's role in therapeutic conversations are synonymous. For one thing, the author of a literary text invites the reader to enter into a storyline, the fundamental shape of which is provided by the author. Therapists, on the other hand, are not the originators of the storyline that is developed in the therapeutic conversation. Although they may be acquainted with many possible stories about life (which makes it possible for them to draw people's attention to significant events that stand outside of the dominant storylines), they are not the primary author in the sense that the author of a literary text is. Rather, therapists privilege the voices of the people consulting them in the attribution of meaning to selected events of their lives, in their interpretation of the links between these events and the valued themes of their lives, in their deduction about what this reflects in terms of what is important to them, and in their conclusions about what this suggests about their own and each other's identities. Whereas the author of a literary text is quite centered in the development of the storyline, the therapist is displaced from the center.

To summarize, in therapeutic conversations that are oriented by re-authoring conversations, the concepts of landscape of action and landscape of identity assist the therapist in building a context in which it becomes possible for people to give meaning to, and draw together into a storyline, many of the overlooked but significant events of their lives. These concepts also guide the therapist in supporting people to derive new conclusions about their lives, many of which will contradict existing deficit-focus conclusions that are associated with the dominant storylines and that have been limiting of their lives.

## Mapping the Re-Authoring Conversation With Liam and Penny

The following review of my conversation with Liam and Penny provides a practical illustration of the therapeutic implications of the concepts of landscape of action and landscape of identity. This review is accompanied by diagrams that chart the therapeutic conversation onto the re-authoring conversations map, which consists of two horizontal timelines—a landscape of action and a landscape of identity (consciousness).

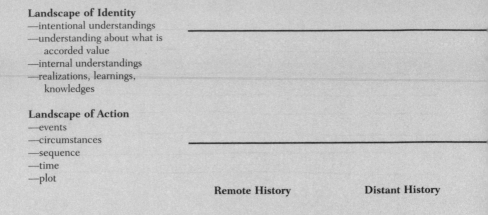

Figure 2.1  Charting Re-Authoring Conversations (Liam)

**Landscape of Identity**
—intentional understandings
—understanding about what is
   accorded value
—internal understandings
—realizations, learnings,
   knowledges

**Landscape of Action**
—events
—circumstances
—sequence
—time
—plot

Remote History          Distant History

**M: (*Figure 2.1*) Liam was more concerned for you than he was for himself, what did this suggest to you about what was important to Liam? Or about what was precious to him?**

Expressions that in some way contradict dominant themes can provide clues to the alternative stories of people's lives. Resignation and the futility of existence were dominant themes in Liam's account of his existence, and yet here Liam expressed significant concern for his mother. I first responded to this contradiction with questions that facilitated the further expression of this concern. I then asked a question that encouraged Penny to reflect on Liam's concerns and to give voice to what this suggested was important to him. This was a landscape of identity question.

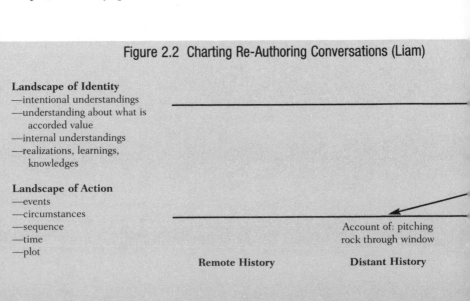

Figure 2.2  Charting Re-Authoring Conversations (Liam)

**Landscape of Identity**
—intentional understandings
—understanding about what is
   accorded value
—internal understandings
—realizations, learnings,
   knowledges

**Landscape of Action**
—events
—circumstances
—sequence
—time
—plot

Account of: pitching
rock through window

Remote History          Distant History

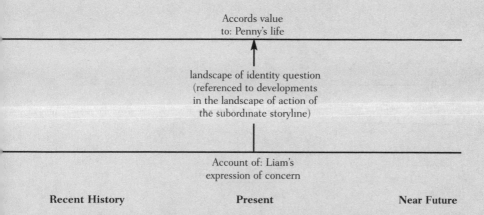

Accords value
to: Penny's life

landscape of identity question
(referenced to developments
in the landscape of action of
the subordinate storyline)

Account of: Liam's
expression of concern

**Recent History**          **Present**          **Near Future**

**M:** (*Figure 2.2*) **Are there any stories that you can tell me about Liam's actions that would be a reflection of what was precious to him? Of what he held precious? Are there any stories you can tell me about him that would help me to understand how you knew this about him?**

Penny asserted that Liam's expression of concern reflected the high value that he gave to her life—that he held her precious. This account of what Liam gave value to can be considered a conclusion about identity. In response to this, I asked Penny for a story about Liam's actions that would reflect this conclusion. This was a landscape of action question, as it triggered an account of specific events of Liam's history that exemplified this conclusion about what he gave value to.

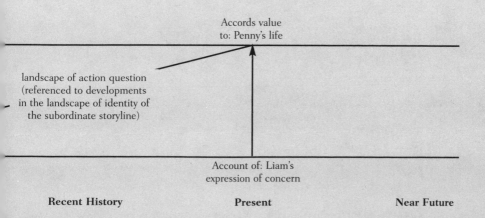

Accords value
to: Penny's life

landscape of action question
(referenced to developments
in the landscape of identity of
the subordinate storyline)

Account of: Liam's
expression of concern

**Recent History**          **Present**          **Near Future**

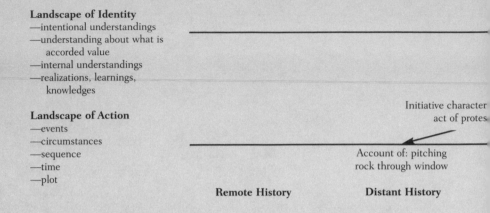

Figure 2.3 Charting Re-Authoring Conversations (Liam)

M: (*Figure 2.3*) **Penny, what sort of step was it that Liam took on that Sunday all of those years ago? How would you name this action of Liam's?**

Upon hearing the story about Liam's distracting his father by pitching a rock through the window, I asked Penny about what sort of name she would give to this action. Although this event was available to her conscious memory, it hadn't been characterized. My question was the first of several that provided the context for the naming of this action as "protest." This was a landscape of action question about the depiction of a neglected but significant event of Penny and Liam's history.

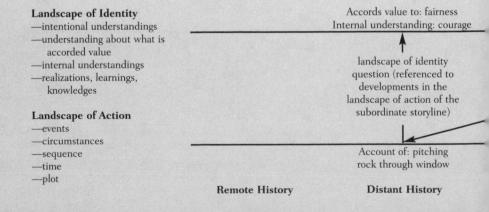

Figure 2.4 Charting Re-Authoring Conversations (Liam)

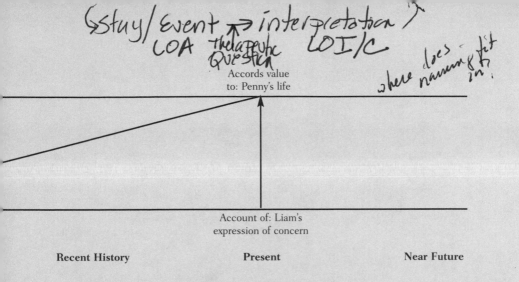

Handwritten annotations: story/event → interpretation ↗ / COA therapeutic question LOI/c / where does naming fit in? / Accords value to: Penny's life

Account of: Liam's expression of concern

Recent History          Present          Near Future

**M: (*Figure 2.4*) Penny, you witnessed Liam protesting what you were being subject to when he was just 8 years old. What did this suggest to you about him? What's your guess about what this reflects in terms of what Liam values?**

Seven years after the event itself, Liam's act of pitching a rock through the window is defined as "protest." Penny led the way with this naming, and at this time Liam was unable to relate to the meaning that she gave to his action. The question about what this action may have reflected about his personhood and about what he valued was one of several landscape of identity questions that provided a foundation for the verification of his bravery and for the voicing of a conclusion about the importance of fairness to Liam.

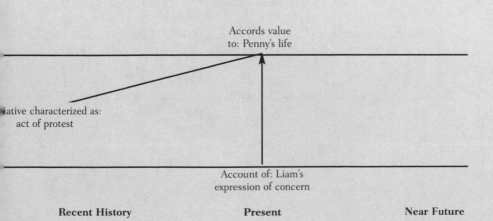

Accords value to: Penny's life

...iative characterized as: act of protest

Account of: Liam's expression of concern

Recent History          Present          Near Future

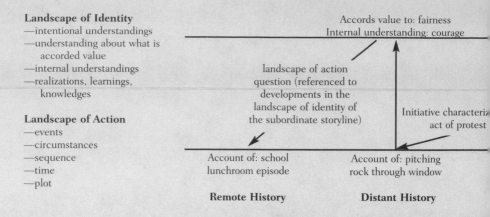

Figure 2.5 Charting Re-Authoring Conversations (Liam)

**Landscape of Identity**
—intentional understandings
—understanding about what is
   accorded value
—internal understandings
—realizations, learnings,
   knowledges

**Landscape of Action**
—events
—circumstances
—sequence
—time
—plot

Accords value to: fairness
Internal understanding: courage

landscape of action
question (referenced to
developments in the
landscape of identity of
the subordinate storyline)

Initiative characteriz
act of protest

Account of: school
lunchroom episode

Account of: pitching
rock through window

**Remote History**

**Distant History**

**M:** (*Figure 2.5*) **Is there anything that you could tell me about Liam, when he was younger still, that would have confirmed what you knew about him? That would fit with what you understood about how important fairness was to him?**

Liam was now more engaged in the development of the subordinate storyline of his life. This was reflected in his willingness to entertain an understanding of how his mother reached these conclusions about his bravery and about the value that he gave to fairness. This question about events in his younger life that might bear out his mother's knowledge about his bravery and his valuing of fairness was a landscape of action question that aroused, in Penny's memory, the story of the school lunchroom.

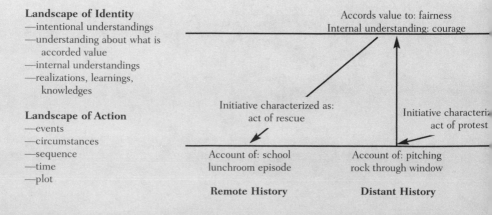

Figure 2.6 Charting Re-Authoring Conversations (Liam)

**Landscape of Identity**
—intentional understandings
—understanding about what is
   accorded value
—internal understandings
—realizations, learnings,
   knowledges

**Landscape of Action**
—events
—circumstances
—sequence
—time
—plot

Accords value to: fairness
Internal understanding: courage

Initiative characterized as:
act of rescue

Initiative characteriz
act of protest

Account of: school
lunchroom episode

Account of: pitching
rock through window

**Remote History**

**Distant History**

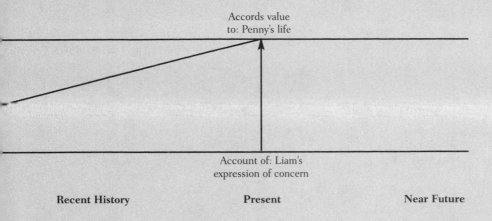

Accords value
to: Penny's life

Account of: Liam's
expression of concern

**Recent History**          **Present**          **Near Future**

**M: (*Figure 2.6*) What sort of step was this? You told me that you thought Liam felt paralyzed in life. It doesn't sound like this fits with paralysis, or with being messed up.**

This was a landscape of action question. Penny responded to it by defining Liam's support of other children as acts of "rescue." Liam was now participating more actively in the development of the subordinate storyline, on this occasion more immediately relating to this naming of his 6-year-old actions.

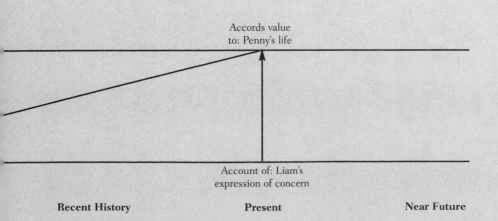

Accords value
to: Penny's life

Account of: Liam's
expression of concern

**Recent History**          **Present**          **Near Future**

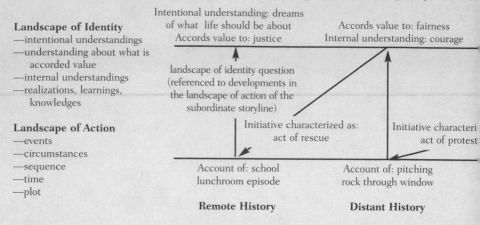

Figure 2.7 Charting Re-Authoring Conversations (Liam)

M: (*Figure 2.7*) **Penny, when I asked you about Liam throwing a rock through the window, about what this said about him, you said that it told you about his courage and about what was important to him in terms of fairness. Thinking back on these events when he was 6 years old, how did this act of rescuing other children shape your picture of him as a person?**

The naming of these 6-year-old actions provided a solid foundation for this question about how this shaped Penny's image of her son. This was a landscape of identity question, and it gave rise to conclusions about Liam's position on justice and his dreams about how life should be. These conclusions were in accord with the emergent storyline and as such were thickening of it. At this point, Liam not only acknowledged that he could relate to these conclusions, but he also actually verified them.

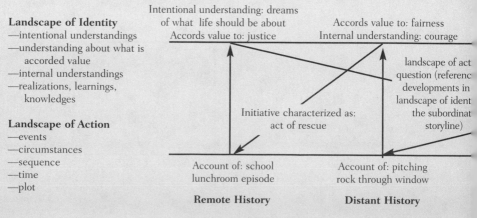

Figure 2.8 Charting Re-Authoring Conversations (Liam)

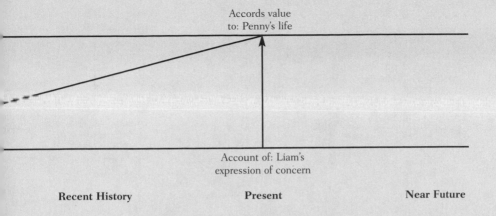

Accords value
to: Penny's life

Account of: Liam's
expression of concern

**Recent History**  **Present**  **Near Future**

**M:** (*Figure 2.8*) **So, the question is: How is it that you are able to relate to what you are hearing? Is there anything that's happened in your life in more recent years that would fit with what we are learning about you? With what I am hearing about where you stand on what is fair and just, with what your mother is telling me about what's important to you, about the dreams of this little boy?**

As Liam had now verified positive conclusions about his identity that were not on his map at the outset of the interview, I sensed that the time was ripe to directly consult him in the further development of the subordinate storyline. This question, which was addressed to Liam, encouraged him to review events in more recent history that might exemplify this conclusion about his position on justice. This was a landscape of action question, and it brought to mind the action he took in talking to his cousin about his history of abuse by his father. This initiative was an expression of his concern for her.

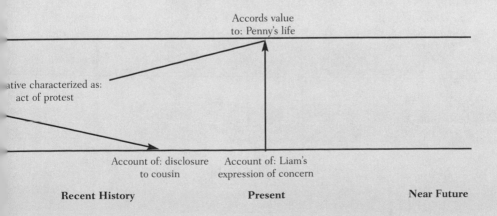

Accords value
to: Penny's life

ative characterized as:
act of protest

Account of: disclosure     Account of: Liam's
to cousin              expression of concern

**Recent History**  **Present**  **Near Future**

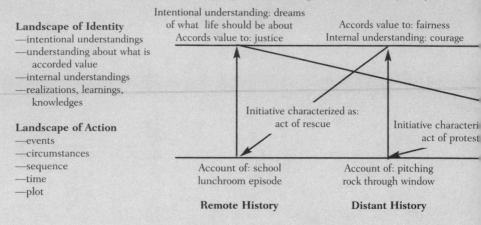

Figure 2.9  Charting Re-Authoring Conversations (Liam)

**M:** (*Figure 2.9*) **Your mum's words were that you "reached out" to your cousin. Would this be a good name for this step, or would some other name fit better?**

Penny had joined Liam in the recounting of the story about the initiative he took with his cousin, and in the context of this she had named it as an act of "reaching out." This question was a landscape of action question that encouraged Liam to participate in this naming.

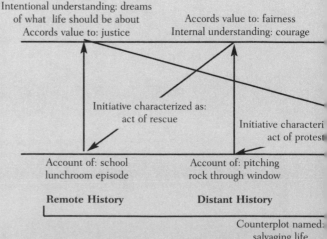

Figure 2.10  Charting Re-Authoring Conversations (Liam)

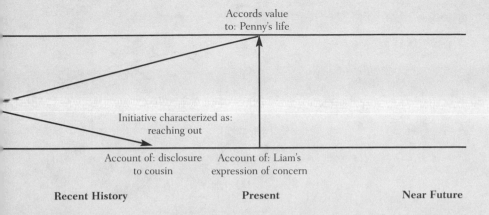

Accords value
to: Penny's life

Initiative characterized as:
reaching out

Account of: disclosure     Account of: Liam's
to cousin                  expression of concern

**Recent History**              **Present**              **Near Future**

**M:** (*Figure 2.10*) **I've learned about actions in rescuing. I've learned about actions that have to do with protest. And I've learned about actions that have to do with reaching out. All of these are part of your history. Putting these actions together, what this all about?**

By this time Penny and Liam had recounted several stories about his actions that were congruent with these positive conclusions about his identity. This question was a landscape of action question that encouraged Penny and Liam to link these stories to a theme and that called for a naming of this theme. The "salvaging life" theme that Liam gave voice to constituted a counterplot, as it contrasted significantly with the plot of the dominant storyline: paralysis in life.

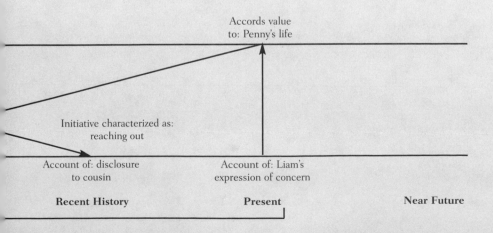

Accords value
to: Penny's life

Initiative characterized as:
reaching out

Account of: disclosure          Account of: Liam's
to cousin                       expression of concern

**Recent History**              **Present**              **Near Future**

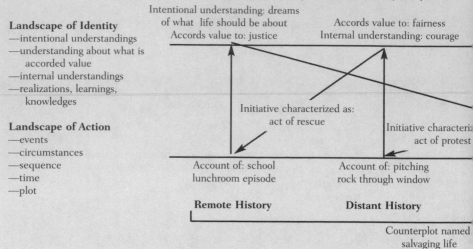

Figure 2.11 Charting Re-Authoring Conversations (Liam)

**Landscape of Identity**
—intentional understandings
—understanding about what is accorded value
—internal understandings
—realizations, learnings, knowledges

**Landscape of Action**
—events
—circumstances
—sequence
—time
—plot

Intentional understanding: dreams of what life should be about
Accords value to: justice

Accords value to: fairness
Internal understanding: courage

Initiative characterized as: act of rescue

Initiative characteri: act of protest

Account of: school lunchroom episode

Account of: pitching rock through window

**Remote History**

**Distant History**

Counterplot named salvaging life

**M: (*Figure 2.11*) Okay. It's about salvaging life. Okay, this says a lot to me. Penny, what's your guess about what this suggests to me about what Liam is aspiring to?**

This was a landscape of identity question that encouraged further reflection on the counterplot of Liam's life in the generation of more of the sort of identity conclusions that were emergent in the subordinate storyline development. The response to this question established that Liam had strong beliefs about what is not okay that he had a knowledge about what makes life worthwhile. This allowed his dreams about what life should be about to become more clearly defined.

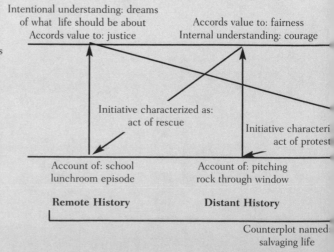

Figure 2.12 Charting Re-Authoring Conversations (Liam)

**Landscape of Identity**
—intentional understandings
—understanding about what is accorded value
—internal understandings
—realizations, learnings, knowledges

**Landscape of Action**
—events
—circumstances
—sequence
—time
—plot

Intentional understanding: dreams of what life should be about
Accords value to: justice

Accords value to: fairness
Internal understanding: courage

Initiative characterized as: act of rescue

Initiative characteri: act of protest

Account of: school lunchroom episode

Account of: pitching rock through window

**Remote History**

**Distant History**

Counterplot named salvaging life

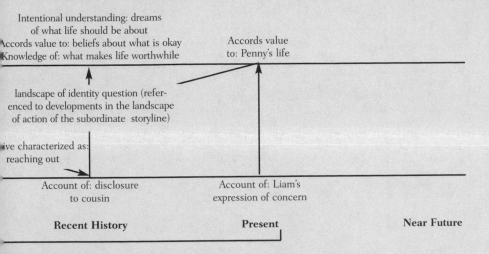

Intentional understanding: dreams
of what life should be about
Accords value to: beliefs about what is okay
Knowledge of: what makes life worthwhile

Accords value
to: Penny's life

landscape of identity question (referenced to developments in the landscape
of action of the subordinate storyline)

...ive characterized as:
reaching out

Account of: disclosure
to cousin

Account of: Liam's
expression of concern

**Recent History**       **Present**       **Near Future**

**M: (*Figure 2.12*) That fits too. I have a question. The things that we've been
learning about you, about what's important to you, about what you've held
onto despite what you've been through, about dreams about what life should
all be about, about how this is all about salvaging life. If you were able to keep
this knowledge about your life close to you, to draw support from this, what's
your guess about what this would make possible for you? What is your guess
about what this would make possible for you to do? What steps could you
take that would fit with this?**

In this question I summarized the identity conclusions that had been named in
the course of our conversation, and I invited Liam and Penny to speculate about
possibilities for action in his life that would be in harmony with these conclusions.
This was a landscape of action question that encouraged the sketching of the subordinate storyline into the near future. In response to this, Liam embraced a proposal to contact Daniel, an old school friend whom he'd not seen for 18 months.

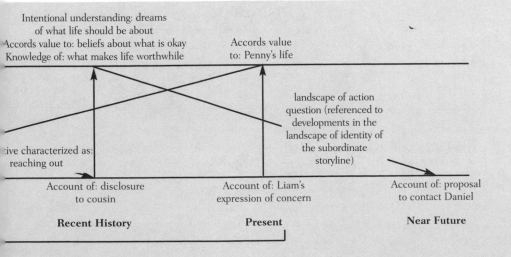

Intentional understanding: dreams
of what life should be about
Accords value to: beliefs about what is okay
Knowledge of: what makes life worthwhile

Accords value
to: Penny's life

landscape of action
question (referenced to
developments in the
landscape of identity of
the subordinate
storyline)

...ive characterized as:
reaching out

Account of: disclosure
to cousin

Account of: Liam's
expression of concern

Account of: proposal
to contact Daniel

**Recent History**       **Present**       **Near Future**

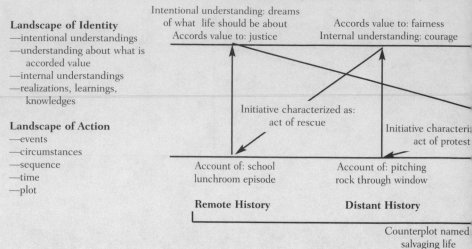

Figure 2.13  Charting Re-Authoring Conversations (Liam)

**M: (*Figure 2.13*) What sort of step would this be if you took it? Would you say it was a step in rescuing, protesting, or reaching out? Or something else?**

This was a landscape of action question that invited Liam to name the step that Penny had proposed and that he had embraced. This was distinguished as a further step in reaching out.

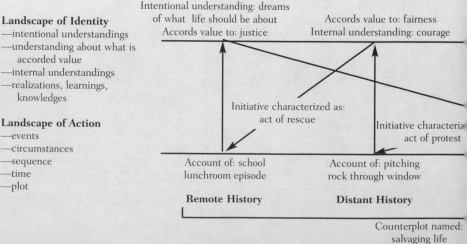

Figure 2.14  Charting Re-Authoring Conversations (Liam)

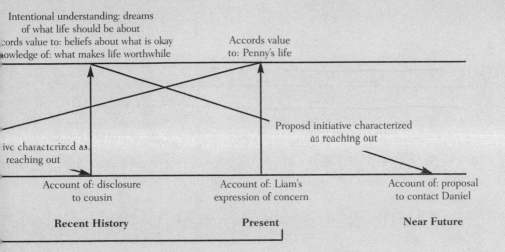

Intentional understanding: dreams
of what life should be about
cords value to: beliefs about what is okay
nowledge of: what makes life worthwhile

Accords value
to: Penny's life

Proposd initiative characterized
as reaching out

ive characterized as:
reaching out

Account of: disclosure
to cousin

Account of: Liam's
expression of concern

Account of: proposal
to contact Daniel

**Recent History**

**Present**

**Near Future**

**M: (*Figure 2.14*) Penny, if you witnessed Liam taking this step to contact Daniel, what would this suggest to you about his purposes in doing this?**

This was landscape of identity question that invited reflection on the reaching-out initiative that had been proposed. This question engaged Penny in the generation of more of the sort of positive identity conclusions that characterized the subordinate storyline.

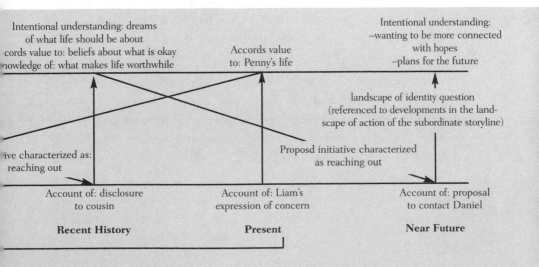

Intentional understanding: dreams
of what life should be about
cords value to: beliefs about what is okay
nowledge of: what makes life worthwhile

Accords value
to: Penny's life

Intentional understanding:
–wanting to be more connected
with hopes
–plans for the future

landscape of identity question
(referenced to developments in the landscape of action of the subordinate storyline)

Proposd initiative characterized
as reaching out

ive characterized as:
reaching out

Account of: disclosure
to cousin

Account of: Liam's
expression of concern

Account of: proposal
to contact Daniel

**Recent History**

**Present**

**Near Future**

This zigzagging movement through time is characteristic of re-authoring conversations. In the context of this movement, subordinate storylines become deeply rooted in history and are thickened.

There is a regularity in this example that is not found in all re-authoring conversations; landscape of action and landscape of identity questions do not always follow each other in such an orderly fashion. There were many other options for rich story development in this conversation with Liam and Penny, and I believe that at various points it would have been equally viable for me to ask a series of landscape of action questions before another landscape of identity question. For example, I might have asked more questions about precursors to the rock-throwing incident that might have provided an account of the foundations of this action. Perhaps this would have provided another route to the story of the school lunchroom. I might have also initiated an inquiry into the specific links between the lunchroom, rock-throwing, and reaching-out incidents—for example, about how each incident was linked to and might have led to the next—before introducing further landscape of identity questions.

These considerations about some of the other options for rich story development underscore the fact that the options I chose were not *the* correct options, but rather just the ones that seemed most available at the time of this conversation. I did not prepare any of my questions in advance; these questions were responses to Penny and Liam's responses. Had I met with Liam and Penny on a different day, the circumstances would not have been identical, and I have no doubt that the route taken in our conversation would have been different.

Regardless of the route taken, the re-authoring conversations map can be a very helpful guide in the journey of therapeutic conversations, leading to destinations wherein subordinate storylines are richly drawn. For Liam, this provided a foundation of knowledge upon which he could proceed with his life. Liam was now in a position to speculate about actions that he might take that would be in harmony with new theme and identity conclusions and that would be congruent with what he gives value to.

Although I have continued to employ the term *subordinate storyline* in the context of this discussion, as our conversations continued over several meetings it was clearly apparent that a shift had occurred in this subordinate status. What had previously been a subordinate story-line began to overshadow the initially dominant account of Liam's life.

## The Benefits and Purpose of Landscape of Identity Questions

As the subordinate storyline in my therapeutic conversation with Liam and Penny was developed, the landscapes of action and identity supporting it were more richly drawn. With regard to the landscape of action, this was achieved by encouraging Liam and Penny to bring together specific events of his life into a sequence that unfolded across time according to a valued theme. With regard to the landscape of identity, this was achieved by inviting Liam and Penny to be witness to these events, to reflect on them, and to give voice to understandings about Liam's life and identity that were derived from this reflection. In this way, the landscape of identity questions I introduced sparked a heightened state of mental activity in Liam and Penny. Among other things, these landscape of identity questions encouraged:

- Reflections that were expressions of subjectivity (what Liam and Penny thought of these events), of attitude (what Liam and Penny felt about these events), of knowledge (what Liam and Penny learned as an outcome of this reflection), of appearance (what Liam and Penny thought these events showed about each other's lives), and of supposition (what Liam and Penny foresaw with regard to the future)*

---

* These terms describe specific transformations of actions in literary-text storylines. These actions occur in the landscape of consciousness. These transformations, defined by Todorov (1977), describe states of mental activity of protagonists, which, according to Bruner (1986, p. 30), "thicken the connective web that holds a narrative together in its depiction of both action and consciousness." In the context of therapeutic practice, questions about what people think of particular events ("subjectivity"), about how they feel about particular events ("attitude"), about what they are learning as they reflect on these events ("knowledge"), about what these events show about each other's lives ("appearance"), and about what these events foretell ("supposition") encourage landscape of identity development and a thickening of the subordinate storyline.

- The derivation of intentional understandings (of a range of purposes, goals, plans, aspirations, hopes, and so on) and of understandings that were centred on considerations of value (of belief, principle, conviction, faith, and so on)
- An account of the manner of engagement with these intentional understandings and with these considerations of value (Penny, and, at a later stage, Liam as well, expressed enthusiasm for some of the intentions reflected in his actions, and they were passionate about the values expressed in this)

Another characteristic of landscape of identity questions is the use of the subjunctive stance (Todorov, 1977). This stance is characterized by terms like *as if, perhaps, maybe, might be, possibly,* and so on. For example: "What conclusions *could be* arrived at in relation to this?" "What are some of the *possible* understandings of this event?" "What *might* this say about what it important to you?" In my conversation with Liam and Penny, this subjunctive stance displaced the mood of certainty and inevitability that was a pervasive feature of the accounts of life that were given by them at the outset of our conversation. I believe that the subjunctive stance of this inquiry had the effect of loosening the interpretive process in Liam and Penny's minds.

Of all the responses that are invoked by landscape of identity questions, it is the intentional understandings and understandings that are centred on considerations of value that are the most significant with regard to rich story development. In the following section I refer to these together as "intentional state understandings" (following Bruner) and contrast them with the "internal state understandings" about human action that are more routinely part of contemporary life.

## Intentional State Understandings Versus Internal State Understandings

In my conversation with Liam and Penny, my landscape of identity questions initially gave rise to internal state understandings of his actions. These internal state understandings featured conclusions about his "bravery," his "strengths," and his "needs." In these understandings, Liam's actions were interpreted as surface manifestations of specific elements or essences that were considered to be the bedrock of his identity—to be emanating from the center of a "self."

However, further questions gave rise to intentional state understandings. Liam's actions were increasingly understood to be shaped by a raft of purposes, values, beliefs, aspirations, hopes, goals, and commitments. These understandings of his actions were not referenced to any concept of an essential self, but instead provided an account of what he was actively and willfully engaging with and embracing in his acts of living. Rather than representing his actions as essences of his identity, these intentional understandings relate to broader considerations of life. The intentional understandings arrived at in these conversations were in harmony with particular themes of life to which Liam and Penny attributed overriding importance. It is these intentional understandings, and understandings that are centred on what people give value to, that are highly significant in rich storyline development.

## Internal State Understandings

Internal state understandings portray human action as a surface manifestation of specific elements or essences of a self that is to be "found" at the center of identity. For example, in the context of internal state understandings, human expression might be interpreted as a manifestation of any number of unconscious motives, instincts, needs, desires, drives, dispositions, personality traits, personal properties (like strengths and resources), and so on. According to this tradition of understanding, these elements or essences are universally present to different degrees in the human condition, and life is derived from either the direct expression of these elements or essences or from distortions of these elements and essences. Such distortions are often called "dysfunctions" or "disorders."

These internal state understandings are often associated with ideas about intrapsychic processes that construct an account of the mechanisms by which the elements and essences of the self are transformed into human expression. At the turn of the 20th century, these conceptions of internal states and intrapsychic mechanisms gave rise to a specific concept of the "unconscious mind." This achievement represented the culmination of a number of "modern" and interlinked developments of the preceding century or two, which included:

- The development of humanist notions of the presence of a human "nature" that is considered to be the foundation of personal existence and that is understood to provide the source of human expression.
- The evolution of the concept of a "self" as an essence that is understood to occupy the center of personal identity. Although this idea of a self is a relatively novel idea in the history of the world's cultures, it has been a hugely successful idea and is today quite taken for granted in the West.
- The progressive development, from the 17th century on, of a new system of social control in which "normalizing judgment" steadily displaced moral judgment.*

Over the past century, these internal state understandings of human expression have become pervasive in Western culture—so much so that internal state understanding have achieved a taken-for-granted status in much of the professional and popular psychology of this current era. It is now routinely believed that these elements and essences of the self are ever-present in people's lives, to be discovered

---

* Michel Foucault, a historian of systems of thought, provided an account of the rise of "modern power" over the past several centuries. He asserted that this has become a principal system of social control in contemporary Western culture. This system of social control incites people to enact "normalizing judgment" on themselves and on others in an effort to reproduce specific norms about life and identity. In other words, *people* become accomplices to a system of social control in which they exercise and act upon judgments about life according to established norms about behavior and identity. According to Foucault, these norms have been principally constructed by the professional disciplines (law, medicine, psychology, and so on). This system of social control has significantly displaced a system of social control that subjects people to moral judgment by representatives of state institutions.

and revealed in the context of personal development and in the context of addressing the problems of living.

## Intentional State Understandings

In contrast to internal state conceptions, intentional state conceptions of identity are distinguished by the notion of "personal agency." This notion casts people as active mediators and negotiators of life's meanings and predicaments, both individually and in collaboration with others. It also casts people as the originators of many of the preferred developments of their own lives: People are living out their lives according to intentions that they embrace in the pursuit of what they give value to in life; they are going about the business of actively shaping their existence in their effort to achieve sought-after goals.

*Are not both true?*

According to Bruner (1990), the significance that is assigned to notions of intention and purpose, the weight that is given to notions of values, beliefs, and commitments, and the emphasis that is given to personal agency constitute a theory of mind that is characteristic of a centuries-old tradition of folk psychology:

> All cultures have as one of their most powerful constitutive instruments a folk psychology, a set of more or less connected, more or less normative descriptions about how human beings "tick," what our own and other minds are like, what one can expect situated action to be like, what are possible modes of life, how one commits oneself to them, and so on. . . . Coined in derision by the new cognitive scientists for its hospitality toward such intentional states as beliefs, desires, and meanings, the expression of "folk psychology" could not be more appropriate. (pp. 35–36)

According to this definition, people routinely employ folk psychology in making their way through everyday life. People put the intentional state notions of folk psychology into service in their effort to understand their own lives and make sense of the actions of others. The intentional state notions of folk psychology equip people with a range of notions about what makes people "tick" and provides a foundation for their responses to the actions of others.

The intentional state notions of folk psychology also come to the fore in people's efforts to make out just what it is that is going on in the world more generally. Bruner (1990) illustrated the way that these intentional state understandings shape people's endeavour to come to terms with the unexpected in life, provide a basis for their effort to address obstacles and crises, and make it possible for them to come to terms with a range of predicaments and dilemmas that confront them in everyday life.

Bruner traced the history of the displacement, in professional and popular psychology, of these intentional state understandings about life and identity through the end of the 18th century and the beginning of the 19th century. In this development, the mind of folk psychology significantly gave way to the "unconscious mind" of the internal state psychologies.

In drawing this distinction between internal state understandings and intentional state understandings, and in privileging the development of intentional state understandings in re-authoring conversations, I am not dismissing internal understandings of life and identity. There are many cherished internal understandings of life that are quite beautiful and that can be seen to have positive consequences. In the context of therapeutic conversations, these understandings can be honored.

However, these internal understandings are unlikely to yield the sort of rich story development that is routinely an outcome of the generation of intentional state understandings. This is because internal understandings tend to:

- Diminish the sense of personal agency (according to internal understandings, people's lives are lived by the elements and essences of the self, not shaped by actions taken under the influence of the intentions and values that one is embracing)

- Be isolating (according to internal understandings, human expression is conceived as one of a singular self, not as an expression of life that is the outcome of the story of one's life being linked with stories of the lives of others around shared and valued themes)
- Discourage diversity (internal understandings are shaped by global norms about life that promote a modern ideal of the "encapsulated self"—one that valorizes notions of self-possession, self-containment, self-reliance, and self-actualization)

Re-authoring conversations usually exhibit a drift toward the generation of identity conclusions associated with intentional state understandings, irregardless of the starting conditions. In my re-authoring conversation with Liam and his mother, this drift was accentuated by the shape of my questions, which were biased toward soliciting the more intentional understandings of Liam's actions: "What did this suggest to you about what was important to Liam? Or about what was precious to him?" "What's your guess about what this reflects in terms of what Liam values?" "Thinking back on these events when he was 6 years old, how did this act of rescuing other children shape your picture of him as a person?" "Penny, what's your guess about what this suggests to me about what Liam is aspiring to?" "Penny, if you witnessed Liam taking this step to contact Daniel, what would this suggest to you about his purposes in doing this?" "What do you think this would reflect about your plans for your future?"

To reiterate, this bias toward intentional state conclusions should not suggest that internal state conclusions are wrong or invariably unhelpful. The internal state conclusions that were generated in the earlier part of my conversations with Liam were positive and validating of him. However, it was the intentional state understandings that significantly contributed to a foundation for:

- The development of a sense of his life being joined with the lives of others around shared themes, which was an anathema to his prevailing sense of isolation

- An experience of being knowledged about his own life, which was an anathema to his sense of being totally lost when it came to matters of living
- The expression of emotional responses to some of the neglected but significant events of his life, which was an anathema to the flatness of affect that was characteristic of his existence
- Speculation about how his life and his identity might appear to others, which was an anathema to his sense of invisibility
- Supposition that included speculation about actions that might be available to him and that would be harmony with what he gave value to, which was an anathema to his sense of hopelessness and futility
- The expression of his manner of engagement with these intentions and values, which was an anathema to his sense of despondency

Apart from this, the intentional state understandings that were generated in our conversation provided Liam with a sense of personal agency, which was an anathema to his prevailing sense of paralysis. They also provided a foundation for the expansion of a preferred sense of identity that was continuous through his past, present, and future, which was an anathema to his conclusions about being messed up and damaged.

## Landscape of Identity: Filing Cabinets of the Mind

Readers might find it helpful to conceive of the landscape of identity as being composed of "filing cabinets of the mind," each one representing a category of identity that is culturally relevant. In Western culture, this would include internal state categories like unconscious needs, instincts, desires, drives, dispositions, personality traits, personal properties, and so on, as well as intentional state categories like purposes, aspirations, quests, hopes, dreams, visions, values, beliefs,

and commitments. It is into these filing cabinets of the mind that people file a range of conclusions about their own and each other's identities. These identity conclusions determine what significance is given
to specific events of people's lives, and they are further developed
through reflection on these events and on the themes that these
events are part of. All of these conclusions, including those of the
internal state categories, significantly influence people's actions; they
are shaping of life. Put another way, it is not actually "things" like
motives and needs that shape life, but socially constructed conclusions about these things.

Re-authoring conversations provide the context for the generation
of many identity conclusions that contradict those associated with the
dominant storylines of people's lives. As these conclusions are entered
into "the filing cabinets of the mind," they deprive the dominant identity conclusions of the space that they previously occupied and of the
influence that they have had in shaping people's existence.

## Further Illustrations

Following are two additional accounts of re-authoring conversations. I
have not, however, provided a narrative commentary on them. Rather,
their inclusion is meant to give readers an opportunity to undertake
their own narrative analysis of these therapeutic conversations, and
then to refer to my charting of them.

### Vivienne

Vivienne, a woman in her early forties, had been referred to me by her
general practitioner. This was one of the few referrals that Vivienne
had followed through on in recent years, and it had been quite an anx-
iety-provoking step for her to take. She had invited her partner, Adel,
to join her for moral support. At the outset of our first meeting,
Vivienne informed me that she was a "long-term sufferer of agoraphobia" and that on account of this she had led a very restricted life. She
had also "endured a struggle with eating disorders for 18 years," chiefly
with anorexia nervosa and bulimia. I learned that Vivienne had been

resigned to living a highly circumscribed life, but that recently, with her partner's encouragement, had decided to embark on renewed efforts "to get her life free" of the forces that "had for so long blighted it."

By the time of our third interview, Vivienne had developed some familiarity with aspects of her life that had previously been invisible to her. Among other things, she had begun to speak of purposes for her life that contradicted those associated with a reclusive existence, personal tastes that contradicted austerity, and desires that were quite discordant with desires incited by anorexia nervosa. It was on this basis that Vivienne had formulated a relatively bold plan. She had decided to initiate contact with some relatives with whom she'd had little to do through her adult life—two aunts, an uncle, and a cousin—and to invite them to join her and her partner for a picnic. Vivienne had chosen these relatives because she had fond memories of her relationship with them in her childhood.

Vivienne had decided on a picnic for three reasons. First, she had warm memories of picnics as a child. Second, this would be in an open space and in defiance of the lifestyle that she'd been restricted to by her agoraphobia. Third, the idea of a picnic was linked to a plan to publicly take sustenance—Vivienne had not consumed food publicly for over 10 years. It was her hope that the nature of the event, a picnic, and the presence of these relatives would contribute to new impetus to recover her life from agoraphobia and anorexia nervosa. However, she was highly apprehensive about this proposed action and was not at all sure that she would be able to follow through with it.

At the fourth interview, 3 weeks later, I learned that Vivienne had followed through on her plan. The picnic had gone ahead, minus the presence of her cousin, who had been away on vacation. Vivienne announced that she'd not fled the open environment and had succeeded in consuming some food. Not only this, but at the end of this event she had announced that this had been the first occasion in which she had publicly taken sustenance in 10 years, that she had carefully chosen the company that she wished to be in for this step, and that she knew that this would be conducive to her success. Her aunts and uncle had spoken of the sense of honor they experienced in being selected for this and about the pleasure they had taken in being present.

Although this had clearly been an achievement in Vivienne's mind, I was concerned that this might not be sustained against all of the forces that had been so containing of her life. So I began to interview her about this initiative with the hope that it might become even more weighty and be taken into the further development of the subordinate storyline of her life.

M: This was quite some picnic! Vivienne, I think I've got a good understanding of the significance of this achievement. Do you have a name for this step that would give it the recognition it deserves?

Vivienne: I don't think so. I haven't really thought about this. I don't know what name would work.

M: I guess it wouldn't be a name that fits with what's been happening around all of that self-doubt? With what you described as "losing your life"?

Vivienne: No, no. Not in any way. I would say that this was more about self-belief.

M: Self-belief! Do you have any thoughts about what this act of self-belief made possible for you?

Vivienne: What do you mean?

M: Do you have any sense of how this act of self-belief affected your life? Maybe in terms of how you felt about yourself? Maybe in terms of new realizations about your life? In terms of your connection with your aunts and uncle? Anything at all.

Vivienne: Well, I do know one thing, and that is that it brought me closer to my aunts and my uncle. I definitely feel reconnected to my two aunts and my uncle. They were so lovely. Yeah. It brought me closer to them, and closer to Adel too.

M: Part of the outcome of this act of self-belief is that it reconnected you to people who are important to you. How do you feel about this sort of development?

**Vivienne:** The only thing I can say is that I'm happy about it, of course.

**M:** Could you say a little about why you are happy about this? Anything at all that would help me understand why this is important to you?

**Vivienne:** This might sound a bit strange to you, especially since I have been so disconnected for such a long time. But I really believe that I am a people person, I really am.

**M:** A people person. Tell me, what sort of things are important to a people person?

**Vivienne:** Well, let's, see . . .

My questions engaged Vivienne in loading with significance the action she'd taken in organizing the picnic and following through on her plan. However, I predicted that the status of these steps would be tenuous if they were not taken into a storyline of her life. For example, the step could be judged to be a "one-off" initiative, perhaps fortuitous or born of chance, or the outcome of unusual circumstances.

This tenuous status renders such steps vulnerable and unlikely to provide the foundation of enduring change. Therefore, I began to ask some questions to encourage Vivienne to take these steps into a storyline of her life. Initially these were very straightforward landscape of action questions that encouraged her to bring forth the recent history of this act of self-belief: "Do you have any idea of what you might have done to pave the way for this act of self-belief?" "Perhaps you might be able to think of something that helped you to prepare the ground for this?" "Would you reflect on events leading up to this step and talk about any that might have been implicated in this?"

Suddenly we were in a conversation about the events and circumstances leading up to the picnic, and this included the steps that Vivienne had taken to keep her anxiety at bay before calling her relatives about the picnic invitation. This review of the recent history of these steps also contributed to a dramatic rendering of the events of the picnic itself, including the moments of crisis that Vivienne went through in the act of joining others in eating and the action that she took to address these moments of crisis. As these steps were being taken into a sequence of events unfolding through time, I asked Vivienne what name she would give to this development in her life: "I am getting a clearer picture of what led up to this act of self-belief. What are your thoughts about what would be a good overall name for this development? If these steps are part of a course in your life, what would you call this course?" In response to these questions, Vivienne concluded that this was about "reclaiming my life."

At the next meeting our conversations again turned to the events of the picnic, and the time seemed ripe to extend our re-authoring conversation:

> **M:** Vivienne, I had some questions about what these developments in reclaiming your life might say about who you are as a person.
>
> **Vivienne:** Well . . . I don't know. I really don't think that I've got an answer to that.
>
> **M:** Perhaps I could ask Adel.
>
> **Vivienne:** Okay, that's fine.
>
> **M:** Adel, I would be interested to have your reflections on the picnic event. You might have some thoughts about what Vivienne was drawing upon in taking these steps. Or maybe some thoughts about what sustained her in following through on this. Or you might have some ideas about what this could say about what is important to Vivienne. Anything like this.
>
> **Adel:** Yeah, actually, I've got quite a few ideas about this. But what comes to me first is that this says a lot about Vivienne's perseverance and willpower.

**M:** Perseverance and willpower. Vivienne, can you relate to Adel's thoughts on this?

**Vivienne:** Well, I guess so. But these wouldn't be my words.

**M:** Do you have some other words?

**Vivienne:** I can't think of any. But I guess I can connect to what Adel is saying.

**M:** Okay. Perseverance and willpower aren't your words, but you can connect to them.

**Vivienne:** Yeah.

**M:** I'm curious about how it is that you can connect to these words. Have you witnessed anything else happening in your life in recent times that might also be a reflection of perseverance and willpower?

**Vivienne:** Well . . . I'm trying to think of . . . maybe . . . .No, that's not an example.

**Adel:** I can think of something. The weekend before last we were talking about what we would do on Saturday afternoon. Michael, we nearly always spend Saturday afternoon together, just the two of us. It's our time. Anyway, I was talking about some gardening that needed to be done, and I remember Vivienne saying something like: "Yes, that is a good idea, but I am a different person, and I have some other ideas." (*turning to Vivienne*) And I don't recall you ever saying anything like that before.

**Vivienne:** No, I haven't. I'm sure I haven't. I mean I am sure I haven't said anything like that before.

**M:** This fits with what Adel was saying about perseverance and willpower?

**Vivienne:** I think it must.

**M:** I wonder what else this "I'm a different person, and I have other ideas" says about you, or about your relationship with Adel. Do you have any thoughts about this? About what this could reflect about what's important to you? Or about your relationship with Adel?

**Vivienne:** I guess . . . yeah, I guess that it maybe says that I am valuing myself a bit. Or beginning to at least. Perhaps that I'm not just totally nowhere.

**M:** You gave your opinion, so . . .

**Vivienne:** So maybe I am valuing my opinions more, that my opinion is worth something at least.

**M:** Like you have a . . .

**Vivienne:** Like I have a mind of my own, and I am valuing this more.

**M:** Adel?

**Adel:** I agree with this. It has to be about Vivienne valuing her opinions more, about valuing her own mind. I think it is also about where we have got to in our relationship.

**M:** In what sense?

**Adel:** The trust, I mean. That Vivienne could trust that she could say this to me.

**M:** So it's also a reflection of trust in your relationship. Of a relationship of trust?

**Vivienne:** Yeah, that's true.

**M:** And trust has always been . . .

**Vivienne:** I honestly can't think of anything that is more important to me.

**M:** Apart from Adel, can you think of anyone else who has recognized this perseverance and willpower in you? Or who has appreciated you valuing your opinions and your mind? Or who would be aware of the importance of trust to you?

**Vivienne:** Helen would have. (*Helen was Vivienne's older sister by 4 years. She committed suicide when she was 16 years old. Until that time, she'd done what she could to protect Vivienne from the abuses that she herself was also being subjected to.*)

**Adel:** Yeah, Helen for sure. From what I know about her at least.

**M:** Would it be okay if I asked some questions about Helen, and maybe about your relationship with Helen? (*I had already learned a little about Helen in my second meeting with Vivienne and Adel.*)

**Vivienne:** This used to be hard for me to talk about, and it might still be. But right now I think it would be okay. No, right now I'd welcome it even if it is hard.

**M:** If Helen could be here and part of this conversation, and if I asked her to tell me a story about you when you were little, a story about your perseverance and willpower, or about you valuing your opinions, or about the importance of trust to you, what do you reckon we would be hearing?

**Vivienne:** Helen really looked out for me, and she would probably tell lots of stories.

**M:** Which one is most present in your mind right now?

**Vivienne:** She'd probably tell you about some of the trouble I got into at school. I remember that everything was just too much for me and I wasn't really coping with anything. All it took to send me over the top was a mean schoolteacher, and I had this really mean teacher in seventh grade, and one day I just lost it. I went totally wild, and I can't even remember much about what I did, except that I just tore everything up and wrecked the classroom. But I do remember that I got sent to the principal and had to stand there for what seemed like hours to think about what I'd said and done and about how I would fix it. But I wouldn't agree that I was the one in the wrong. And then suddenly Helen turned up. How she found out about this I don't know, because the senior school was a whole block away. Anyway, she started going for the principal. You know what I mean. Telling the principal where to go and how to manage his teachers, about what a disgrace his school was, and so on. Then she went to hit him, and wow, before long it was like a riot. I'd joined in too, and there were people everywhere all of a sudden and all sorts of things happening, and it seemed to go on forever. We sure got into a lot of bother over this, from my father as well.

**M:** That's a very moving story.

**Adel:** Yeah. I haven't heard all of these details before.

**Vivienne:** It hasn't been in my mind. Maybe I haven't wanted to think about it because things just went from bad to worse after that.

**M:** What's your guess about what Helen appreciated about you back then?

**Vivienne:** I don't have to guess. I know that she appreciated how determined I was not to give in.

**M:** And about your mind?

**Vivienne:** Yeah. I'm sure she'd say that she appreciated the fact that I had my own mind.

**M:** What do you think this event might have told Helen about what is important to you, or about what you wanted for your life?

**Vivienne:** About what I would have wanted? About what's

important to me? Well, I'm thinking about the trust thing. It was so strongly there between the two of us. And maybe the fact that I wouldn't give in. Helen would say that this meant that I was holding onto some fantasy about what life could be.

**M:** Fantasy? Any other word?

**Vivienne:** Yeah. "Hope" would be better.

**M:** Could I ask some questions about that hope?

**Vivienne:** Sure.

The details about the events surrounding the crisis at school, and about how they might have confirmed some of Helen's conclusions about Vivienne's identity, marked the beginning of a deeply moving re-membering conversation. I will not provide the details of this here, as the subject of re-membering conversations is covered in the next chapter of this book.

At the end of this conversation, I asked Vivienne to speculate about what might be possible for her if what Helen knew about her identity was more available to her to draw on in taking further steps in the reclaiming her life. I also consulted both Vivienne and Adel about

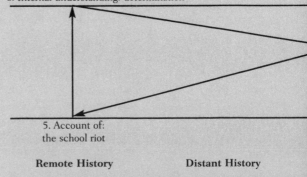

Figure 2.15  Charting Re-Authoring Conversations (Vivienne)

8. Intentional understanding:
   –holding onto a fantasy about life
   –maintaining relationship with hope

**Landscape of Identity**
—intentional understandings
—understanding about what is accorded value
—internal understandings
—realizations, learnings, knowledges

7. Accords value to: one's own mind
6. Internal understanding: determination

**Landscape of Action**
—events
—circumstances
—sequence
—time
—plot

5. Account of:
the school riot

**Remote History**          **Distant History**

what circumstances might be arranged that would be favorable to Vivienne's desire to stay in touch with this knowledge about her identity. In response to these questions, Vivienne named three steps that would be congruent with what Helen knew about her, and they both had some thoughts about what would make it possible for Vivienne to keep this knowledge about her identity close to her in the coming weeks. At the next meeting I learned that Vivienne had taken two of these steps.

Over a period of 18 months we had many more conversations that contributed to the further development of the landscapes of action and identity of the subordinate storyline characterized by the "reclaiming my life" theme. This took in many of Vivienne's initiatives in challenging the restrictions of agoraphobia and the dictates of anorexia nervosa. At the 18-month follow-up I learned that Vivienne had established a life for herself "out there in the world" from which she was drawing pleasure, and although she still struggled at times with insecurity in open spaces and with "discouraging thoughts" about food and weight, they were no longer preoccupying concerns.

Figure 2.15 shows my charting of the re-authoring conversation with Vivienne and Adel. The up arrows indicate landscape of identity questions and the down arrows indicate landscape of action questions.

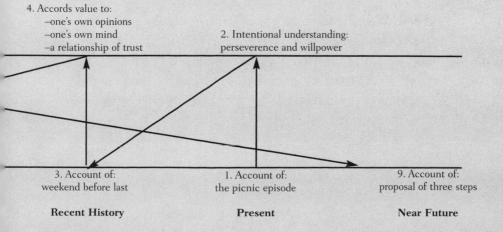

## David

David, age 11, and his parents, Pauline and Fred, were referred by a social service agency that had had extensive involvement with this family. In response to yet another crisis precipitated by David's actions, Pauline and Fred were close to the conclusion that nothing more could be done to resolve this situation, and they were seriously considering "bailing out"—seeking alternative living arrangements for David, away from the family home. Early in our first meeting there was an opportunity to engage in an externalizing conversation about trouble and its effects on the lives and relationships of these family members. In this conversation Pauline and Fred, and then David as well, spoke fully of their experience of this trouble.

Once this externalizing conversation was well established—when "trouble" was not collapsed so solidly onto David's identity—circumstances were right for the identification of some of the events of his life that contradicted trouble's agenda. In response to my questions about this, Fred told me a story about a recent family visit to the beach. Fred had met an old friend there, and they'd been locked in absorbing reminiscences for some time. Toward the end of this exchange, Fred suddenly become aware of the circumstances that had made this possible—he wasn't constantly being called upon to address the trouble that David usually got into on these occasions.

> **M:** Please say a bit more about why you are telling me about this?
>
> **Fred:** Well, I hadn't seen Geoff for nearly 20 years, and he'd been my best friend when I was young. The only reason we got to have such a good talk about old times was that David wasn't so much into trouble. This didn't really occur to me until the end.
>
> **M:** David, do you remember this? This day at the beach?
>
> **David:** Yep.
>
> **M:** So, what was going on for you?

**David:** Dunno.

**M:** What do you think, Fred? What's your guess about what was going on for David?

**Fred:** Well, maybe it was just one of those things that come along once in a while. For some reason David was just getting along with everyone. It just seemed to come out of the blue. But it sure was nice.

**M:** Pauline, what do you think about this?

**Pauline:** I don't know. I wasn't there at the time.

**M:** David, on this day at the beach, were you there for trouble, or were you there for something else?

*David shrugs.*

**M:** (*turning to Fred*) Do you think that David was there for trouble, or do you think that he was there for something else?

**Fred:** Something else, I guess.

**M:** Pauline?

**Pauline:** Yeah. I'd say that. He was there for something else.

**M:** (*referring to understandings derived in the earlier externalizing conversation*) Let's go back to what we figured out about trouble, about what trouble was out for. To wreck friendships with other kids. To paint a negative picture of David in everybody's eyes, and in his own eyes. To build a bad reputation for him that puts everyone off. To create hardship in David's connection with his mum and dad. To demoralize David's father. To . . .

**Fred:** Well, obviously it didn't succeed this time, so that's something. But then, it was only for one day, and then not even a whole day. Just an hour or two.

**M:** However long it was, if David wasn't there for trouble, what was he doing there?

**Fred:** Well, I guess what happened is that David just resisted trouble for a while. He must have resisted the trouble.

**M:** That's your guess. That this was about resistance?

**Fred:** On this occasion I would say so. Yes, I'd say it fits. But I'd sure like to see more of this.

**M:** David, does this fit for you? Were you resisting trouble on that day at the beach?

*David nods yes.*

**M:** Do you know what your father means by using the word *resistance*?

*David shakes his head no.*

**M:** Would you define this for David? Would you spell it out for him?

**Fred:** Well, its like this David . . .

Fred provided David with an account of what he meant by resistance, which included some practical examples of actions that typified this. It became quickly apparent that David was rather taken with this description. I then asked him if he thought that "resisting trouble" was a reasonable characterization of his actions at the beach, and he didn't hesitate in confirming this. This response led us into a conversation about the actual and potential consequences of this expression of resistance in David's life and in his relationship with his parents and others.

As the events of this recent visit to the beach had now been rendered newly significant, I began to ask questions that I hoped would assist David and his parents in taking these events into a storyline:

**M:** I'm curious, David. How did you manage to resist trouble at the beach in the way that you did?

*David shrugs.*

**M:** Can you think of anything that happened before this that could have prepared the way for you to resist trouble? Can you think of anything that might have helped you get ready to resist trouble?

*David shakes his head no.*

**M:** (*turning to Pauline and Fred*) Did you see anything in David's life in the lead-up to this that might have paved the way for him to resist trouble at the beach? Anything that might have given him a foundation for this, that would have helped him to get ready for this?

**Pauline:** Nothing that I can think of. We have had a hell of a rough ride with David, and it has been even worse over the last year or so. We haven't seen any real smooth patches, if that's what you're looking for.

**M:** Fred?

**Fred:** I can't think of anything either. Like I said, it's just one of those things, I guess.

**M:** So neither of you saw anything that could have prepared you for what David did at the beach?

**Pauline:** No, not me.

**Fred:** Nope.

**M:** David, if no one saw anything, could it be that you secretly got ready to resist trouble, and then just surprised everyone with this?

*David shrugs.*

**M:** I am asking you about any secret preparations, because it was a surprise to everyone, wasn't it?

*David now grins and nods yes.*

**M:** What does that nod mean, David?

**David:** It was a secret.

**M:** Well who would have guessed that?!

**Fred:** We should have! (*Pauline laughs.*)

**M:** Okay, David, let us in on the secret. How did you get ready for this? What did you get up to?

**David:** Well, I . . . um . . . I . . . Actually it was on the Sunday before. I'd got into the worst trouble on Saturday, and I'd got up late.

**Pauline:** Yeah, that's right. We'd had the police around and everything. It was terrible!

**M:** Sure doesn't sound good. Back to you, David.

**David:** It was the Sunday, and I'd got up late, see. And I looked in the mirror in the bathroom, and there I was looking back, and I sure didn't look too good. So, I looked down at the sink, and then up at the mirror again, and said to myself: "Son, you've got to do something about this, your life is going down the drain."

*Pauline and Fred look at each other quizzically.*

**M:** And that was the start of it!

**David:** Yep.

**M:** That's something! And how did this prepare you for resisting trouble at the beach?

**David:** Don't know. But it must have.

**M:** (*turning to Pauline and Fred*) What do you think was the link between what David did on that Sunday morning and what he did in resisting trouble at the beach a week later?

In response to this question, Pauline and Fred began to speculate about the possible links between these two events. David subsequently confirmed some of this speculation. It was in this speculation, and in David's confirmation, that his actions in resisting trouble at the beach were taken into a sequence of events unfolding across a week's time. These actions at the beach were no longer singular, but had been incorporated into an emergent storyline. With this development, the time seemed ripe for me to ask David to name the associated theme or plot.

> **M:** All right, we're now all getting a little more clarity on these events in David's life. David, I know that for you the word *resistance* is a good word for what you did at the beach. But is there another word that would be a good word for all of this, from what you did on the Sunday morning right up to resisting trouble at the beach? Maybe there is another word for what you were doing for your own life.
>
> *David shrugs.*
>
> **M:** This wasn't about going along with trouble. It wasn't about going in trouble's direction, was it?
>
> **David:** Nope.
>
> **M:** Well, if it was a different direction, what would be a good name for this direction? Just a guess?
>
> **David:** Um . . . um . . . it's about, I think it's about making a comeback. That's what I'd say.
>
> **M:** Making a comeback from trouble. So that's what it is all about!
>
> **David:** Yeah.
>
> **M:** (*turning to Fred and Pauline*) Did you know this?
>
> **Fred:** Sure didn't.
>
> **Pauline:** Neither did I. This is something that I thought I'd never hear.

**M:** So, it's a surprise, and because of this my next question might be a bit difficult to answer.

**Fred:** Okay. Let's have it.

**M:** What does David's decision to make a comeback say to you about him? Does it affect your picture of him in any way? Or does it suggest something to you about what he really wants for his life?

**Pauline:** It says something to me about his determination, which I know he's always had. He's really a pretty gritty kid. But the difference is that he had this working for him, not so much against him. Yeah. And not so much against us, either.

**M:** What are your thoughts on this, Fred?

**Fred:** Well, I don't know . . . but I'll take a punt on it. It is about David trying for something. I guess trying to make something of his life so that he can get ahead, so that he can have friends, so that he can make something different happen in his life.

**M:** David, how's that? Do you think that your mum and dad are getting this right about your determination working for you, not against you and them? And what do you think of what your father said about making something of your life?

**David:** Yep. That's it.

**M:** What's this like for you? I mean, what's it like for you that your parents are getting things right about you?

*David grins.*

**M:** (*turning to Pauline and Fred*) What is it like for the two of you to find that you are getting some things right about David?

**Pauline:** This is a surprise too. It'd take us a long time to get used to this. But it's good, really good. If only there could be more of it.

**Fred:** Yeah, I'd say that.

**M:** I was just wondering whether the developments we've been talking about are totally new in David's life, or whether they can be traced back to other events.

**Fred:** What are you thinking about?

**M:** Well, I was wondering whether you could tell me any stories from David's younger life that might fit with this determination and this wish to make something of his life. Or perhaps other stories about secret preparations, or perhaps about making an earlier comeback? Anything like this.

**Fred:** Hearing you ask this makes me think of a time when he was just a little kid, 5, maybe, or nearly 6 years old. You'd remember, Pauline. I think it was on a Sunday, around lunchtime. I was cooking lunch, and we heard David calling out for us from the street. He was yelling. I thought, what trouble is he in now? So we ran out there, and what did we see? David was riding this enormous two-wheeler bike up the street, swinging all over the place, looking as dangerous as hell. And then what does he do? He lets go of the handle bars and calls out, "Look, no hands!" We were petrified.

**Pauline:** And we were surprised, too, because we didn't know he could ride a two-wheeler.

**M:** Secret training?

**Pauline:** Yeah, secret training again. And a whole lot of determination for something.

*David was grinning and clearly enjoying the recounting of this story.*

**Fred:** There was something else about that that we won't go into right now.

**M:** What's that?

**Fred:** (*endeavouring to be gracious*) We won't talk about where the bike came from. It wasn't David's, and he didn't have any friends with bikes like this.

*David now looks sheepish but clearly is still delighted with the recounting of this story.*

**M:** David, was it your plan to surprise your parents?

**David:** I think so.

**M:** And do you agree with them that this shows how you can get your determination working for you, and that you can make something of your life?

*David grins and nods.*

**M:** Okay, let me ask you some more questions about what this says about you, and about how you want your life to be. And I'll ask your mum and dad to help out as we go along.

These questions prompted a conversation that gave rise to several more identity conclusions that contradicted those shaped by all of the trouble that had so closely pursued David's life. These conclusions provided a foundation for questions about more stories of David's life that were confirming of them. David also began to initiate some of this storytelling. Before long I was engaging David and his parents in specula-

Figure 2.16  Charting Re-Authoring Conversations (David)

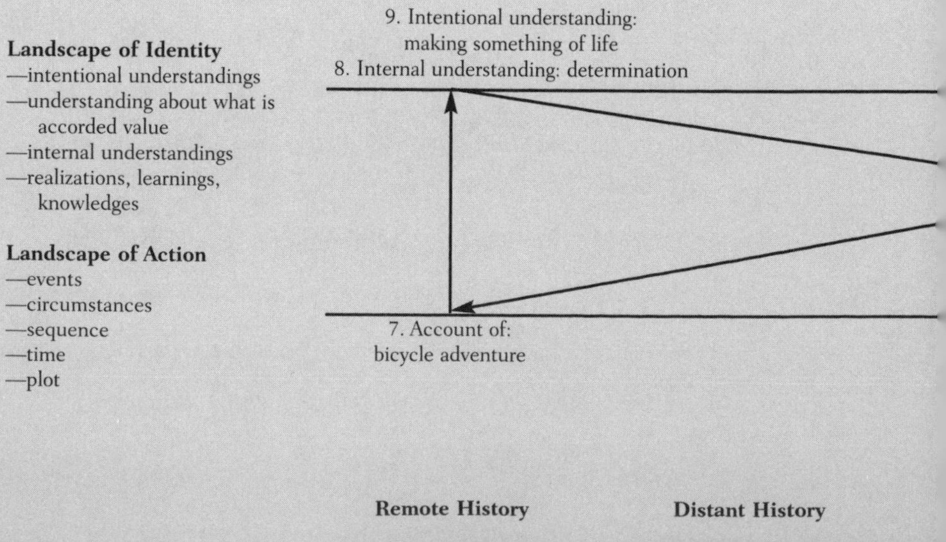

9. Intentional understanding:
making something of life

8. Internal understanding: determination

**Landscape of Identity**
—intentional understandings
—understanding about what is
    accorded value
—internal understandings
—realizations, learnings,
    knowledges

**Landscape of Action**
—events
—circumstances
—sequence
—time
—plot

7. Account of:
bicycle adventure

Remote History                    Distant History

tive conversations about the near future of these developments: "David, if you were going to build on this comeback, if you were going to go further with it after leaving here, what do you reckon your next step could be? And if it is okay with you I will ask your mum and dad to help us out with their ideas. But in the end, it will really be up to you."

With his parent's assistance, David came up with a number of ideas about how to extend his comeback from trouble. He also said that he had some other ideas, but that these were secret. I asked Pauline and Fred for their thoughts about what they might do to provide a good climate for David to get to work on these ideas for extending his comeback from trouble, and then I checked this out with David. I made it clear that I had no expectation whatsoever with regard to David's acting on any of these ideas.

Over a series of meetings, David did extend on these initiatives and succeeded in his comeback from trouble. Along the way, Fred and Pauline took a turn in surprising him—they undertook some quite unexpected and positive actions in ensuring that he had a supportive climate that was favorable to the pursuit of this comeback. At the 6- and 18-month follow-ups, I learned that, apart from a few hiccups, things were working out well for David and his parents.

Figure 2.16 shows my charting of the re-authoring conversation with David and his parents. The up arrows indicate landscape of identity questions and the down and horizontal arrows indicate landscape of action questions.

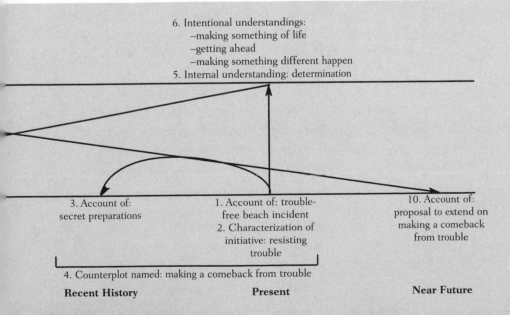

6. Intentional understandings:
   —making something of life
   —getting ahead
   —making something different happen
5. Internal understanding: determination

3. Account of: secret preparations

1. Account of: trouble-free beach incident
2. Characterization of initiative: resisting trouble

10. Account of: proposal to extend on making a comeback from trouble

4. Counterplot named: making a comeback from trouble

**Recent History**            **Present**            **Near Future**

## Conclusion

In this chapter I have presented a re-authoring conversations map of narrative practice. This map is founded upon a text analogy that represents stories as composed of a "landscape of action" and a "landscape of consciousness." This re-authoring conversations map provides therapists with a guide for shaping therapeutic conversations that redevelop the subordinate storylines of people's lives. It is the redevelopment of these subordinate storylines that provides people with a foundation to proceed to address their predicaments and problems in ways that are in harmony with the precious themes of their lives. These precious themes become more richly known in the course of re-authoring conversations.

The re-authoring conversations map has been a mainstay of my therapeutic practice for many years. I have never been short on curiosity about the events of life, or on enthusiasm for rich conversations about life. The narrative analysis of story-making has continued to fuel this curiosity and I find that I am ever-more intrigued by life and enthusiastic about therapeutic practice.

In writing this chapter it was my hope to provide a relatively comprehensive account of "the imaginative application of the narrative mode" in therapeutic practice. As I have drawn significantly from the work of Jerome Bruner in developing this map, it seems fitting to close this chapter with the following quote, which captures the sentiment associated with the narrative practices that I have been describing here.

> The imaginative application of the narrative mode leads . . . to good stories, gripping drama, believable . . . historical accounts. It deals in human or human-like intention and action and the vicissitudes and consequences that mark their course. It strives to put its timeless miracles into the particularities of experience, and to locate the experience in time and place. Joyce thought of the particularities of the story as epiphanies of the ordinary. (Bruner, 1986, p. 13)

# 3
# Re-Membering Conversations

Re-membering conversations are shaped by the conception that identity is founded upon an "association of life" rather than on a core self. This association of life has a membership composed of the significant figures and identities of a person's past, present, and projected future, whose voices are influential with regard to the construction of the person's identity. Re-membering conversations provide an opportunity for people to revise the memberships of their association of life: to upgrade some memberships and to downgrade others; to honour some memberships and to revoke others; to grant authority to some voices in regard to matters of one's personal identity, and to disqualify other voices with regard to this.

Re-membering conversations are not about passive recollection but about purposive reengagements with the history of one's relationships with significant figures and with the identities of one's present life and projected future. There are many options with regard to the identification of figures and identities that might be re-membered in people's lives. These figures and identities do not have to be directly known in order to be significant in re-membering conversations. For example, they may be the authors of books that have been important or characters from movies or comics. Nor do these figures and identities have to be people; they could be the stuffed toys of a person's childhood or a favorite pet.

## Jessica

Jessica, a woman in her forties, consulted me about the consequences of the abuse that she was subjected to by her parents during her childhood and adolescence. She had been isolated in her experience of the abuse, and her struggle to deal with its consequences had been a major theme of her life. These consequences included highly negative conclusions about her identity: that she was worthless as a person and that her life was hopeless. Because of the despair that had been constantly with her, Jessica had come very close to abandoning her life on a number of occasions. However, she had survived, and as an outcome of my effort to understand what had at least minimally sustained her through these times of crisis, I learned that Jessica had managed to hold onto a faint hope that her life might be different at some future time.

In response to learning this, I began to interview Jessica about this hope. I was keen to understand how she had managed to maintain a relationship with this hope despite everything she'd been through. I was also keen to learn of any experiences that might have verified, for Jessica, that these hopes were valid for her life. In response to my questions, she began to tell me a story about a neighbor whom she thought might have played a part in verifying and sustaining this hope. For a period of about 2 years, until Jessica's family relocated when she was age 9, this neighbor had taken Jessica in when she was hurting. Among other things, this neighbor had physically comforted Jessica, had fed her when she was hungry, and had introduced her to sewing and knitting, which were this neighbour's favorite hobbies. After encouraging Jessica to more fully draw out this neighbour's contribution to her life, I encouraged her to reflect on what this contribution might say about who she was in the eyes of this neighbor—about what this might say with regard to what this neighbor appreciated about her identity.

- "Do you have any understanding of why this neighbor took you in like this?"
- "What is your guess about why she contributed to your life in this way?"

- "What could it be that she appreciated about you that your parents seemed oblivious to?"
- "What do you think she was recognizing about you that wasn't visible to your parents?"
- "Do you know what she valued in you that was overlooked by others?"

In response to these questions, Jessica began to voice some very different understandings about herself that included positive conclusions about her own worth. At first these positive conclusions were tentatively stated, and it was quite clear that she was surprised to hear herself speaking about her own identity in this way. As our conversation unfolded these conclusions about her own worth became much firmer. This marked the first step in a reconstruction of Jessica's identity.

After reviewing this neighbor's contribution to Jessica's life, our conversation turned to an account of the inverse—that is, to Jessica's contribution to the neighbor's life. The very idea that she, as a young girl who had been so traumatized, may have made a contribution to the life of this neighbor was startling to Jessica. She had always assumed that she had simply been the passive recipient of what the neighbor had to give her, that she was simply a passenger in this connection. Because of this entrenched one-way account of her connection with this neighbor, it was necessary for me to provide, through my questions, a scaffold that would make it possible for Jessica to become knowledged about her contribution to the life of the neighbor. This scaffold was provided by questions including:

- "Did you accept this neighbor's invitation for you to join her in what was clearly precious to her—that is, her knitting and sewing? Or did you reject this invitation?"
- "In response to this invitation, did you join her in this precious interest, or were you closed to this?"
- "In joining with her in this way, were you honoring what she could give to you that was precious to her, or did your response dishonor this?"

- "What is your guess about what it was like for this neighbor to experience your joining her in this interest in knitting and sewing?'
- "Do you have any thoughts about what this honoring might have brought to her life?"
- "How might her life have been different on account of your responsiveness?"

In response to questions like these, Jessica began to develop an account of her contribution to the life of this neighbor. There was some delight for Jessica in this, but she also experienced many other strong emotions. At times during this part of our conversation she was in tears and quite lost for words.

The development of this account of Jessica's contribution to the life of this neighbor provided a foundation for questions that encouraged further reflection, this time on how Jessica's responses might have touched the neighbor's sense of identity. This reflection was aided by questions about how Jessica's contribution might have affected the neighbor's sense of who she was and of her sense of purpose, about how this might have validated and reinforced the purposes and values that this neighbor treasured, and about how this might have enriched the neighbor's understanding of what her life was about.

- "What is your guess about how this shaped your neighbor's sense of what her life was about?"
- "How do you think this might have affected her sense of purpose?"
- "Could this have reinforced any values that might have been precious to her?"
- "If so, what's your speculation about which values were reinforced?"
- "How might this have affected what your neighbor believed to be important about life?"
- "Do you have any thoughts about how her sense of her own life might have been different for knowing you in the way that she did?"

Jessica was powerfully moved by these and other similar questions, and she was tearful for much of this part of our conversation. The idea that she could have made such a contribution to the neighbor's life and sense of identity was quite overwhelming for Jessica. Because she had assumed that her connection with this neighbor was an entirely one-way phenomenon, the understanding that it might have been two-way in its consequences was, to Jessica, quite awesome: "I thought I was just a burden to everyone. Who would have thought that as a 7 year-old girl I could have given anything back? There is something strange that's been happening to me as we have been talking. I am not sure what this is about, but I think that it is because for the first time I am feeling respect for the little girl that I was."

Months later, when reviewing the course of our meetings, Jessica remarked that she considered this first therapeutic conversation to be a turning point in her life. The conversation had made it possible for her to give meaning to aspects of her life that she had previously neglected: She was now able to understand many aspects of the way that she lived to be a testimony to this neighbor's sentiment of living, and to conclude that many of her initiatives of living were in honor of this neighbor's contribution to her life. This included some recent initiatives Jessica had taken in searching out and assisting other women who had been subject to abuse in childhood. This conversation had been a turning point around which the highly negative conclusions that she had held about her own identity were eroded and displaced by more positive conclusions. From this point on Jessica gradually became less vulnerable to the critical understandings that she had held about her own life and that had been overwhelming her.

## Saying Hullo Again

No matter how often I witness these dramatic turning points in therapeutic conversations, the difference that can be made by the appropriate question at the appropriate time never fails to surprise me. What was it that shaped my questions in this conversation with Jessica? To a significant extent, these questions were shaped by a map that I refer to as a "re-membering conversations map." The development of this map has its genesis in my consultations with people experiencing loss and grief, and I will say a little about this history here.

In 1988 I published an article titled "Saying Hullo Again: The Incorporation of the Lost Relationship in the Resolution of Grief." This article gave an account of the work that I had developed through my consultations with people who were experiencing what at the time was frequently referred to as a "delayed grief reaction" or "pathological mourning." Most of these people had already received intensive and lengthy treatments that had been oriented by normative ideas about grieving. Many of these normative ideas sponsored the "saying goodbye" metaphor, which was associated with the goal of achieving acceptance of the loss of the loved one and the development of a desire to get on with a new life that is detached from the loved one.

In my first meetings with these people, it was clear to me that they had already lost too much. It was apparent that they had not only lost a loved one, but that they had also lost a substantial part of their own sense of self, of their own identity. Without prompting, these people put me in touch with the consequences of these losses, freely relating details of their subsequent sense of emptiness and desolation, of their feelings of worthlessness and of despair.

It was also clear to me that, under these circumstances, any further grief counseling shaped by a normative model—that is, one that specifies the stages of the grief process according to the saying goodbye metaphor—would only complicate the situation further, that this would only serve to exacerbate their sense of emptiness and desolation and their feelings of worthlessness and despair. The incorporation of the lost relationship seemed a far more appropriate goal than further encouraging these people to forfeit this relationship. My therapeutic explorations of the "saying hullo" metaphor were prompted by this consideration.

Guided by the saying hullo metaphor, I formed and introduced questions that I hoped would open up the possibility for people in these circumstances to reclaim their relationship with the lost loved one. Surprised by the effect of these questions in the resolution of the sense of emptiness and desolation, and in the resolution of the feelings of worthlessness and despair, I decided to explore the metaphor further. I expected that a fuller understanding of the processes involved would enable me to more effectively assist people to reposition themselves in relation to the death of a loved one, a repositioning that would bring the relief so strongly sought after.

In the "Saying Hullo Again" article I outlined some of the categories of questions that seemed particularly effective in contributing to this reincorporation of the lost relationship in the resolution of grief. These were the sort of questions that I asked Jessica when inviting her to witness her identity through the eyes of her neighbor—when I invited her to speculate about what this neighbor's contribution to Jessica's life might say about what she appreciated and valued about Jessica.

Also included in the article were categories of questions I had developed that were effective in encouraging people to:

- Explore the real and potential effects of these preferred understandings about their identity on their daily life
- Contemplate ways in which these understandings might be resurrected and circulated within the context of their social networks, which could include exploring possibilities for recruiting an audience to these understandings about their identity
- Speculate about how this might provide a foundation for them to proceed with their lives

Additionally, the article touched on the contribution that the person had made to the life of their lost loved one and on how this contribution might have shaped the sense of identity of the person who had died. After writing this article I more fully developed this aspect of the therapeutic inquiry. This development is evident in the questions I asked Jessica when inviting her to speculate about how this connection with her neighbor might have affected the neighbor's sense of who she was and her sense of purpose, about how this connection might have validated and reinforced the values that this neighbor treasured, and about how this connection might have enriched the neighbor's understanding of what life was about.

## The Benefits and Purpose of Re-Membering Conversations

Through further explorations of the saying hullo metaphor, and upon reading the work of Barbara Myerhoff (1982, 1986), a cultural anthropologist, I began to refer to therapeutic conversations that focused on the resolution of grief as "re-membering conversations." In Chapter 4 I give a short description of Myerhoff's fieldwork with an elderly Jewish community in Venice, Los Angeles, in which she introduces the re-membering metaphor. Here, I will briefly touch on the significance that Myerhoff (1982) attributes to the re-membering of lives in the identity projects of the members of this community:

> To signify this special type of recollection, the term re-membering may be used, calling attention to the reaggregation of members, the figures who belong to one's life story, one's own prior selves, as well as significant others who are part of the story. Re-membering, then, is a purposive, significant unification, quite different from the passive, continuous fragmentary flickerings of images and feelings that accompany other activities in the normal flow of consciousness. (p. 111)

This definition of re-membering evokes the image of a person's life and identity as an association or a club. The membership of this association of life is made up of the significant figures of a person's history, as well as the identities of the person's present circumstances, whose voices are influential with regard to how the person constructs his or her own identity. Re-membering conversations provide an opportunity for people to engage in a revision of the membership of their associations of life, affording an opening for the reconstruction of their identity. Myerhoff (1982) draws out some of the social mechanisms that contribute to re-membered lives:

> Private and collective lives, properly re-membered, are interpretive. Full or "thick description" is such an analysis. This involves finding linkages between the group's shared, valued beliefs and symbols, and the specific historical events. Particularities are subsumed and equated with grander themes, seen as exemplifying ultimate concerns. (p. 111)

Re-membering, as defined by Myerhoff, contributes to the development of a "multivoiced" sense of identity and facilitates activity in making sense of one's existence and achieving a sense of coherence through the "ordering" of life. It is through re-membering that "life is given a shape that extends back in the past and forward into the future" (p. 111).

This concept of re-membering gave me another perspective on "saying hullo again" conversations and a fuller understanding of some of the mechanisms of these conversations that were contributing to the very positive outcomes that I was consistently encountering in consultations with people. The concept of re-membering also inspired me to extend these conversations, and they have since become more prevalent in my work generally, not just in consultations over experiences of grief and loss.

I believe that these re-membering practices are generally relevant to therapeutic conversations because they open opportunities for people to challenge what has been so isolating of them—that is, opportunities for people to challenge the dominant notions of identity in Western culture that are associated with the construction of an encapsulated self, one that emphasizes norms about self-possession, self-containment, self-reliance, self-actualization, and self-motivation. These contemporary Western social and cultural forces that promote isolated, single-voiced identities actually provide the context that generates many of the problems for which people seek therapy. Re-membering conversations provide an antidote to these forces. They also provide alternative ways for people to understand their identities and alternative avenues of identity formation.

In the therapeutic context, re-membering conversations:

- Evoke "life" as a "membered" club and "identity" as an "association" of life, in contrast to notions of identity that construct an encapsulated self. These re-membering conversations encourage the development of notions of identity that emphasize the contributions that others make to our lives and to our understandings of self.

- Contribute to the development of a multivoiced sense of identity, rather than the single-voiced sense of identity that is a feature of the encapsulated self. In this multivoiced sense of identity people find that their lives are joined to the lives of others around shared and precious themes. This is a sense of identity that features positive but non-heroic conclusions about one's actions in life and about who one is.

- Open possibilities for the revision of one's membership of life, which is mostly achieved by the upgrading and honoring of some memberships. In this upgrading, certain voices are granted more authority with regard to matters of one's personal identity, and this has the effect of disqualifying other voices. It can also have the effect of revoking some memberships.

- Richly describe the preferred versions of identity and the knowledges of life and skills of living that have been cogenerated in the significant relationships of people's lives. In reviewing these memberships, these accounts of identity and these knowledges and skills can be explored in their particularities. This contributes significantly to people's sense of being knowledged about their life, which provides a basis for them to develop specific proposals about how they might proceed with their lives.

- Provide for a two-way understanding of a person's relationship with the significant figures of their lives. This two-way understanding displaces "passive recipient" conceptions of one's identity, and emphasizes a mutuality of contribution in which the sense of one's personal agency is resurrected.

- Encourage not passive recollection of one's past, but deliberate reengagements with the significant figures of one's history and with the identities of one's present life that are significant or potentially significant. These figures and identities do not have to be directly known in order to be considered significant.
- Are often initiated through two sets of inquiry. The first part of this inquiry invites:
  - A recounting of what the significant figure contributed to the person's life
  - The person to witness his or her identity through the eyes of this figure, initiating a rich description of the ways in which this connection shaped or has the potential to shape the person's sense of who he or she is and what his or her life is about

  The second part of this inquiry invites:
  - A recounting of what the person contributed to the life of this figure
  - The person to richly describe the ways in which this connection shaped or has the potential to shape this figure's sense of who he or she was and what his or her life was about

Figure 3.1 shows charting of the re-membering conversation with Jessica onto a map that is informed by these categories of inquiry.

I will now introduce another story about a re-membering conversation. In doing this I hope to illustrate some of the considerations relevant to developing a context that is favorable to introducing re-membering conversations. In Jessica's story there was an opportunity to introduce a re-membering conversation in the first interview. However, circumstances are not always as straightforward, and on these occasions careful attention to the appropriate preparation is required before initiating these conversations.

Figure 3.1 Charting Re-Membering Conversations (Jessica)

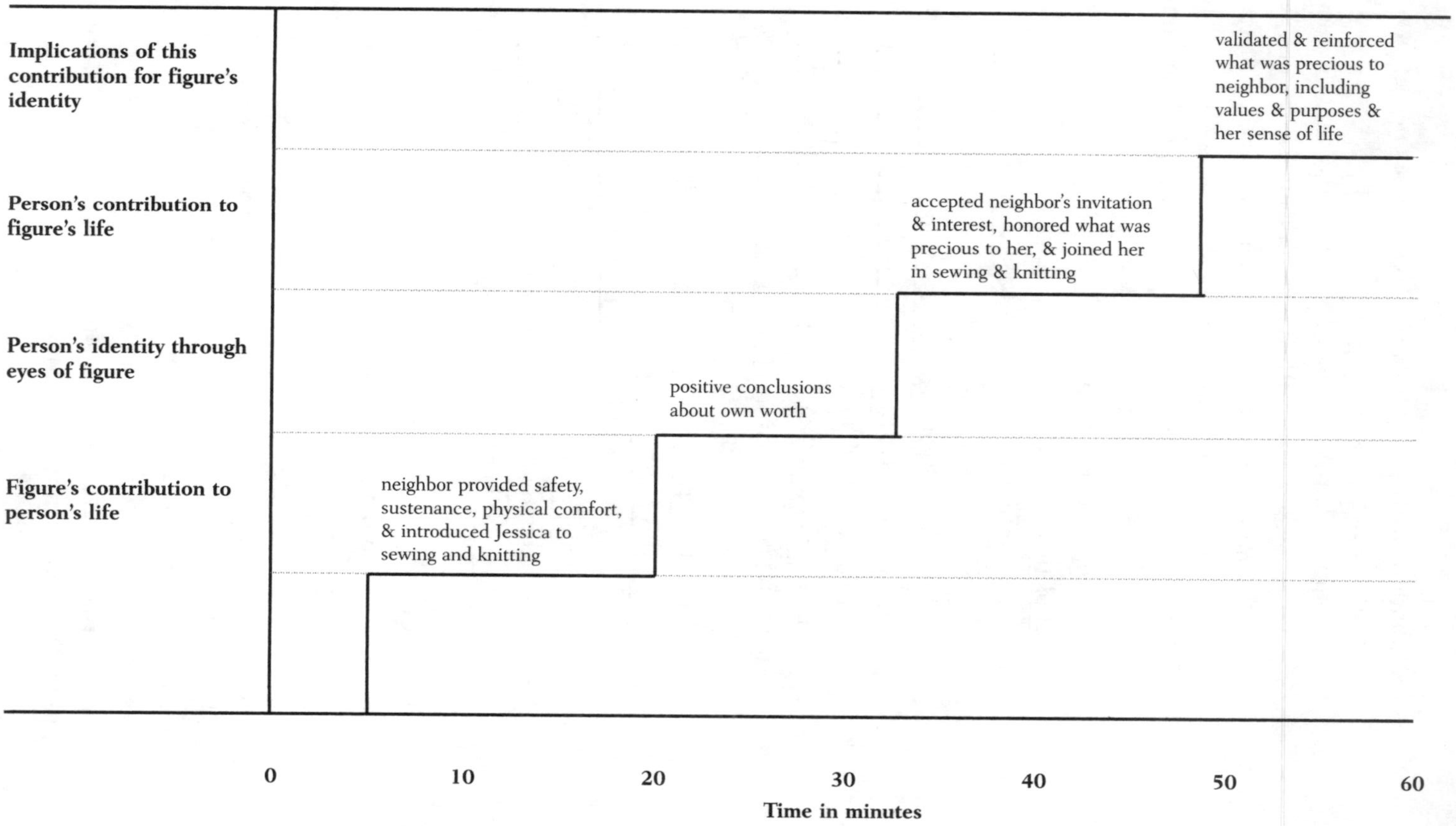

## Thomas

Thomas had been meeting with Cheryl, a counselor, over a period of 5 months. He had initially agreed to consult Cheryl at the insistence of an accommodation service. This was part of a contract that had been worked out with Thomas—the accommodation service would take him off the street and provide him with the accommodation that he was seeking if he agreed to counseling. Thomas had no interest in meeting with a counselor but acquiesced to this with the knowledge that he could be quite skilled in "stonewalling" and in discouraging other people's interest in his life, especially the interest of counselors. He had assumed that he would be able to use these skills to win a quick discharge from therapy while at the same time appear to be acceding to the requirements of the accommodation service.

Thomas arrived at his first meeting with Cheryl 35 minutes late but was surprised to see that she was entirely unruffled by this. He told her that she was "quite frankly wasting her time" with him, that he was "a lost cause," that he lived "in an emotional wilderness," that there were "no possibilities for his future," that he predicted he would not be in this world for very much longer, and that she wouldn't find him very responsive. Despite things getting off to a familiar start in his conversation with Cheryl, over the 25 minutes of their meeting something went profoundly wrong with the plans laid by Thomas. His tactics of discouraging Cheryl's interest didn't appear to be working well at all in the first part of the meeting, and he had a vague sense that she was "somehow getting at him." By the end of this first brief meeting, Thomas was quite disconcerted. He felt off balance and at a loss as to how to proceed with his original plan. After leaving Cheryl's office, he found himself standing motionless for a while on the sidewalk, not knowing which way to turn.

Before long he managed to put this experience out of his mind and began to recognize his own life again. Then, suddenly, a week later, he again found himself disconcerted. He had arrived early for the second meeting with Cheryl and hadn't called in sick as had been his intention. He was now perplexed. He had no understanding of how he had gotten to this place, and he began to worry about his mental status.

Then things seemed to deteriorate even further. He found himself wanting to linger in his conversation with Cheryl. At the end of this second meeting, Thomas was "quite puzzled," felt on "unsteady ground," and was "dizzy" and "at a loss" as to how to understand his experience.

This time it was more difficult for him to put this experience out of his mind, and he found himself looking forward in anticipation to his next meeting with Cheryl. He continued to keep his appointments with her. Then, suddenly, Cheryl learned that she would have to relocate for family reasons. Thomas was devastated upon hearing this. He couldn't understand this devastation and thought that he was going mad. He felt that he now had no choice but to tell Cheryl about the strange experiences he'd been having in the context of their meetings, hoping that she would make sense of them. They talked for a while about this, and, as Cheryl had planned to refer Thomas to me before her move, she suggested that they meet together with me for a consultation about this. Thomas agreed.

This was the story I heard upon meeting with Thomas and Cheryl. In an effort to assist Thomas to make sense of what was happening to him in these meetings with Cheryl, I interviewed them both about their experiences of their conversations with each other. About 20 minutes into this exploration, Thomas had a significant realization: "It's acknowledgment, that's what it is! This is the first time that I've put my finger on it. It's acknowledgment! It is Cheryl's acknowledgment of me that's been so bewildering! I've never had anything like this before, and I don't know how to take it. I really don't know how to take it."

I asked Thomas why he thought he was drawn to this acknowledgment. "Surely you would know! Surely it's something that is only human. Don't you know that it is only human to long for acknowledgment?" replied Thomas. I said that I wasn't sure that I did know this, and I asked if he would care to expand on this understanding. This he did, evoking human nature as an explanation for what he was relating to in his meetings with Cheryl. I then interviewed Thomas about Cheryl's responses to the stories of his life, and before long I had an account of some of her special skills of acknowledgment.

Thomas had evoked human nature as an explanation of his response to Cheryl's acknowledgment of him. In these contemporary times, it is not at all uncommon for people to evoke "human nature" in this way (see Chapter 2). On account of this habit of thought, it is only to be expected that people will go "naturalistic" in their effort to understand the developments of their lives. Although many of these naturalistic understandings are quite beautiful, and although they can be powerfully honored in the therapeutic context, they obscure the social and relational history of the significant developments of people's lives. It is because of this that these naturalistic understandings are quite thin and take us into conversational culdesacs.

In order to make way for re-membering conversations, it is important that these culdesacs be circumvented and that thoroughfares be opened to the social and relational history of the significant developments of people's lives. For example, a person might invoke hope as an explanation of her survival of historical trauma and give this a "naturalistic" status—that is, to propose that it is human nature to have hope in the face of what is personally devastating. This is a very beautiful notion, but it does not promote rich story development. In the context of therapy, it is possible to honor such understandings and at the same time circumvent them through the introduction of questions like:

- How were you able to hold onto hope in the way that you have despite everything you have been through?
- Do you have any ideas about how you have been able to maintain your relationship with hope through these difficult times?
- Of all of the people who have known you, who would be least surprised to learn that you have held onto hope in the way that you have?
- And what is your guess about what these people witnessed that made it possible for them to predict that you could do this?
- Can you recall any experiences that might have been validating of these hopes?

- Experiences that might have verified that it was reasonable for you to hold these hopes for your life?

Questions like these create openings for an appreciation of the developments of people's lives that go beyond naturalistic understandings and that provide the foundation for rich story development. They also provide the foundation for the introduction of re-membering conversations. When Thomas went naturalistic in his understanding of his response to Cheryl's expressions of acknowledgment, I introduced the following reflections and questions:

- "At some level you recognized this acknowledgment when it was offered to you."
- "What experiences of life can you tell me about that would help me to understand how you recognized this acknowledgment when it came your way?"
- "Do you have any sense of why this acknowledgment was familiar to you? About what made it possible for you to recognize it for what it was?"
- "This acknowledgment didn't just bounce off you. Rather, you responded to it. You let this acknowledgement touch you, and you took it in. I am very curious about how you knew how to relate to this acknowledgment."
- "Is there anything that you can tell me about your life that would help me to understand how you knew what to do with this acknowledgment?"
- "Are there any stories of your history that would make it possible for me to comprehend your ability to take this acknowledgment in and to let it touch you in this way?"

It was in response to these and other reflections and questions that Thomas for the first time mentioned his mother:

**Thomas:** You will probably want to know about my mother. Other counselors do. She committed suicide when I was 7 years old. I don't remember much about it. All I know is that I was home at the time. I can remember looking around the house for her. I found her in the bath. She was still. Everything went fuzzy then. The next thing that I can remember is that I was running somewhere and kept falling down. I never saw her again. And no one ever said much about her after that. I wasn't told very much, except that she killed herself, which I couldn't understand. Much later I found out that she'd done this by cutting her wrists. I also found out that she'd asked my uncle to take me out, but this didn't happen because he was passed out on the front lawn from drinking too much booze. For a while after that I lived with an aunt and uncle. This aunt was my mother's cousin, but it was terrible there. Eventually I couldn't take it anymore, and I ran away to the streets when I was 14. Then I was in a couple of foster homes that didn't work out. Anyway, I don't want to talk about this, and I am just telling you because counselors always want to know this stuff.

**M:** You don't want to talk about this?

**Thomas:** I am tired of talking about it. I am tired of all this.

**M:** Okay, but what are you tired of?

**Thomas:** About how this caused my problems. You know.

**M:** I'm not sure that I do.

**Thomas:** You know. About how all my problems and my drug abuse is about my anger. You know, about my anger turned against myself.

**M:** Anger?

**Thomas:** You know. Over what my mother did. The anger that I had toward my mother for rejecting me like this. For what she did to my life. Anyway, I have done all of this and I just want to drop it. I just want to let the past be.

**M:** Are these understandings about what has happened to your life honoring of or dishonoring of your mother?

**Thomas:** What?

**M:** Would you say that these understandings are honoring or dishonoring of your mother's life, and of her relationship with you?

**Thomas:** What? I don't think I have . . . Uh!

**M:** Take your time.

**Thomas:** Well, I haven't thought much about this. But I suppose they put her in a pretty bad light. Yeah.

**M:** So, would you say dishonoring or honoring?

**Thomas:** Well, putting it like that, I'd have to say dishonoring.

**M:** I wouldn't want to have any conversations that were dishonoring of your mother, or dishonoring of her connection with you. And I wouldn't want to encourage you to rage against her for any reason.

**Thomas:** You wouldn't! Okay. Okay.

**M:** But I would like permission to ask you some more questions about her, and about you when you were a child. I would like to do this because when I was asking about the history of your familiarity with acknowledgment, your mother's name came up, and I have a sense that there is more to the story of her connection with you.

**Thomas:** (*seeming surprised*) Okay.

**M:** I would be more interested in any memories of your connection with her that are presuicide memories.

**Thomas:** Presuicide memories? Look, I'd really like to

answer your question, but I honestly don't have any clear memories of that time of my life.

**M:** Okay. What about vague memories then?

**Thomas:** Nope. I'm afraid not. Not even vague memories.

We talked for a while longer, but I was unsuccessful in my effort to evoke earlier memories of Thomas' relationship with his mother that would explain his reference to her in response to my questions about the history of his familiarity with acknowledgment. But I did have some thoughts about the building of a context that might be favorable to the recovery of some of these memories.

About 8 months before meeting with Thomas I had been consulted by Juliet, a mother of three children. Juliet had been referred to me following a suicide attempt that nearly claimed her life and had necessitated admission to the hospital. A single parent, Juliet had been experiencing hard times of the sort that Thomas' mother, also a single parent, probably would have encountered. It was in the context of these hard times, and due to how they had influenced her actions, that Juliet had reached a conclusion that she was hindering her children's development and that she might destroy their lives. She was anguished about this. She wanted so much for them to have a better life than she had experienced as a child, and she decided that they would be better off without her—that if she wasn't around they would be better off being raised by her older sister.

In my first meeting with Juliet it became apparent that her decision to take her own life was born of her love for her children; this attempted suicide was an act of love. Following this, I had some highly memorable meetings with Juliet and her three children, for whom this understanding of their mother's desperate action had made a world of difference. At the end of my meetings with Juliet and her children she had volunteered to enter her name into one of my outsider-witness registers, to be available to join me in my work at some future point should this seem appropriate.

At the end of my first meeting with Thomas, I shared some thoughts about options for how we might proceed in our conversa-

tions. I said that I knew a woman named Juliet who had nearly succeeded in doing what his mother had succeeded in doing—taking her
own life. I said that I was sure that Juliet would be interested in joining us for a meeting or two if Thomas thought this option might be
helpful.

> **M:** Of course, Juliet couldn't stand in for your mother—I
> doubt that anyone could do this. But it would be my idea
> to interview you about what we have been talking about
> today with Juliet present as an audience. I'd then ask you
> to sit back while I interviewed her about what she had
> heard in your story. It is my guess that she will hear things
> in your story that I haven't heard, and perhaps even things
> that you haven't heard. Following this, it would be my plan
> to interview you about what you heard in Juliet's reflec-
> tions. Now, it isn't necessary for us to do this in order to
> proceed with our work together, but what do you think of
> the idea?

> **Thomas:** Well . . . I don't know . . . It's not anything that I
> would have thought of. But, hey! Why not? You know, I'm
> really at a point in my life where I have nothing to lose.

I called Juliet that afternoon and informed her that I had been
meeting with a young man who'd been through some very hard times
in his life and who had tragically lost his mother at an early age. When
I asked Juliet if she would be willing to join us, there was no hesita-
tion in her response—this was something that she wanted to do and
we could count her in. Juliet then called back 3 days later. I have
reconstructed our telephone conversation:

> **Juliet:** I have been talking to my kids about coming to your
> next meeting with Thomas. When I told them this, they
> said that they wanted to be there too. In fact, Craig said
> that he *should* come with me. So would it be okay if they
> came along as well?

**M:** It is fine with me, but it is a pretty heavy topic of conversation, and I'm not sure if it's going to be good for them to . . .

**Juliet:** My kids know a lot about this from my own crisis. And we've became good at talking about things that are hard to talk about, and this has been important to all of us. Besides, when I told them what you told me, they were all sad for Thomas, and they'd like to help.

**M:** Okay. I'll call Thomas about this and get back to you as soon as I can.

I called Thomas about this proposal to include these children. His response was: 'Well, it isn't anything I would have thought of doing. Sounds a bit wild. But then hey! I'm in this far already! I've got nothing to lose, have I!'

Soon I was meeting with Thomas, Juliet, and her three children, Craig, 13, Robert, 9, and Corinda, 6. We talked over the proposal for how the meeting might be structured. My plan was to first interview Thomas about the story of his life. At this time Juliet, Craig, Robert, and Corinda would be present as an audience to this conversation. Second, I would interview Juliet, Craig, Robert, and Corinda about what they had heard in Thomas's story. Thomas would be strictly an audience to this retelling. Third, I would interview Thomas about what he had heard in the retellings of Juliet, Craig, Robert, and Corinda. At this time, Juliet, Craig, Robert, and Corinda would be back in the audience position, listening to Thomas's account of their retellings. This plan for our meeting was acceptable to everyone.

In the first part of this meeting Thomas and I reproduced the conversation of our initial meeting. It was then time for Thomas to sit back and for me to interview Juliet and her three children about what they had heard. This turned out to be a very powerful retelling for everyone:

**M:** (*addressing everybody but looking toward Juliet out of concern over the possibility of burdening the children*) Let's start with what it was that caught your attention. Was there something that Thomas said that particularly stood out for you? Or was there something that you noticed about him that you would like to talk about?

**Craig:** One thing that he said was that his uncle was supposed to take him out, so she (Thomas's mother) didn't want him to be the one to discover this.

**Robert:** Yeah.

**Corinda:** I think that too.

**M:** What did this . . .

**Craig:** And another thing was that Thomas didn't show us that he was sad about this.

**Robert:** Yeah, that's right. Maybe he's already cried a lot about it and doesn't have anything left.

**Corinda:** I think that too.

**M:** Craig, you said that Thomas's mother didn't want him to discover this. What did this say to you about his mum? What did this say to you about her relationship with him?

**Craig:** Let's see . . . Maybe that she really did care about him. Yeah. Maybe that she really cared about him. What do you think Rob?

**Robert:** Yeah, I agree with that. She would've have cared about him. For sure.

**M:** What do you think Corinda?

**Corinda:** My mom loves me, and, and . . . Thomas's mum loves him. Yes, she does too. It made me sad, and . . . and it made Thomas sad too.

**Craig:** I think Corinda could be right about that.

**M:** Juliet?

**Juliet:** (*in tears*) Right now I think that I'd just like to sit here and keep listening to what my kids have to say if that's okay.

**M:** Sure, sure. Craig do you know why you understood things in the way that you did?

**Craig:** What do you mean?

**M:** What you heard from Thomas gave you the idea that his mother really cared for him, and you agreed with Corinda that she could have loved him. Did you hear anything that touched on what you've been through? Did this strike a chord with anything that has happened to you?

**Craig:** Yeah, yeah. (*tears welling in his eyes*) You could say that.

**M:** Would you say something about this or would you prefer not to?

**Craig:** No, I want to. I think I know a bit about what Thomas went through. I mean it is not really the same, it really isn't. But it might have been the same. We nearly lost our mum too. And we thought that she didn't really care about us any more. But it wasn't true, it really wasn't true, was it, Mum?

**Juliet:** No, Craig, it wasn't true, because . . .

**Craig:** We found out that she thought that she was just making things hard for us, just messing everything up. We found out that she thought that we would be better off without her. Didn't we? (*turning to Jerry and Corinda*)

**Corinda:** Yeah.

**Robert:** Yeah. It was real hard at the beginning. Everybody was real upset. I mean real upset. We couldn't stop Corinda from crying all the time, and she wouldn't let go of me and Craig, and in the end, even when we knew Mum was going to be okay, and when I went back to school, the teachers had to let Corinda stay with me in the classroom. That was fine though, wasn't it Corinda?

**Corinda:** (*with tears*) Yeah. Robert looked after me.

**Juliet:** I want to say something. I was having a really difficult time, and I was making a mess of the things that were most important to me. I was so low, and I thought that I was ruining everything that was precious to me. I thought that I was a pathetic excuse for a mother, I really did. Like Craig said, I thought the kids would all be better off without me. I now know that this was crazy thinking, but that was the space that I was in back then.

**M:** Are you saying in some way that your suicide attempt was an act of love?

**Juliet:** Yeah. I know it seems a bit weird to say this, but it really was. It really was.

**M:** I am going to ask you all to sit back in a minute and listen to me talking with Thomas about what he heard as he listened to you. Before I do that, though, I would like to ask you all about what it has been like for you to be here helping us out in this way.

**Juliet:** It has been lots of things for me. I don't know anything about Thomas's mother, but I have been feeling a connection with her. I have been thinking about the turmoil that she was probably going through. I am sure that she wasn't perfect. I know that I haven't been perfect with my kids. But I think that, as a mother, I might have some understanding about what it would have been like for her to give up her son. My heart goes out to her. My heart really goes out to Thomas for his loss. But it also goes out to his mother for her loss.

**M:** Where does this leave you right now?

**Juliet:** (*tearful*) Feeling sad. But I am also feeling the power of mothers' love for their children. I am feeling the power of my love for these three. And I am also feeling proud of these three for speaking up in the way that they have today. I just hope that Thomas gets something from this.

**M:** What's it been like for the three of you to play this part today?

**Robert:** I am glad we came.

**Corinda:** Me too. Aren't you Craig?

**Craig:** We've been through a lot, and if talking about what we have been through is going to help anyone else, that's great. Mum and us kids have been talking about how sad lots of people are, and about how they don't have to be so sad. So us kids feel good about doing this, don't we?

**Robert:** Yeah.

**Corinda**: Yeah.

**M:** Okay, thanks for all that you have done in our meeting today. I am now going to talk with Thomas about what he heard as he listened to us talking.

Tears had been streaming down Thomas's face for a good part of the retellings of Juliet, Craig, Robert, and Corinda. I invited him to put words to these tears, and to say what had been happening for him as he was listening. Thomas was so choked up with emotions that he was unable to respond. I wondered if a time-out might be helpful, and he nodded. He headed to the courtyard for a smoke, and Juliet and her children headed for the kitchen for refreshments. We reconvened our meeting about 15 minutes later, at which time Thomas was still under the sway of powerful emotions. But he was able to speak.

**Thomas:** I was . . . I was just so unprepared for this.

**M:** Would you say a little about what you were unprepared for?

**Thomas:** It was the way that Craig and Robert and Corinda and Juliet related to what I'd said. I'd thought partly, you know, that maybe this was simply one of those things to go through. And to be honest, I'd also been humoring you a bit in going along with this idea in the first place. But this turned out to be totally something else. Yeah, totally something else.

**M:** What was it about how Craig and Robert and Corinda and Juliet related to your story that made this so totally something else?

**Thomas:** Everything. Everything. Right from the start with Craig picking up on my mother caring about me. And with what Robert and Corinda said. Corinda really got me going when she said my mom loves me. Right now I am trying not to think about what Corinda said, because if I do I won't be able to speak again. And what Juliet said, including that part about her heart going out to my mother over her loss. Look, I don't understand why this had such an enormous impact on me, but it did. It sure was powerful. Phew! Here I go again. (*more tears*)

**M:** As you were listening to this did anything in particular come to mind? Any mental pictures? Any realizations? Whatever? Perhaps about your mother? Perhaps about her relationship with you? Perhaps about what you meant to her?

**Thomas:** Yeah, I guess so. I guess so. I will have to sit with this for a while though. There were lots of thoughts rushing at me, and they all got into a jumble. It would be hard for me to tease out anything in particular. But there were some flashes among all of this.

**M:** Flashes?

**Thomas:** That's the best word I can think of. Like short flashes of light being thrown onto my history. I can't say much more about this, and I can't get them back right now.

**M:** Do you have any sense of why these retellings of Juliet, Craig, Robert, and Corinda touched you in the way that they did? Do you have any sense of what they might have struck a chord with?

**Thomas:** I can't think of anything in particular right now. I don't know if what Juliet and her children said about my mother is right. But I am thinking there must be some truth in this because of the impact this had on me. Wow! I really have never had an experience like this before, and that's no exaggeration. It's really no exaggeration.

**M:** We are coming to the end of our time together. Where has this exercise taken you to? Where are you right now?

**Thomas:** In what way do you mean?

**M:** Sometimes these events are like journeys, and people arrive at a place in their life that wasn't visible to them at the outset of the event. Do you have any sense of standing in a place right now that . . .

**Thomas:** Okay, I know what you mean. This has turned some parts of my life upside down. It's been quite unsettling. And I don't know for sure, but I think that this might be important.

Juliet and her children joined us again for the next meeting. It was in the context of this meeting that Thomas recalled some faint memories of his mother that hadn't previously been available to his consciousness. One of these memories was of walking home with her from a shopping center, and Thomas guessed that this was in the year leading up to her suicide. He had some recollection that she had been away and a vague sense that she had been in the hospital for reasons that he couldn't understand. On this walk they happened across a dead dog—he thought it was a terrier—that had been hit by a car. He thought he could recall his mother saying something like: "Kids around here have to see enough bad things already." She then cradled the dog in her arms, carried it onto a derelict building allotment, and had Thomas help her scrape a hole in the ground. She lowered the terrier into this shallow grave, and then she and Thomas covered it with building rubble. Although he couldn't remember her words, he could recall his mother "giving the terrier last rites" and bidding farewell to its spirit. They then walked back to the street together, she holding his hand. But they didn't immediately recommence their homeward journey. Instead, they sat on the gutter, his mother looking at him and crying. This seemed to go on for a long while, with Thomas asking his mother time and again what was wrong, and with her unable to respond.

This memory provided the foundation for a rich re-membering conversation that was structured by the two categories of inquiry that I have described in this chapter. Before introducing this inquiry, I asked some general questions that I hoped would prepare the way for the initiation of this re-membering conversation:

> **M:** Thomas, you've recalled your mother saying something like: "We have to do something. Kids around here already have to see enough bad things."
>
> **Thomas:** Yeah. That's about it.
>
> **M:** And then the two of you buried the terrier. Does this suggest anything to you about the value that she put on children's lives?
>
> **Thomas:** Yeah. I suppose she must have known of lots of kids who were having a hard time. And she must have been worried about this. So she must have believed that kids were important. Yeah, she must have valued kids.
>
> **M:** And you also recall her giving the dog last rites and bidding farewell to its spirit.

**Thomas:** Yeah. That's right.

**M:** Does this gesture suggest anything to you about her attitude toward life?

**Thomas:** I guess so. Well, it must. But I'm not sure how to say what it meant. Maybe, maybe something about respecting there's something unique about every life. Something that's to be valued. I'll have to think more about this to find the right words.

I then proceeded with the re-membering conversation by asking questions that helped Thomas to recount what his mother contributed to his life:

**M:** She included you in every step of this ritual in ways that children often don't get included.

**Thomas:** Yeah. That's my memory of it.

**M:** Do you have any sense of what being included in this way might have brought to the life of that little boy?

**Thomas:** Ask me that again.

**M:** Do you have any sense of what being included by your mother in this way could have contributed to your life?

**Thomas:** Well, I can only guess that it must have made me feel a bit warm inside, and maybe a little bit important, like I was grown up enough to handle this. Like I was worthwhile.

**M:** You also said that your mother held your hand at times during this ritual.

**Thomas:** Yeah. I'm sure she did.

**M:** What's your guess about how this touched the life of that little boy?

**Thomas:** (*tearful*) The only thing that I can think of right now is that this must have made me feel alive on the inside. That's the only thing I can think of right now. Maybe later I'll find some other ways of saying it.

My next set of questions encouraged Thomas to witness his identity through the eyes of his mother:

**M:** How do you explain this inclusion of you in something in which children are often not included?

**Thomas:** I don't know if I have an answer for this.

**M:** Well, what does this inclusion suggest about what she was respecting in you?

**Thomas:** That I was a kid who could be counted upon? Maybe that's what it was. You know, that I was the sort of kid who could be trusted to handle this. That there was something a bit solid about me.

**M:** A bit solid?

**Thomas:** Yeah. That I was a kid who didn't need to be shielded from these things, I guess. But hey, all this is taking me right out of the square, and I need to think more about this.

**M:** Okay then. Can I ask a different question?

**Thomas:** Sure, sure. As long as it's okay that I don't have many answers.

**M:** What understanding do you have of your mother's physical touch at this time? What does this suggest about what she valued in you and appreciated about you?

**Thomas:** That it was good to be with me at this time? Yeah. That I was good to be with, that I was good company even when I was little, and that because . . . perhaps because even though I was little, I could understand what she was doing?

**M:** And afterwards, you were sitting on the gutter together, and she was in tears just looking at you. What's your guess about what she was seeing in you at this time?

**Thomas:** (*tearful*) I dunno. Maybe something about the spirit in me? (*now quite choked up, indicating that talking was not possible and that he needed some time out*)

**M:** (*later, after a break*) You have been bringing me up to speed on what it is that your mother might have appreciated about you. Would it be okay if we went back a step or two, and I asked some more questions about what she contributed to your life? Getting clearer about this could give us an even better foundation for figuring out what she valued in you.

**Thomas:** Sure, sure. Go for it.

Following this I asked questions that would help Thomas to recount what he had contributed to the life of his mother:

**M:** You responded to her inclusion of you, and you joined her every step in the ritual of burying the dog.

**Thomas:** Yeah, you could say that I did that. Yeah.

**M:** What's your guess about what it was like for your mother to have your company in this way?

**Thomas:** Boy, these are big questions! Well, maybe it gave her a sense of security. Like a sense of being joined, like . . . I'm trying to find the right word. There's a word for this.

**M:** We've got lots of time.

**Thomas:** Dammit! It's frustrating. It's a word like . . . solidarity! That's it! Maybe it gave her a sense of solidarity.

**M:** Solidarity?

**Thomas:** Yeah, maybe it gave her a sense of solidarity in caring about what lots of people don't care about.

**M:** And what's your speculation about what it was like for her to have this little boy's hand to hold at this time? What is your guess about how this might have touched her?

**Thomas:** (*tearful*) A warm feeling?

**M:** A warm feeling. You brought warmth to her life?

**Thomas:** I think so . . . maybe . . . yeah.

**M:** Are there any other guesses that you could make about how your mother's experience of this event was different on account of your presence?

**Thomas:** Yeah. But I have to leave this question for now if that's okay, and just sit for a while with what's already going on for me.

**M:** Fine, fine.

These last questions were intended to help Thomas, richly describe the ways in which this connection with his mother had shaped his mother's sense of who she was and what her life was about:

**M:** To have you joining her in this burial ritual in this way, what's your guess about how this might have affected her sense of what was important in life? Could this have been validating of what she believed, of what she held precious? Or do you think that it might have been irrelevant to her sense of what life was all about?

**Thomas:** No, no. I can only think that it must have supported what was precious to her.

**M:** That it would have supported what was precious to her?

**Thomas:** Yeah. I'm only just getting to figure out what she stood for, you know. Or even . . .

**M:** I know . . .

**Thomas:** Look, I would never have known this, but maybe there were some things that my mum was passionate about, that are really important.

**M:** And your response supported this. Or what would you say? Validated this? Confirmed this? Verified this? Or . . .

**Thomas:** Yeah, maybe it would have to be all of these.

**M:** Your mother had her little son's hand to hold after bidding farewell to the spirit of the dog. What's your guess about how this might have affected her sense of being a mother?

**Thomas:** I don't know for sure. I want to say the word "proud," but I'm not sure . . .

Over several meetings we came back to these and other similar questions. In the course of this, Thomas became more convinced that the source of this familiarity with acknowledgment was to be found in his relationship with his mother, and he began to develop a much stronger sense of their mutual contributions to each other's lives and to each other's sense of identity. This had a profoundly positive effect on Thomas's conclusions about his own worth. And the development of some appreciation of his contribution to his mother's life as a 6-year-old boy significantly resurrected his sense of personal agency and eroded his conception of himself as a passive subject of life's forces.

These re-membering conversations also had the effect of reconnecting Thomas to the sort of values and purposes that he came to believe linked him with his mother's life. As this link became more richly known through some archaeological work on his family of origin, he developed the ability to evoke his mother's presence in his life, and this he found highly sustaining. This was an antidote to the sense of emptiness and desolation and the feelings of worthlessness and despair that had been so overwhelmingly present for such a significant period of his life. It was in the context of these conversations that Thomas suddenly became aware of some new possibilities on the horizons of his life, and over a period of time he began to step into these possibilities. He also discovered an aunt (his mother's second cousin) who had been fond of his mother when they were young women. Thomas found delight in building a connection with this aunt, whose family came to adopt him.

Figure 3.2 shows my charting of the initial re-membering conversation with Thomas.

## Conclusion

This chapter described some of the ideas that shape re-membering conversations. These conversations can act as an antidote to the powerfully isolating understandings of identity that are so pervasive in contemporary Western culture. Considering life as an association with a membership, and introducing practices specifically shaped by the acknowledgment that identity is wrought by important figures of a person's past and present, opens diverse possibilities for the reconstruction of identity in the context of therapeutic conversations.

In retelling the stories of my conversations with Jessica and with Thomas, Juliet, and her family, I have endeavored to provide a comprehensive account of the form of therapeutic inquiry associated with the re-membering conversations map. I have also described some of the groundwork that must at times be undertaken before the initiation of these re-membering conversations. On many occasions, it is only after significant preparation that it becomes possible for people to reincorporate their relationship with the significant figures of their past and their present.

Over many years of meeting with people about the predicaments of their lives, this re-membering metaphor has touched my own life in a multiplicity of ways. For example, these consultations have encouraged me to reflect more fully on my connections with the significant figures of my own history and on their contribution to the shaping of

## Figure 3.2 Charting Re-Membering Conversations (Thomas)

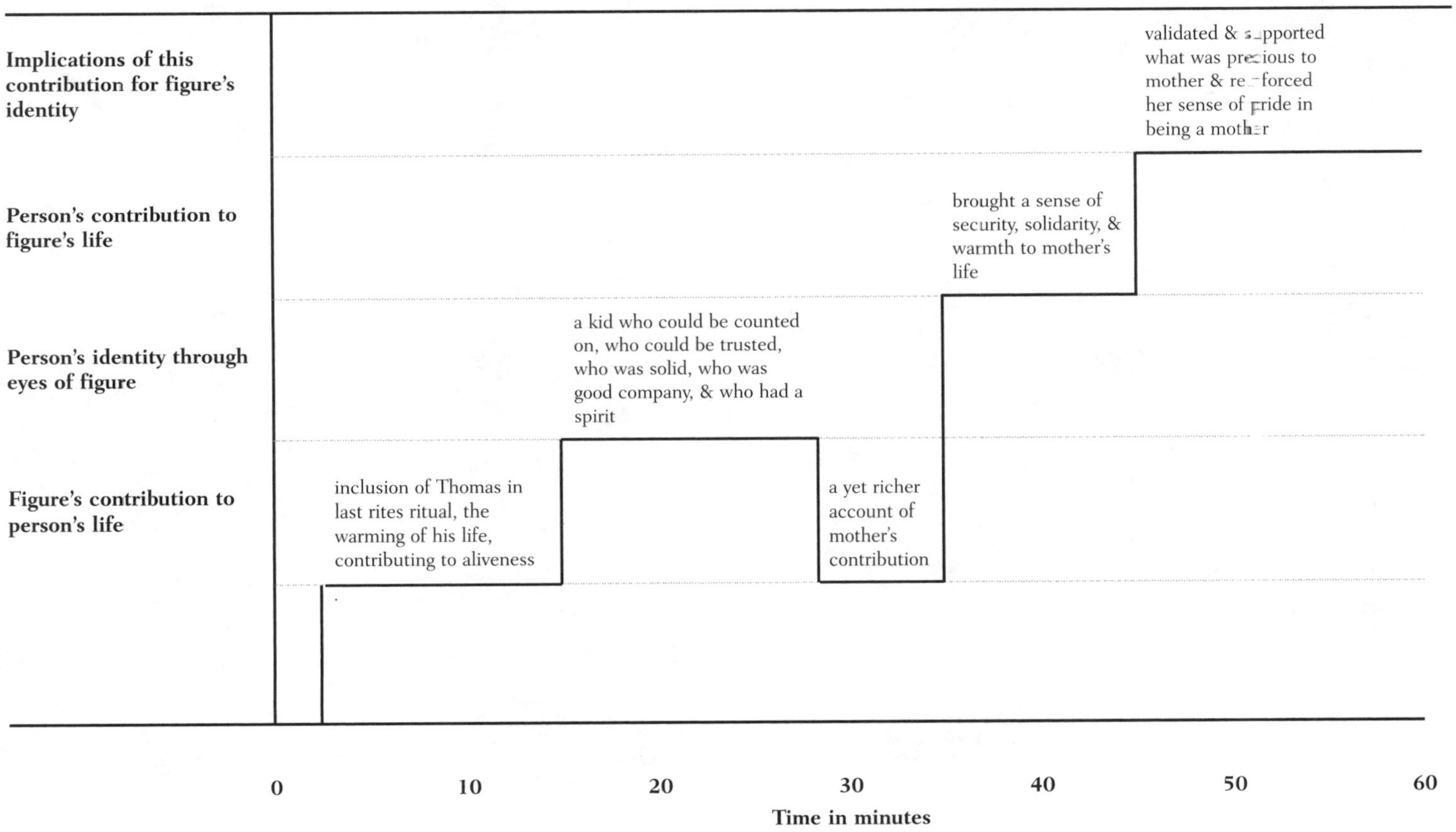

my own life and work. This has also prompted rich conversations with my family and friends that have opened possibilities for the revision of the membership of my own association of life. And routinely engaging with this re-membering metaphor has also contributed to a greater consciousness of the part that the people who have consulted me have played in the development of my work and to a stronger sense of what my work is about in terms of what is precious to me. Needless to say, this has been very sustaining.

# 4
# Definitional
# Ceremonies

Structuring therapy sessions as definitional ceremonies provides a context for rich story development. These ceremonies are rituals that acknowledge and "regrade" peoples' lives, in contrast to many rituals of contemporary culture that judge and degrade people's lives. In many of these degrading rituals, peoples' lives are measured against socially constructed norms, and they are judged to be inadequate, incompetent, disordered, and often a failure in terms of their identities. Definitional ceremonies provide people with the option of telling or performing the stories of their lives before an audience of carefully chosen outsider witnesses. These outsider witnesses respond to these stories with retellings that are shaped by a specific tradition of acknowledgment.

The responses of the outsider witnesses are not shaped by contemporary practices of applause (giving affirmations, pointing out positives, congratulatory responses, and so on) or by practices of professional evaluation and interpretation. It is not the place of outsider witnesses to form opinions, give advice, make declarations, or introduce moral stories or homilies. Rather, outsider witnesses engage one another in conversations about the expressions of the telling they were drawn to, about the images that these expressions evoked, about the personal experiences that resonated with these expressions, and about their sense of how their lives have been touched by the expressions.

In these outsider witness retellings, what people give value to in their acts of living is re-presented in ways that are powerfully resonant and highly acknowledging. Additionally, it is through these retellings that people experience their lives as joined around shared and precious themes in ways that significantly thicken the counterplots of their existence.

## Alison, Fiona, Louise, and Jake

I was between appointments late on a Friday afternoon when the receptionist asked if I would be able to take a call from a young woman who said she wouldn't keep me on the line for long. I took the call, and I have recounted our telephone conversation here:

> **Alison:** Hi, Michael! It's Alison! I don't know if you'll remember me. I came to see you with my mum and dad a while back. Actually it was quite a long time ago.
>
> **M:** Alison, let me have your family name.
>
> **Alison:** Johnston, Alison Johnston, and I think that I came to see you about . . .
>
> **M:** Would that be about 10 years ago?
>
> **Alison:** Yeah. Actually it was about 12 years ago. When I was 15. I'm 27 now.
>
> **M:** And you have a brother a couple of years older who was into athletics.
>
> **Alison:** Yeah, you've got it. So you do remember me!
>
> **M:** Well, Alison, it's great to hear from you after all this time. Twelve years!
>
> **Alison:** Yeah, I've been meaning to give you a call for some time. You know, just to catch you up. Things are sailing

along pretty well in my life and I just thought that you'd like to know.

**M:** How's Henrietta? (*One of the stuffed toys I use in my practice, whom I hadn't seen for 12 years. At times I introduce stuffed toys to people who consult me. These stuffed toys are attributed to a range of lived experiences, personal character-istics, sentiments of life, and problem-solving skills that peo-ple can strongly identify with. Stuffed toys can provide people with a sense of solidarity and inspiration in their efforts to address problems and predicaments (White, 2006).*)

**Alison:** Actually, that's the other reason that I called you. Henrietta and I did have some ups and downs back then, and we've seen each other through some hard times. I feel very attached to her. But lately I've been feeling a bit self-ish about hanging on to Henrietta, mostly because I imag-ine that there are other kids out there who could do with her help. You, know, kids following in my footsteps who could find it helpful to connect with her. I know that she meant so much to me. So I've been thinking that it's about time that she returned to work with you.

**M:** This sounds like quite a big step for you to be taking.

**Alison:** Yeah, it is. And I know I'll be a bit sad about it. But it's the right thing.

**M:** Okay. Why don't we meet for a handing-over ceremony, one in which we could celebrate what you have con-tributed to each other's lives. What do you think?

**Alison:** Great! Shall we do this over coffee?

**M:** Sounds good to me.

Alison said that it would be her preference to meet in a local café for this handing-over ceremony. It was good to see her again and to have the opportunity to catch up on the developments in her life over the past 12 years. It was also good to see Henrietta again and to hear about the part that these two had played in each other's lives over this time. Alison had given me permission to take notes about their team-work, and at the end of our conversation I asked if she would be prepared to sign what I had written. This, I said, could be a new reference for Henrietta's portfolio. Alison was delighted to do so. She also included her telephone number. When I commented on this, Alison said that she would welcome calls from anyone who was introduced to Henrietta in the course of my work. She'd be more than happy to share stories about her connection with Henrietta and about what this had made possible in her life.

This made me realize that I hadn't invited Alison to enter her name into one of my "outsider witness" registers. These registers list the names and contact details of people who volunteer to join me in my work with others. I took this opportunity to describe to Alison the role of the outsider witness, and I asked her if she was interested in signing up. Alison promptly reminded me that there had been two outsider witnesses present at one of our meetings 12 years ago. She recalled that she'd found this especially helpful and said that she would be happy to play this part for others.

Approximately 5 weeks later I was consulted by Louise, Jake, and their daughter, Fiona. Fiona was 16 years old, and she'd had a 15-month struggle with anorexia, which had already hospitalized her on two occasions. In some respects, Fiona reminded me of Alison. In the course of our first meeting I perceived an opportunity to introduce Fiona to Henrietta. I also lent Henrietta's portfolio to Fiona and remarked on the recent reference from Alison. At this time I also informed Fiona that Alison would be happy to talk about her connection with Henrietta if she was interested in giving her a call.

At my second meeting with this family, I learned that Fiona had called Alison, and that this had been helpful. Among other things, Fiona found Alison to be particularly understanding. In response to this, I raised the possibility of Alison joining us for a meeting and described the role that she would be taking if she did so: Alison would first be an audience to my conversation with Fiona and her parents. Then they would sit back and listen closely as I interviewed Alison about what she'd heard in their story. Then it would then be time for Alison to return to the audience position, and for Fiona and her parents to speak of what they had heard in Alison's retelling of their story. I mentioned that it was my experience that structuring such meetings in this way often contributes to an acceleration of positive develop ments and that if Fiona and her parents decide to proceed with this, they would need to let me know about what sort of questions they would be happy for me to ask in Alison's presence and which they would like me to avoid. Fiona was enthusiastic about this idea, and her parents were supportive of this.

Alison joined us for our fourth meeting. During my interview with Fiona and her family, with Alison in the audience position, much of the focus was on the influence and the operations of the anorexia in the lives and relationships of the family members, on their experience of this, on aspects of their lives that they'd managed to hold apart from anorexia's sphere of influence, and on initiatives that were challenging of its status. Alison was the "outsider witness" to this conversation—a term I have borrowed from Barbara Myerhoff (1982, 1986). Alison was not an active participant in this conversation, but rather witnessing it from the outside.

When the time seemed right, the positions were switched, and I interviewed Alison about what she'd heard, with Fiona and her parents now in the audience position. Alison's retelling of the stories she'd heard turned out to have considerable effect on the lives of Fiona and her parents. In the third stage, the positions were again switched, and I interviewed Fiona and her parents about what they'd heard in Alison's retelling of their stories.

The following transcript provides an account of the second stage in this meeting, Alison's response to the stories shared by Fiona and her parents. Alison's response was structured by my questions.

**M:** Alison, would you begin by talking about what you heard that you were most drawn to?

**Alison:** I just think that Fiona and her parents are just the most amaz—

**M:** Alison, could we stay with what you heard that most caught your attention, and then we can get on to your reflections.

**Alison:** Okay. Okay. Well, there were quite a few things. Fiona talked about how she's becoming more aware of all of the expectations about perfection that have got so big in her life, and about how she is now talking about these with her mum. And now with some other people, too. She said that she has started to say these expectations out loud when she's having a hard time with them. Someone used the words "unmasking anorexia," and that's what she's doing. I reckon it's a pretty big step for Fiona to let other people in like this. Fiona could have just given in to anorexia and if she'd done this she would have become totally alone. Then anorexia would find it quite easy to take her life away from her.

**M:** There was this, and other things as well? You said "quite a few things."

**Alison:** Yeah. It wasn't just that Fiona was saying these expectations out loud. She also said that her mum has been asking her about what anorexia is saying to her when things are going badly. I know that Fiona doesn't always answer her, but her mum keeps the opportunity there for her, and even guesses out loud about what anorexia is up to when Fiona doesn't answer. And another thing is that her mum has started to talk to Fiona about all of the expectations that are on her as well, and about how she is always hearing this little voice in her own head that goes, "Are you being a good wife?" or "You are supposed to be here for the kids" or "But you haven't done the cleaning yet" or "You look too much like this or like that." I know her mum has been feeling pretty terrible, like she's responsible for what's been happening to Fiona, that she feels like she's failed Fiona, but she hasn't let this get in the way of getting together with Fiona in this.

**M:** Okay. Was there anything else that you . . .

**Alison:** I've got one more thing. This one's about Fiona's dad.

**M:** Okay.

**Alison:** He said that he was getting a bit of an education in listening to Fiona and her mum talking like this. So, he's been interested. And he's also been open to what they've been saying.

**M:** Thanks, Alison. You've been catching me up on what really caught your attention here. What came to your mind while you were listening to this?

**Alison:** What came to my mind while I was listening?

**M:** How did what you heard shape your sense of these people? How did this effect your picture of who they are?

**Alison:** Well, what actually came to my mind was a storm. I had a picture of Fiona and her mother weathering this huge storm, something really massive, like a cyclone. I think it was because I was watching the news last night about this big cyclone off Darwin. Only with Fiona and her mum, it's a cyclone made of all of these expectations about who they should be and shouldn't be. I had this picture of this cyclone bending their lives like trees, bending them so far that they are almost flat to the ground. But they won't break. They are weathering this with each other, and they are starting to spring back up at times.

**M:** This is a very strong image.

**Alison:** Yeah. Her dad is there too, but in a different way. Let's see. If I think about it, yeah, that's it, he's finding ways of bending that will give the best chance of everyone getting through this.

**M:** What did you hear from Jake that set off this image of him?

**Alison:** It was when he said that he was getting an education when he was listening to Fiona and her mum, when they were, you know, taking off anorexia's mask. He was open to what he was hearing, and I noticed that he wasn't crowding in on them with his own agenda.

**M:** This is quite an image of these people weathering this cyclone. What does this suggest to you about what is important to Fiona and her parents?

**Alison:** What's important to them?

**M:** Yeah. What's your guess about what Fiona and her parents value, or about what is precious to them?

**Alison:** Well, with Fiona and her mum, they are both women who are talking about what's going on for them on the inside. You know, about all of these expectations about who they should be, and about what they are up against. So, maybe this is something about their hopes. Or maybe about their dreams. Dreams that they haven't ever had the chance to talk about before.

**M:** Maybe about what sort of dreams?

**Alison:** Dreams about having different lives, about not just having all of these frustrations to live with. About having a life where they have space to breathe clear air. Maybe dreams about being . . . being entitled to a bit more. That sort of thing.

**M:** Your guess is that it is about these hopes and dreams. Did you hear anything in particular that might relate to these hopes and dreams?

**Alison:** I think this was about when Fiona's mum talked about how she knew that Fiona really hungered for lots of things that anorexia was getting in the way of, and that she herself, Fiona's mum, was only just starting to think about some of the things she also hungered for, things that had been pushed out of her mind for a very long time, nearly forever.

**M:** And you also had this image of Jake being with them in weathering the cyclone, about finding ways of bending that will give the best chance of everyone getting through this. What does this suggest to you about what is important to Jake?

**Alison:** Well, like I said, he's hanging in there to. And I reckon that some of these new directions aren't going to be easy for him because he's also going to have to make changes too. I think he's going to have to do different things, things that he hasn't done before, particularly with Fiona's mum getting clearer about all of the expectations and things that she's hungered for. I think it could be a really big stretch for him.

**M:** You talked about him hanging in with this. What does this suggest about what's important to him?

**Alison:** There's something about, maybe about being able to be out of his comfort zone a bit and to see this through. I don't think I'm being very clear. . . .

**M:** Like a principle of seeing things through, of not letting—

**Alison:** Yeah, something about seeing through what has to be seen through.

**M:** You have talked about what you heard that really stood out for you, and about how this shaped your sense of Fiona and her parents. Would you say a little about what this struck a chord with in your own life?

**Alison:** I know the answer to this. It took me right back to my own struggle with anorexia. Anorexia really had me in a corner. I was down on my knees, and it nearly had me dead. I was nearly a goner. I know this now. For a while nearly everyone had given up on me, and I was almost totally alone. And the more alone I became the worse the situation got. But I still had these lifelines that I hadn't really realized had been there all the way along, and one of these was with my own mum. I remember that learning that we weren't so different was really important. I mean we were different, but we were dealing with lots of the same things. And we drew a lot from each other in this.

**M:** How do you mean?

**Alison:** Well, I can say it better these days. Mum and I started to talk more about what was happening on the inside of us, and even though she didn't have anorexia, what was happening on her inside was pretty similar. You know, being hammered by all of these expectations, day in, day out, night in, night out.

**M:** Okay, I understand. Another question?

**Alison:** Okay.

**M:** You've been an audience to a story about aspects of these people's lives. And you've given a retelling of what you heard in their story. When people are an audience to important stories, and when they have the opportunity to respond in the way that you have, they often go on a journey in their own lives. Being present to these stories takes them to a place that they wouldn't have arrived at if they'd been at work or out shopping. So I'd be interested in any reflections that you might have about where this has taken you. Maybe to new thoughts about your own life. Maybe to some realizations. Anything.

**Alison:** Well one thing that I do know is that I've got a better understanding of how I got through this, about how I got my life back from anorexia. I did know that it was important that my mum didn't let me get isolated, even though her guesses about what was going on inside my thoughts often really irritated me. And I mean *really* irritated me. But I think I am clearer about how me and my mum did this together, and about how important it was for me to hear about what was going on inside of her thoughts.

**M:** Having a better understanding. Do you have any ideas about what this better understanding will bring to your life?

**Alison:** I think even a better appreciation of my relationship with my mum, and this gives me a really warm feeling inside. And I also got more of a realization of my dad's part in this, and how hard it must have been for him to make lots of the changes that had to be made. I know that he'd say that he's a better person for this, but it must have been pretty tough at times. I think I'll go and have a good talk with him about this.

**M:** What's your guess about the outcome of doing this?

**Alison:** I don't know, but I think it would be good for him and me in our relationship with each other.

**M:** It is nearly time for you to switch places with Fiona and her parents. But before we finish, would you again just return to what you heard from Jake that has opened up this possibility for this conversation with your father? And also about what you heard from Fiona and her mother that has given you an even stronger appreciation of your relationship with your mother, and that has given you such a warm feeling inside?

**Alison:** Okay . . .

After this retelling, Alison returned to the audience position. At this time I began to interview Fiona and her parents about what they'd heard in this retelling that had caught their attention, about any images that this had evoked of their own lives and identities, about any realizations regarding their own lives that might have been set off by this, about their understandings of why they were drawn to particular aspects of Alison's retelling, and about what they had arrived at on account of being an audience to this retelling. In response to these questions I learned that Alison's retelling had been a very profound experience for all three family members.

The metaphor of the cyclone had been deeply resonant for them, as were Alison's reflections on what this suggested about what they gave value to in life. Alison's reflections provided a foundation for them to further embroider upon what life was about for them, to refamiliarize themselves with the purposes and values that were of central importance in their lives, and to reinvigorate these.

Fiona talked about how the retelling had helped her to get clearer about what anorexia was up to and had given her a glimmer of what a future apart from anorexia would be like. This, she said, had fueled her hopes. Although she was at a point where it was still difficult to distinguish thoughts that were favorable to anorexia from thoughts that were favorable to her making a stronger appearance in life, she felt that Alison's reflections had "helped to lift some of the fog."

Louise talked quite emotionally about how this retelling had taken some weight off her shoulders, as she'd felt so burdened by a sense of failure and guilt. The validation that she'd experienced in the retelling had been almost overwhelming and was not something she would have ever expected to be the recipient of.

Both Fiona and Louise spoke of how touched they had been by Alison's reflections on their relationship, and they were in tears for a time as they talked about the frustrations associated with their new teamwork and about some of the breakthroughs they felt they were beginning to achieve in their project to free Fiona's life from the clutches of anorexia and to free Louise's life from expectations associated with impoverishing gender-role prescriptions.

Louise spoke of the inspiration that she'd drawn from Fiona in her initiative to speak up about her internal experience of the expectations for perfection—about how this had made it possible for Louise to begin to give voice to what she'd never given voice to and begin to challenge some of the forces of life that were in league with these prescriptions. Fiona was speechless for a time upon hearing this—that she was a source of inspiration for her mother was a huge piece of news for her to take in. I had a sense that taking in this news was something of an antidote to the sense of desolation and emptiness that she had been feeling.

Jake was quite taken by Alison's reflections on his own contribution in "bending in directions most favorable to getting through" what had to be gotten through. He acknowledged that he had been finding this challenging and that it had required him to do things he'd never done before. For example, it had required him to challenge old habits in his relationship with Louise, including those that were a reflection of the taken-for-granted assumptions that contributed to the forces that she'd been up against. He spoke of the defensiveness that he had felt within himself and that he had been struggling with, but also of some of the ways that he had managed to "loosen up a bit." He was feeling some pride in the fact that he thought he was becoming "less uptight."

At the end of our meeting, as we were saying goodbye, I asked Alison if she thought that her own parents would be interested and available to join her in a future meeting as an audience to another conversation with Fiona and her parents and to participate with her in another retelling. Alison thought that they would be quite motivated to do this. Fiona, Louise, and Jake were also enthusiastic about this idea, and three meetings later Alison's parents joined us.

It was clear from the feedback I received and from information about subsequent developments that these two meetings—first with Alison as an audience, and then with her and her parents as an audience—contributed to significant turning points in Fiona's recovery from anorexia nervosa. I believe that Alison and her parents' contribution to these turning points far outweighed any contribution that I could have made in my role as therapist. This is usually the case when an audience is recruited to play this part. However, it is very unlikely that such an outcome can be achieved if the therapist doesn't develop questions that are effective in structuring the audience retellings. The questions that I asked were shaped by categories of inquiry that I have developed over many years in my exploration of these retellings.

In the following sections I describe the history of this practice of engaging an audience, the ideas that have contributed to the refinement of this, and the categories of inquiry that structure these retellings. I also discuss a range of considerations relevant to successful outcome in the employment of this practice.

## Engaging an Audience: The Lead-Up to the Use of Definitional Ceremonies in Therapeutic Practice

In the 1980s, along with my friend and colleague David Epston, I began to actively engage audiences in my work with families. This was partly inspired by our observations of the extent to which many of the children we met with spontaneously recruited audiences to the preferred developments of their lives. For example, in the context of our meetings with families, children would be awarded certificates that acknowledged significant achievements in their effort to reclaim their lives from troublesome problems. Invariably these children would show this certificate to others—perhaps to their siblings, cousins, friends, or peers at school. This usually had the effect of prompting questions from the "audience," which provided an opportunity for these children to give an account of the feats signified by the certificate and at times to actually demonstrate their prowess. These questions and responses from the "audience" were clearly influential in acknowledging the preferred developments in these children's lives, in contributing to the endurance of these developments, and in extending them.

The practice of engaging audiences in our work with families was also inspired by our explorations of the narrative metaphor. We had developed a strong appreciation of the extent to which people's lives are shaped by their personal narratives, and of the extent to which these personal narratives are coauthored in the context of people's relationships with those significant to them. In our work we had become aware of the vital importance of rich narrative development in opening to people a range of possibilities with regard to addressing their problems and concerns. These were possibilities not previously recognized. It was obvious to us that the audience played a critically important role in this rich story development.

A third factor influencing this development in the recruitment of an audience was our awareness of the degree to which personal narratives are shaped by the socially constructed norms of culture, by the institutions of culture, and by the power relations of these institutions. Very often, we found that our therapeutic conversations were contributing to the development of personal narratives that contradicted these socially constructed norms and that shaped action that challenged these power relations. In these circumstances we found that it was very important to engage an audience that would play a role in verifying these alternative personal narratives. Apart from other things, this contributed to building a sense of solidarity with regard to the values and aspirations for life reflected in these personal narratives. This was highly sustaining in circumstances that could otherwise diminish any story development that might be at odds with what was expected.

These observations about the role of the audience, dispelled any thought that audience engagement should be a secondary consideration in therapeutic practice. However, at this time we rarely involved the audience directly in therapeutic conversations. Rather, we encouraged the people consulting us to identify others whose response might be significantly supportive of preferred developments in their lives, and we assisted them in seeking this audience out. We often took recourse to written means of achieving this—certificates, "to whom it may concern letters," and so on.

Over many years this audience engagement was a consistent theme in our work. Initially these audiences were drawn from family and friendship networks, from school and workplace environments, from pools of acquaintances including neighbors and shopkeepers, and from communities of people unknown to those seeking consultation. As we further explored this practice, we began to draw on the people who had previously consulted us, asking them if they'd be interested in joining us in our work at some future time in ways that might contribute to the resolution of other people's problems and concerns. These invitations have mostly been met with strong enthusiasm—people have been more than willing to have their names and contact details entered into our registers. I can count on one hand the number of times, over the years, that this invitation to join one of these registers has been declined.

## The Origin of Definitional Ceremonies

The work of cultural anthropologist Barbara Myerhoff (1982, 1986) provided us with a fuller understanding of the significance of the audience's contribution. Her understanding of the role of the "definitional ceremony" in people's identity projects also encouraged us to further explore and develop options for recruiting audiences to our therapeutic conversations and to research the sort of audience responses that seemed most effective in contributing to rich story development and to the endurance and expansion of the preferred developments of people's lives. Myerhoff described the definitional ceremony when providing an account of the identity projects of a community of elderly Jews in Venice, Los Angeles. This community was the focus of her anthropological fieldwork in the mid-1970s.

As children and infants, at the turn of the 20th century, many of the elderly Jews of this community had left the shtetls of Eastern Europe and migrated to North America. Later in life, in their retirement, they had been drawn to the mild climate of Southern California, which was kind to their health, and to the inexpensive housing in Venice, a beachside principality of Los Angeles. A large number of these elderly Jews had become relatively isolated as a consequence of losing their extended families to the Holocaust and as an outcome of outliving their own children. For many of these people, this isolation had led to the development of uncertainty about their very existence, an uncertainty fueled by a sense of invisibility in the eyes of the wider community, in the eyes of those in their more immediate network, and in their own eyes.

With the assistance of a highly devoted and talented community organizer named Maurie Rosen, these elderly Jews built a sense of community in Venice. It was in the context of this community that they recuperated and reenergized their sense of existence. Of all of the mechanisms that contributed to this recuperation and reenergizing, the definitional ceremony played the primary role. *Definitional ceremony* was the term employed by Myerhoff to describe the forums,  convened by this community, in which community members would have the opportunity to tell and retell, and to perform and to reper-

form, the stories of their lives. It was in these forums that these elderly Jews had the opportunity to reappear on their own terms in the
eyes of community members and in the eyes of the outsiders who
were invited to participate.

> When cultures are fragmented and in serious disarray,
> proper audiences may be hard to find. Natural occasions
> may not be offered and then they must be artificially
> invented. I have called such performances "Definitional
> Ceremonies," understanding them to be collective self-def-
> initions specifically intended to proclaim an interpretation
> to an audience not otherwise available. The latter must be
> captured by any means necessary and made to see the truth
> of the group's history as the members understand it.
> Socially marginal people, disdained, ignored groups, indi-
> viduals with what Erving Goffman calls "spoiled identities,"
> regularly seek opportunities to appear before others in the
> light of their own internally provided interpretation.
> (Myerhoff, 1982, p. 105)

These definitional ceremonies provided an antidote to the effects
of the isolation experienced by the people of this community and to
the sense of invisibility that was a chief outcome of this isolation. In
drawing attention to the role of definitional ceremonies, Myerhoff
(1986) asserted that:

> Definitional ceremonies deal with the problems of invisi-
> bility and marginality; they are strategies that provide
> opportunities for being seen and in one's own terms, gar-
> nering witnesses to one's worth, vitality, and being. (p. 267)

Participation in these definitional ceremonies fostered an ethos of
living that was centered on the displacement of "thin" conclusions
about identity and on the recuperation of "thick" conclusions—for the
people of this community, life was an identity project. These identity
projects were characterized by a special self-reflexive consciousness.

In this consciousness, community members were aware of their participation in the ongoing construction of their own and each other's identities. In this consciousness, they were alert to the life-shaping effect of their own contributions to the production of their own lives. In this consciousness they were able to "assume responsibility for inventing themselves and yet maintain their sense of authenticity and integrity" (Myerhoff, 1982, p. 100). This made it more possible for community members to intervene in the shaping of their lives in ways that were in harmony with what was precious to them.

Myerhoff (1982) drew attention to the exceptional nature of this phenomenon.

> Sometimes conditions conspire to make a generational cohort acutely self-conscious and then they become active participants in their own history and provide their own sharp, insistent definitions of themselves and explanations for their destiny, past and future. They are then knowing actors in a historical drama they script, rather than subjects of someone else's study. They "make" themselves, sometimes even "make themselves up," an activity which is not inevitable or automatic but reserved for special people in special circumstances. (p. 100)

As part of this self-reflexive consciousness, the actions of the members of this community reflected an understanding of the extent to which identity is:

- A public and social achievement, not a private and individual achievement
- Shaped by historical and cultural forces rather than by the forces of human nature, however this human nature might be conceived of
- The outcome of deriving a sense of authenticity through social processes that acknowledge one's preferred claims about one's identity and history (this is in contrast to the idea that it is through the identification and expression of

the essences of the "self" through introspection that one
finds authenticity in life)

The prominence given to "collective self-definitions," to the imperative of "appearing before others," to "garnering witnesses to one's
worth, vitality, and being," and to "proclaiming an interpretation to an
audience not otherwise available" emphasises the central significance
of the contribution of the audience in these definitional ceremonies.
It was the audience response to the stories told and performed in
these forums that was verifying of these stories. It was the audience's
acknowledgment of the identity claims* expressed in these stories
that was authenticating of these identity claims. It was the audience
recognition of these stories that so significantly contributed to the
community members' achieving a sense of feeling at one with their
claims about their lives. In the context of these forums, the audience
found themselves "participating in someone else's drama" and becoming "witnesses who push a plot forward almost unwittingly":

> These old Jews . . . separating the curtains between the real
> and unreal, imagined and actual, to step across the thresh-
> old and draw with them, pulling behind them, witnesses
> who find, often to their surprise, that they are somehow
> participating in someone else's drama. . . . Having stepped
> over the threshold, they become the "fifth business," wit-
> nesses who push a plot forward almost unwittingly; their
> story is not wholly their own but lives on, woven into the
> stuff of other people's lives. (Myerhoff 1986, p. 284)

Myerhoff stressed the significance of the active participation of the
outsider witnesses in these definitional ceremonies. It was the audi-

---

* The term claims is not used here in a pejorative sense. Rather, it reflects the idea that
all conclusions about identity begin as identity claims that are socially constructed, and
that it is the social verification of these claims that lends veracity to them. In the context
of this social verification, a truth status is allocated to identity claims, which has a powerful shaping effect on a person's life and on the responses of others to the actions of this
person.

ence retellings of the stories that most powerfully authenticated the identity claims expressed in those stories. It was the audience retellings that lent "greater public and factual" character to these claims, serving to amplify and authorize them. It was the audience retellings that fostered in community members a sense of being at one with their claims about their lives. It was the audience retellings that played the principal role in the renewal of one's sense of personal authenticity.

## Definitional Ceremonies in Therapeutic Practice

Myerhoff's description of the role of the witnesses in these definitional ceremonies struck a chord with some of the discoveries we had made in our therapeutic practices—discoveries about the relevance of the audience to rich story development, to the building of thick conclusions about identity, and to the endurance and expansion of preferred outcomes in the lives of the people who were consulting us. Just as with the members of this community of elderly Jews in Venice, we perceived that the audiences that we were recruiting in our work were providing an opportunity for the people who were consulting us to:

- Re-appear on their own terms in the eyes of community members and in the eyes of the outsiders who were invited to participate
- Experience an acknowledgment of the identity claims expressed in their stories
- Experience the authentication of these identity claims
- Intervene in the shaping of their lives in ways that were in harmony with what was precious to them

It was clear that the audiences that we were engaging in our work played the role of witnesses who lent "greater public and factual" character to people's identity claims and who pushed "a plot forward almost unwittingly."

Understanding the significance of audience participation in our therapeutic practices, we more strongly focused on eliciting from audiences retellings of what they had heard in people's accounts of the preferred developments of their lives. However, at this time the audience was still mostly engaged indirectly in our work.

Tom Andersen's (1987) development of "reflecting-team work" provided the inspiration to more directly engage the audience in therapeutic conversations. At first these more directly engaged audiences were drawn from the networks of the lives of the people consulting us and from the networks of our own lives. Later these audiences were also drawn from the professional disciplines. At this time I set about exploring what aspects of the retellings of the outsider witnesses were most effective in contributing to rich story development in therapeutic conversations. In the following section I describe some of the findings of these explorations, focusing on the structure of meetings shaped by as definitional ceremonies and on the specifics of the tradition of acknowledgment associated with these audience retellings.

## The Definitional Ceremony Structure

In therapeutic practice, definitional ceremonies are divided into three distinct stages:

1. The telling of the significant life story by the person for whom the definitional ceremony is for.
2. The retelling of the story by the people invited to be outsider witnesses.
3. The retelling of the outsider witnesses' retelling, which is done by the person for whom the definitional ceremony is for.

### The Telling

In this first stage, the therapist interviews the people seeking consultation while the outsider witnesses listen as an audience. In the context of this interview, the therapist finds opportunities to ask questions that encourage the telling of significant stories of people's lives that are relevant to matters of personal and relationship identity. The outsider witnesses listen carefully to the stories told and prepare to engage in a retelling of what they have heard.

In my meeting with Fiona, her parents, and Alison, I first interviewed Fiona and her parents. This interview provided the context for further explorations of the operations of anorexia nervosa in the lives and relationships of family members, of their experiences of this, and of the many forces that supported anorexia nervosa. It also provided the context for further explorations of developments that were not favorable to anorexia nervosa, of the foundations of these developments, of what these developments reflected about what family members accorded value to, and of the history of what they accorded value to. Alison was in the audience position during this time, as an outsider witness to this conversation that I refer to as the *telling*. Alison was not an active participant in this conversation, but rather witnessed it from the outside.

## The Retelling

When the time seems right, the outsider witnesses switch positions with the people whose lives are at the center of the definitional ceremony. These people now form an audience to the retelling of the outsider witnesses. This retelling is usually shaped by the questions of the therapist. It is not a retelling of the whole content of the telling or a summary of what the outsider witnesses heard. Rather, it is a retelling of those aspects of the original telling that the outsider witnesses were drawn to, a retelling that encapsulates and embroiders upon these aspects of the telling so that the retelling exceeds the boundaries of the original telling in significant ways. This contributes to the rich description of the relationships and personal identities of the people whose lives are at the center of the ceremony. These outsider witness retellings also contribute to the linking of the stories of people's lives around shared themes, and they are powerfully resonant in that they vividly represent what people accord value to in ways that are highly acknowledging.

When the story of Fiona and her parents had been sufficiently drawn out to provide Alison with a foundation to respond, I asked them to sit back while I interviewed Alison about what she had heard. My questions supported Alison in the development of a retelling that vividly re-presented what it was that Fiona and her parents accorded value to. These questions encouraged Alison to identify the aspects of the telling that had particularly caught her attention and aroused her interest. They also invited Alison to speak of the images or mental pictures that were evoked by the expressions of the telling, of what these expressions struck a chord with in her own experience, and of the ways in which she had been personally moved by these expressions. In this manner, Alison's retelling encapsulated elements of the original telling, but also exceeded the boundaries of it in various ways. This retelling contributed significantly to the sort of rich story development that was redefining of the relationships between Fiona and her parents and of their identities. This retelling also contributed to rich story development through a linking of all the participants' lives around specific themes that related to what they intended for their lives and what they accorded value to. In a subsequent meeting, when Alison's parents joined her as outsider witnesses, the stories of their lives were also linked to these themes.

A key part of outsider witness retellings is their adherence to a tradition of acknowledgment. This tradition of acknowledgement can be described in terms of four principal categories of inquiry. I use the term *inquiry* to emphasize the fact that retellings are not conducted according to an "anything goes" sentiment, but rather are guided by questions from the therapist. Specifically, these retellings are not about giving affirmations, offering congratulatory responses, pointing out positives, focusing on strengths and resources, making moral judgments or evaluating people's lives against cultural norms (whether these judgments and evaluations are positive or negative), interpreting the lives of others and formulating hypotheses, delivering interventions with the intention of resolving people's problems, giving advice or presenting moral stories or homilies, reframing the events of people's lives, imposing alternative stories about people's lives, trying to help people with their predicaments and dilemmas, or expressing worry for the lives of others. Further, outsider witness responses are not so much about empathy and sympathy but about resonance—outsider witness responses that are most effective are those that re-present what people give value to in a way that is highly resonant to these people.

In defining what these outsider witness retellings are not, it is not my intention to suggest that all that routinely goes in the name of acknowledgment is inappropriate with regard responding to the events of people's lives. I am not questioning the validity of these responses in daily life; I can think of many occasions in which congratulating, giving affirmations, advising, and so on is appropriate and valuable. However, in the context of definitional ceremony conversations, these responses are unlikely to contribute to rich story development and may even promote thin conclusions about life

Additionally, many of the responses listed above involve acts of judgment—for example, congratulating a person implies that the person has performed well according to a particular criterion and that the audience occupies a position of knowledge that makes it valid for them to make such an assessment. The therapeutic context is not an everyday life context, and in this context people can easily be and feel patronized by congratulatory responses, or feel that the audience doesn't understand and takes lightly their circumstances or predicaments, or that the audience is insincere, or that the audience is ridiculing and mocking them. Because there is a power relationship in the therapeutic context, any of these experiences will lead to a sense of alienation from the therapist and from the outsider witnesses.

Therapists have an ethical responsibility for the consequences of the audience participation in therapeutic contexts. This responsibility can be best observed if the therapist structures the retellings of the outsider witnesses. In speaking of this structuring, I don't mean to imply that it restricts the audience participation. Rather, in my experience, this structuring provides conditions under which outsider witnesses find themselves thinking beyond what they routinely think and giving voice to what they would not otherwise be giving voice to. In general, retellings are not constricted by familiar and taken-for-granted responses to the stories of people's lives.

Retellings structured according to the four following categories of inquiry have the potential to be highly resonant for the people whose lives are at the center of the definitional ceremony. It is this resonance that contributes significantly to rich story development, to a stronger familiarity with what one accords value to in life, and to the erosion and displacement of various negative conclusions about one's life and identity. This resonance also facilities an experience of being knowledged about how to proceed in addressing the dilemmas and predicaments being faced.

Before I discuss the four categories of inquiry, however, I will provide a brief overview of how I prepare outsider witnesses for the definitional ceremony.

## Outsider-Witness Preparation

In most cases, I talk briefly with the outsider witnesses before they participate in the meeting. At this time I inform them that, in their retelling, I will be inviting them to:

- Play a part in a tradition of acknowledgment that I understand to be particularly relevant to rich story development
- Engage in retellings that are the outcome of close listening and that are composed of particular aspects of the stories that they were drawn to
- Express these retellings in ways that will not be imposing
- Respond personally in speaking of their understanding of why they are drawn to what they are drawn to and about how this has affected them
- Step back from many of the common ways that people respond to the stories of other people's lives, including from giving opinions or advice, making judgments, and theorizing

I then negotiate with the outsider witnesses the option of my interjecting with a question if I have a sense that this might contribute to responses more favorable to rich story development, or if I think that the retelling is entering into territories of acknowledgment that contradict the tradition that we are intending to reproduce in these

retellings. I also make it clear that this option of interjection is necessitated by the fact that I will be taking full ethical responsibility for the
consequences of the outsider witness retelling. This arrangement is
invariably welcomed by outsider witnesses, for it helps to reduce
apprehension and allay fears and concerns about the task ahead. It is
also relieving, for it offers outsider witnesses the freedom to respond
to my questions without having to get into the sort of self-monitoring
that would be entirely restrictive of them in their responses.

I then usually describe the four categories of inquiry that will shape
my interview of the outsider witnesses, being careful to use language
that is familiar to them and taking into account cultural considerations and the age and stage of development of the outsider witnesses.
At this time, copies of the following description (or a version of it) can
be handed out.

*The Four Categories of Inquiry*

1. First, the focus will be on the expression. I will be asking you to
   identify and speak about what you heard that you were most drawn
   to: what caught your attention or captured your imagination. At this
   time I will be particularly interested in the expressions that provided you with a sense of what it is that the person accords value
   to in life. These expressions may be specific words or phrases or
   particular moods and sentiments. In speaking of the expressions
   that you are most drawn to, you will be signaling that your interest
   in the person's life is particular and distinct—not a general human
   interest or a global interest. This focus on the person's specific
   expressions will lend a precision to your retelling.
2. Second, the focus will be on the image. I will ask you to describe
   any images that came to your mind as you listened—images that
   were evoked by the expressions that you were drawn to. These
   images might take the form of certain metaphors about the person's
   life, or they might be mental pictures of the person's identity or
   relationships. Or they might be in the form of a "sense" that you
   derive from the person's life. After you describe these, I will
   encourage you to speculate about what these metaphors and mental pictures might reflect about the person's purposes, values,

beliefs, hopes, aspirations, dreams, and commitments—about what the person intends for his or her life and accords value to. At this time I will ask you questions that place the stress on what these images might say about the person's life and identity; I will not be asking you to formulate any solid conclusions about this matter.

3. Third, the focus will be on personal resonance.* I will encourage you to provide some account of why you were so drawn to these expressions, with a specific focus on your understanding of what these expressions struck a chord with in your own personal history. In placing your interest in the person's expression within the context of your own experiences of life, your interest becomes what I often refer to as "embodied interest," not disembodied interest. Another way of saying this is that your interest will be clearly established as personal interest, not academic interest; engaged and vital interest, not distant, armchair interest. What will be most relevant at this time will be for you to speak of what experiences in your own history lit up and came into memory on account of these expressions. For those of the professional disciplines, this can include experiences of therapeutic conversations had with others.

4. Fourth, the focus will be on transport. I will invite you to identify and speak of the ways in which you have been moved on account of being present to witness these stories of life. It is rarely possible to be an audience to the powerful dramas of other people's lives without this moving us in some way. I mean "moved" in a broad sense of the word. It might help for you to think about the places that this experience has taken you that you would not have arrived at had you been out gardening or shopping at this time. This can help you to prepare for my questions about where this experience has taken you with regard to your own thoughts, including your reflections on your own existence, your understandings of your own

---

* In this chapter I use the term *resonance* to describe two different phenomena. First, I employed this term to characterize the retellings of the definitional ceremony, understanding these to be powerfully resonant with what people give value to in life. Second, I have employed this term to characterize the personal resonances experienced by the outsider witnesses. These resonances are experienced in response to people's expressions.

life, or your perspectives on life more generally. Or about where this experience has taken you with regard to ideas about conversations that you might have with figures of your own life, or about options for action with regard to predicaments in your own life and in your relationships. This acknowledgement will be an account of how your life has been touched in ways that have contributed to your becoming someone other than who you were before you witnessed the person's expressions and had the opportunity to respond to them.

After describing these four categories of inquiry in terms that will be clear to the outsider witnesses, I suggest that, while listening to the telling, outsider witnesses simply endeavour to be aware of what they are drawn to and to be conscious of what images, reflections, or thoughts this is evoking for them. I inform the outsider witnesses that the material that provides a foundation for responses to the third (resonance) and fourth (transport) levels of this inquiry will be generated in response to my questions during the course of the retelling.

To further illustrate these categories of inquiry, I have charted Alison's retelling onto a "definitional ceremony conversations map" (Figure 4.1). This is a generalized charting that depicts the journey of this conversation as progressive and incremental in its movement through the four stages of outsider witness inquiry. However, Alison's retelling was not actually this linear in its progression, for time and again I encouraged her to recenter the expressions of Fiona, Louise, and Jake. This constant recentering of the expressions of the people who are the center of these therapeutic conversations ensures that all outsider witness responses are grounded in these expressions. This authenticates these responses and this is a characteristic of the definitional ceremonies of narrative practice.

I developed the expression, image, resonance, and transport categories of inquiry in response to my explorations of audience participation in therapeutic practice. I also put other categories of inquiry, mostly derived from narrative conceptions of life, to the test, and although many of these were influential, I found the four categories that I have described here to be most effective in promoting rich story development. These findings are based on my own direct observations

Figure 4.1 Charting Outsider-Witness Retellings (Alison)

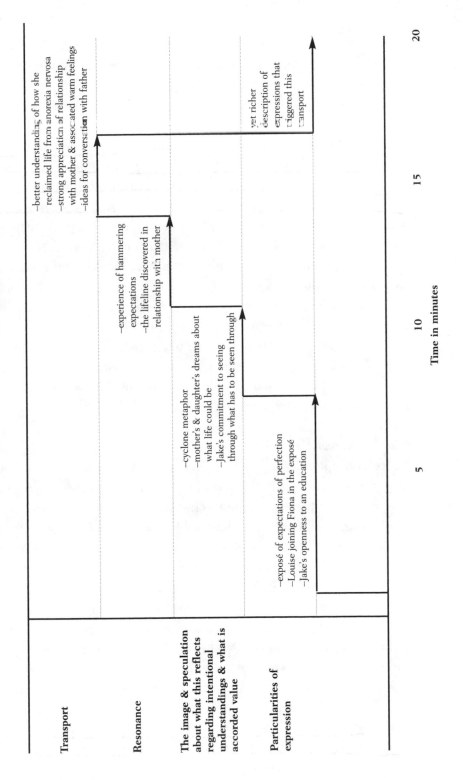

**Transport**
- better understanding of how she reclaimed life from anorexia nervosa
- strong appreciation of relationship with mother & associated warm feelings
- ideas for conversation with father

**Resonance**
- experience of hammering expectations
- the lifeline discovered in relationship with mother

**The image & speculation about what this reflects regarding intentional understandings & what is accorded value**
- cyclone metaphor
- mother's & daughter's dreams about what life could be
- Jake's commitment to seeing through what has to be seen through

**Particularities of expression**
- exposé of expectations of perfection
- Louise joining Fiona in the exposé
- Jake's openness to an education

- yet richer description of expressions that triggered this transport

Time in minutes

5          10          15          20

of the effects of these retellings, as well as on feedback I have received from the people whose lives are at the center of the definitional ceremonies

I also found that the retellings that seemed most seamless and that were most significant to outsider witnesses were those that were structured by these four categories of inquiry. For outsider witnesses, attending to what they are most strongly drawn to in people's expressions usually heightens awareness of their associative thoughts and of the images of life and identity that are triggered by these expressions. These images of life and identity are often rich in metaphor, analogy, and simile. Such images have the potential to set off reverberations into the history of their lives. Much in the way that the surface of the eardrum resonates when touched by the reverberations of sound waves, aspects of our own personal experiences can resonate in response to these reverberations of the image. These experiences, many of which have previously been neglected, "light up" and come into memory. We therefore experience a sense that, in some way, the stories of our lives are joined with the stories of the lives of the people at the center of the ceremony.

### Image, Reverberation, Resonance, and Katharsis

These concepts of image, reverberation, and resonance are drawn from the work of Gaston Bachelard (1969), a philosopher of science who wrote about the images of reverie and the poetics of the image. I have considered many of his ideas highly relevant to therapeutic practice in general, and to outsider witness inquiry in particular. Having these three concepts in mind when interviewing outsider witnesses has significantly shaped the questions that I have generated.

Another concept that I have found strongly influential, and that is implicit in the fourth category of outsider witness inquiry (transport), is the concept of *katharsis*. I spell this with a *k* to distinguish it from contemporary notions of catharsis associated with metaphors of discharge, release, abreaction, and so on. By katharsis I am referring to what I understand to be a central classical understanding of this concept—katharisis as a phenomenon that one experiences in response to witnessing powerful expressions of life's dramas, a phenomenon particularly associated with one's response to the performance of Greek tragedy. According to this classical definition, an experience is kathartic if one is moved by it—moved not just in terms of having an emotional experience, but in terms of being transported to another place in which one might:

- Achieve a new perspective on one's life and identity
- Reengage with neglected aspects of one's own history
- Reconnect with revered values and purposes for one's life
- Make new meanings of experiences of one's life that were not previously understood
- Experience a familiarity with knowledge of life and skills of living that one was previously barely aware of
- Initiate steps in one's life otherwise never considered
- Think beyond what one routinely thinks

I believe that the employment of this concept of katharsis is very much in accord with the priority that is given in outsider witness practices to the description of the particularities of the expressions of the people whose lives are at the center of these definitional ceremonies. This is because the phenomenon of katharsis relates to specific expressions of life that strike a chord for us, that we are drawn to, that most capture our imagination, that fire our curiosity, and that provoke our fascination.

The katharsis concept fosters inquiry into the identification of the ways in which one has been transported by the stories of the people whose lives are at the center of the definitional ceremony. And it encourages the acknowledgment of this—acknowledgment of the way that these stories have taken us to places that we could not have predicted. It helps us to find appropriate ways of acknowledging that these powerful expressions of life have shaped our own lives and that we have become someone other than who we would have been if we had not been present to witness these expressions. These acknowledgments are made even more powerful by their grounding in the specifics of their influence—they are not grand or ingratiating.

It should also be noted that the concept of katharsis does not apply

solely to outsider witness retellings. I believe it is an appropriate concept through which to understand our own responses as therapists to
the everyday dramas of life that we witness in our therapeutic conversations, in teaching contexts, and in working with communities.

There are occasions in which outsider witnesses have difficulty
identifying katharsis. At these times therapists can introduce explorations of the potential ramifications of the outsider witness's experience of resonance. For example, in acknowledging resonance, an outsider witness might give an account of the contribution of a favorite
aunt who saw the person through difficult times but find it difficult to
identify any katharthic response. The therapist can briefly interview
this outsider witness about whether the aunt knew how significant her
contribution was, and if not, about what it would mean for her to
know this and about how the direct acknowledgment of this might
touch the life of the outsider witness. Another example: An outsider
witness might give an account of a yearning that he or she experienced
in the context of resonance but then find it difficult to trace any element of katharsis. In response, the therapist might inquire about the
experience of publicly declaring this yearning: What has it been like
for you to speak openly of this yearning here? What are the effects of
taking this step? Will this make it any easier for you to make this
yearning visible to others? If so, what might be the consequences of
this?

### The Retelling of the Retelling

After the retelling, the outsider witnesses return to the audience position, and the people whose lives are at the center of the ceremony are
interviewed about what they have heard in the retelling. In this way,
they are engaged in the second of the retellings, this time in a retelling
of the outsider witnesses' retelling

This interview is conducted according to the same four categories
of inquiry (expression, image, resonance, and transport), except that
the focus of the second category of inquiry (image) remains on the
images of the person's life and identity rather than on images of the
life and identity of the outsider witnesses. In other words, the person
is interviewed about the metaphors or mental pictures of his or her

*own* life that were evoked by the retellings of the outsider witnesses.

People are interviewed about:

- The expressions of the outsider witnesses that they were drawn to
- The images or mental pictures evoked by these expressions (this time, the images or mental pictures pertaining to their own lives, not the lives of the outsider witnesses) and what this reflects about what they intend for their lives and what they accord value to in life
- The personal experiences that these expressions touched on
- Where these expressions of the outsider witnesses had taken them to in their thoughts on, understanding about, and perceptions of their own lives and in their reflections on possibilities for action

In this stage of the meeting with Alison, Fiona, Louise, and Jake, I began by interviewing Fiona and her parents about what they had heard in Alison's retelling that had particularly caught their attention and aroused their interest. They were then interviewed about what these expressions had evoked for them: for Fiona, a vision of new hope for a future apart from anorexia; for Louise, an image of a mother who had persevered in the face of powerfully discouraging forces and of the inspiration that she drew from Fiona's initiatives in reclaiming her life from anorexia, for Fiona and Louise, a portrait of their life-giving teamwork and of women who were challenging inequitable expectations for their lives; for Jake, a stronger sense of his commitment to values of fairness expressed in his willingness to face the challenges associated with negotiating a new relationship arrangement with Louise and Fiona.

I also interviewed Fiona and her parents about their personal experiences that had resonated with these aspects of Alison's retelling and about the destinations that they might have arrived at in their understandings and in their reflections on possibilities for their lives on account of being an audience to this retelling and as an outcome of participating in a retelling of this retelling. I learned that, apart from other things, Fiona had arrived at a greater clarity about the operations of anorexia nervosa and about aspects of her teamwork with Louise; Louise had felt freed from some of the burden of guilt and had new realizations about challenges and developments in her own life that paralleled those that Fiona was experiencing; and Jake had some proposals for how he might modify some of his previously taken-for-granted ways of responding to Louise and Fiona.

## Shifting Between the Three Stages of Telling and Retelling

The shifts between the telling, the retelling, and the retelling of the retelling are distinct and relatively formal movements. For example, when engaging in the retelling, it is important that outsider witnesses do not bring the audience into this circle; they do not directly address those in the audience position, but rather talk with each other (or with the therapist) about what they heard during the telling. To directly address the people whose lives are at the center of the ceremony would be to deprive them of their audience status. This would have profound implications with regard to the listening orientation of the audience, limiting what they might otherwise hear. Degeneration of these distinct positions would compromise the conditions that give rise to rich story development.

To facilitate these distinct shifts of position, one-way screens and closed-circuit television can be utilized. However, this is not necessary, and in many of the contexts in which I employ definitional ceremony structures, including in work with communities, such facilities are rarely available and often not appropriate. In these circumstances, those in the audience position sit apart from those who are engaging in the tellings and retellings, and those who are engaging in the tellings and retellings form a circle with the therapist.

In providing an account of this structure of definitional ceremony in therapeutic contexts, I have emphasised three stages of telling and retelling. However, given the appropriate circumstances, the luxury of time, and the interest and energy level of participants, these positions may be switched time and again in the facilitation of multiple levels of telling and retelling. There can even be a fourth stage in which all

parties meet together to talk about their experience of the exercise. I
have discussed this fourth stage in detail elsewhere (White, 1995).

## The Extended Performance of Katharsis

Another variation on the stages of definitional ceremonies may be
appropriate when the person seeking consultation has found the
katharsis aspect of the conversation extremely beneficial. This is particularly the case when the person seeking consultation has little
sense of personal agency, as is common among people who have been
through significant trauma. When people have little sense of personal
agency, they often feel irrelevant, empty, desolate, and paralyzed—as
if their life is frozen in time. Outsider witnesses' acknowledgment of
katharsis—their explanations of how they have been transported by
the stories they have heard from the person—can be a potent antidote
to this.

·When therapists sense that outsider witness retellings have been
particularly resonant for the person seeking consultation, they can talk
with the outsider witnesses after the definitional ceremony about the
possibility of extending the performance of katharsis. These "extended
performances" are are intended to provide outsider witnesses with an
opportunity to acknowledge the continuing effects of the katharsis on
their lives. This acknowledgment can be in the form of notes, letters,
audiotapes, or videotapes sent to the person whose life was at the center of the definitional ceremony, or they can be other gestures that
convey the significance of the katharsis with regard to events following the definitional ceremony. Here is an example of of this.

Marianne had a history of significant and recurrent trauma, and
she had struggled with the consequences of this over a long period of
her life. In our second meeting I interviewed Marianne in the presence of three outsider witnesses. Two of them were people who had
previously consulted me about the effects of trauma in their lives. The
third, Hazel, was a counselor who had a special interest in working
with people who had been subject to trauma.

In the first part of this second meeting I interviewed Marianne
about her experience of trauma, about the consequences of this to her
life, about her responses to trauma, and about the foundation of these

responses. I then interviewed the outsider witnesses and noticed that Marianne seemed particularly drawn to Hazel's acknowledgment of katharsis. In this acknowledgment, Hazel had spoken of some new realizations that she had come to about what might be helpful in her work with two women who had been consulting her about the effects of trauma on their lives. Hazel said that until this moment she had felt somehow constrained in her consultations with these two women and frustrated that she couldn't find a way of proceeding that was to her satisfaction. She also said that over the last month or so she had become concerned that she was failing these two women. In the context of the outsider witness retelling, Hazel spoke of these new realizations and of the possibilities that she thought these might bring to her therapeutic conversations with these two women. She rounded off this acknowledgment of katharsis with: "Because of what I've heard from Marianne, I now have some clear ideas about how to proceed in my consultations with these two women." When I interviewed Marianne about her response to the retellings of the outsider witnesses, she dwelled for some time on this account of her potential contribution to Hazel's work. She seemed a little awestruck: "I always think of myself as something that is useless and just a burden to others. Who would have ever thought that I could do anything that might help someone else? This is a big thing to get my head around, it really is. It is going to take a while!"

At the end of this meeting Hazel was acutely aware of the significance of her acknowledgment of katharsis. Three weeks later I received two letters addressed to Marianne via my office, along with a note from Hazel. In this note Hazel explained that these two letters had been cowritten by her and the women she'd mentioned, and that these letters provided an account of the ways in which Marianne's story had opened new avenues for them to address the consequences of trauma in their lives. Hazel also suggested that I read these letters to Marianne during my next meeting with her.

Marianne was so moved by these letters that she had to take a time-out in the courtyard on two occasions in order to, in her words, "get myself together again." She was also powerfully touched by the gifts that we had discovered in the two envelopes. One of the letters was accompanied by a beautiful hand-crafted card with an inscription that honored Marianne's contribution. The other letter was accompanied by five coupons for espresso and cake at a café.

Some time later Marianne informed me she had never experienced anything even close to this sort of acknowledgment in her entire life; that this was "light-years" away from anything that she'd ever known. She also said that it had been important that this acknowledgment wasn't in a form that she could refute or deny; she hadn't experienced it as an attempt to point out positives but rather as a factual account of the ripples produced by her own expressions. This provided her with a platform for new initiatives to recover from the trauma of her history. I also learned that this experience had affirmed a long-held secret hope that all she had been through would not be for nothing.

As I mentioned earlier, extended performances of katharsis can be particularly significant for people who have been subject to trauma. It is common for these people to hold onto a secret longing for the world to be different due to what they have been through or a secret hope that all that they endured wasn't for nothing, a hidden desire to contribute to the lives of others who have had similar experiences or a fantasy about playing a part in relieving the suffering of others, or a passion to play some part in acts of redress in relation to the injustices of the world. Extended performances of katharsis can be powerfully resonant with these longings, hopes, desires, fantasies, and passions and can serve as antidotes to a sense of personal emptiness and desolation.

## Outsider Witness Selection

As previously mentioned, when I first began conducting definitional ceremonies, I drew outsider witnesses principally from people's family and friendship networks, from school and workplace environments, and from pools of acquaintances including neighbors and shopkeepers. I also drew from communities of people unknown to the people seeking consultation, including from our my personal and social networks or from others of the professional disciplines visiting us for training and consultation.

In my continued development of these ceremonies, however, I have increasingly drawn from my registers of people who have previously sought my consultation and who volunteer to join me in my work with others who might follow in their footsteps. Invitations to join these registers are invariably received enthusiastically. I believe that this enthusiasm is partly due the fact that many of these people have had direct experience with outsider witness retellings in the context of their own therapy sessions with me. Thus, they understand that their contribution to the life of others has the potential to be quite profound. They also understand that they will not be taking responsibility for the problems of the people they help and that their participation will be time-limited.

## Repositioning

When outsider witnesses are recruited from within people's families, especially when these family members are in significant dispute with those whose lives will be at the center of the definitional ceremony, it is usually necessary to help them to "reposition" themselves before their participation as outsider witnesses. This is because the definitional ceremony will require them to disengage from their habitual ways of responding to the people who will be the subjects of their retellings. These habitual responses can seem almost hard-wired with regard to the tensions in family relationships, making them very difficult to break.

Disengaging from these habitual responses often can be best achieved by inviting the family members to separate, for the duration of the definitional ceremony, from their usual sense of being in relationship with each other. One effective way of achieving this is for them to adopt an alternative position from which they will find it easier to reproduce the tradition of outsider witness response. To help them establish this alternative position, therapists can invite family members to share stories about life experiences in which they were the subject of significant acknowledgment, understanding, compassion, or acceptance and to identify the figures who extended this. Family members can then reposition themselves as one of these figures during the outsider witness retelling. It is important that the figures chosen by family members are acceptable to those who are the focus of the definitional ceremony. The figures chosen should not be ones that these people have had a negative experience of or feel alienated from in any way. If a figure chosen is unknown to those who are the focus of the definitional ceremony, it is important that the identity of this figure is drawn out before it is sanctioned as an acceptable choice.

This repositioning inquiry is usually prefaced by some discussion of the difficulties that can be predicted in trying to respond in ways that are not dictated by usual habits of response. It is also prefaced by the observation that although many things can be uniquely achieved in the context of family relationships, some things are better achieved in the context of other forms of relationship. This observation is followed up with the suggestion that family members not reposition themselves as each other, or as other members of the immediate family.

As figures who are candidates for this repositioning are identified, the therapist can inquire about the ways in which they went about expressing acknowledgment, understanding, love, compassion, or acceptance. In this inquiry, the therapist encourages family members to spell out the sort of skills employed by these figures in these expressions. In this way, the relationship know-how associated with these expressions is richly described and becomes easier to reproduce in the context of outsider witness retellings. If it seems necessary, the therapist can further this outsider witness preparation by encouraging family members to provide an understanding of what these expressions suggest about the figures' sentiments of living, about their perspectives on life, and about their purposes, values, and beliefs. Drawing out the skills and sentiments of these figures should not be rushed; an entire meeting can be devoted to this if necessary.

Once this is achieved, the therapist informs family members that he or she will assist them in maintaining the position they have chosen for the definitional ceremony. An agreement should be reached about how the therapist might interject if it becomes apparent that family members are falling back into habitual responses. Further, family members are informed that on such occasions they will be consulted about options for proceeding. These options may include a simple reminder to reengage with their chosen positions, a second repositioning interview (to better understand the skills associated with the figures' expressions of acknowledgment), a temporary suspension of the exercise to gain clarification on hurdles to engaging with the chosen positions or to explore what might make it more possible to assume these positions, or a permanent abandonment of the exercise to pursue other approaches.

Repositioning of family members is not required in all situations, but it is invariably necessary when there is significant tension between family members and the people whose lives are the focus of the definitional ceremony. Readers who are interested in reading an illustration of the repositioning of family members can refer to my article "Narrative practice, couple therapy and conflict dissolution" (White, 2004).

## Therapeutic Responsibility in Guiding Definitional Ceremony Conversations

Regardless of the source of outsider witnesses, the therapist assumes ultimate responsibility for the shaping of retellings. If this responsibility is not taken up from the outset of outsider witness retellings, it is relatively certain that other traditions of responding to the stories of people's lives will be enacted. This is even the case when the outsider witnesses have been familiarized with the categories of inquiry relevant to rich story development.

### Responding to Superlatives

It is not at all uncommon for outsider witnesses to immediately engage with superlatives at the commencement of their retellings: "I think that Joan is the most amazing person," or "Wow, Harry is just one extraordinary guy." When this happens, the therapist immediately refocuses the outsider witness on the first category of inquiry: their retelling of the aspects of the expression that struck a chord with them. For example, the therapist could say, "Okay, I can see that you are appreciative of Joan. Tell, me what is it that you heard or experienced in Joan's story that you were most drawn to?" or "I'd like to hear what you actually heard that shaped your impressions of Harry. Could we start with what it was that Harry said that really struck a chord for you?"

## Responding to "Going Autobiographical"

Another common tendency for outsider witnesses is to "go autobiographical" when acknowledging resonance. In response to the invitation to embody their interest in a person's life, outsider witnesses often share a small personal narrative about an episode of their own histories. These mini-narratives are not just a recounting of the experience that resonated with aspects of the person's story but also a description of how the outsider witnesses responded to the experience, about what this meant to them, about what this made possible in their lives, and so on. If this goes unchecked, the outsider witness retelling will quickly enter the territory of advice-giving through moral story and homily, or of the sort of sharing-experience-for-the-sake-of-sharing-experience that will displace the experiences of the person who is at the center of the definitional ceremony.

When outsider witnesses go autobiographical, therapists can encourage them to more richly describe the resonant experience: "You have been catching us up on how you responded to this experience in your own history and on what this made possible for you. But I would like to know more about the actual experience itself. Would it be okay if we went back a step or two, and I asked you some questions about this?" Another option is to re-focus on the expressions of the people who are the focus of the definitional ceremony: "It is obvious that the story that you heard profoundly touched on your own experiences. Could you say more about which aspects of the story that you heard were so powerful for you?"

The following transcript provides an example of an outsider witness retelling that become autobiographical and how the conversation was successfully redirected toward the expressions of the people who were the focus of the definitional ceremony. This retelling was in response to a conversation with a single-parent mother, Leanne, and her two children, Amy, 7, and Rebecca, 4. Leanne's primary concern was about what she understood to be a delay in Amy's development, about what she perceived to be the failure of her relationship with Amy, and about her sense of failure as a mother. One of the outsider witnesses participating in this meeting was a therapist named John. He began his account of personal resonance as follows:

> **John:** There were so many echoes in this for me. It took me back to when I was just a boy who was like Amy in so many ways. I also didn't relate much to other kids. I got easily bored. I was a bit of a handful at times. Actually lots of the time. And if the diagnosis of ADHD was around then, I know I would have gotten it, just like Amy has. But my mother, she was wonderful. She said to the world out there, this is my son, and I know there are some things about him that are different, and lots of these things can be appreciated if you just know how to approach them. Let me tell you about the things that are different about him that you can learn to appreciate. She was just wonderful. And she would also say to everyone, I'll tell you how to—
>
> **M:** What was it like for you to revisit this image of your mother?
>
> **John:** It was powerful. And it was really beautiful. (*smiling*) This is how my mother lived. She had these principles of—
>
> **M:** I would like to understand more about what you heard or witnessed in Leanne's story that so powerfully evoked this image of your mother. What was it that you witnessed as you listened to Leanne's story that mirrored your mother's ways?
>
> **John:** Oh! That's easy. It was when Leanne . . .

John's telling of his experience of resonance had become autobiographical—it was an account of his identification with Amy in her predicament, of his mother's wonderful response to this, of the principles that shaped her response, and of how this was a reflection of her ways in life. I strongly appreciated John's recounting of this resonance, but I was concerned about its autobiographical nature—there was a risk that it could be received by Leanne as a moral story or homily and could consolidate some of Leanne's negative conclusions about her identity by giving her an opportunity to judge herself poorly in relation to this other woman who was being revered. In encouraging John to speak more of what he witnessed in Leanne's telling, that had evoked this image of his mother, this hazard was circumvented. Instead of experiencing an unfavorable comparison between her actions and the actions of John's mother, she experienced parallels being drawn between her identity as a mother and the identity of another mother who was being revered. This recentering of Leanne's expressions was also a prelude to my questions about the transporting or kathartic aspects of her story:

> **M:** I understand that listening to Leanne's story was a powerful experience for you—that in this Leanne evoked the image of your mother and that this was beautiful. What's your guess about what it is going to be like for you going away from here today having had this experience?
>
> **John:** I'm in a great place and would just like to sit with this a bit.
>
> **M:** Could I ask you a question about your work?
>
> **John:** Sure, sure.
>
> **M:** Do you sometimes get consulted by women who are single-parent mothers?
>
> **John:** Sure I do. And I think I know what you are asking. I think there are things to hear in my work that I don't think I have been hearing well enough.
>
> **M:** Are you saying that there is something that has come of hearing Leanne's story and of talking about what this touched on for you that will contribute to your hearing things in other women's stories that you might not have fully heard?
>
> **John:** You're right on it. That's what I'm saying.

Leanne was quite emotional as I interviewed her for the retelling of the retelling. John's account of resonance, the parallels drawn between her expressions and those of his mother, and his acknowledgment of katharsis deeply touched her. It was clear that this was an antidote to her conclusions about being a failure. Leanne said that she felt less burdened and that she could see some possibilities for proceeding with her effort to address her concerns about Amy. I have charted John's retelling in Figure 4.2.

The tendency to go autobiographical can be countered if therapists suggest, when orientating outsider witnesses to the tradition of acknowledgment associated with retellings, that outsider witnesses endeavor to prioritize not the events of their lives that are well known and familiar, but the experiences that might have been outside of memory or only dimly perceived before listening to the stories of those whose lives are the focus of the definitional ceremony.

### Responding to "Going One-Down"

When asked to to acknowledge katharsis, outsider witnesses may respond by "going one-down." For example: "In hearing about how Joan got through what she was put through in the way that she did, I had this realization that I didn't do nearly as well in coping with some things that what I went through. Joan really did so much better than I ever could have done." "Going one-down" in this way represents a diminishment of one's life for the sake of the elevation of another, and it is invariably experienced as unhelpful because it leads to a sense of being misunderstood and to the erosion of joining around shared themes. Another hazard of going one-down is that it constructs a heroic identity of the person whose life is at the center of the definitional ceremonies. Although heroic accounts of identity have become quite popular in contemporary culture, they can be very isolating and alienating of the people who are construed as heroes.

### Responding to Expressions of Anguish

Because of the way it is structured, the first stage of the definitional ceremony usually yields conversations in which people begin to give meaning to some of the neglected initiatives of their lives and reveal

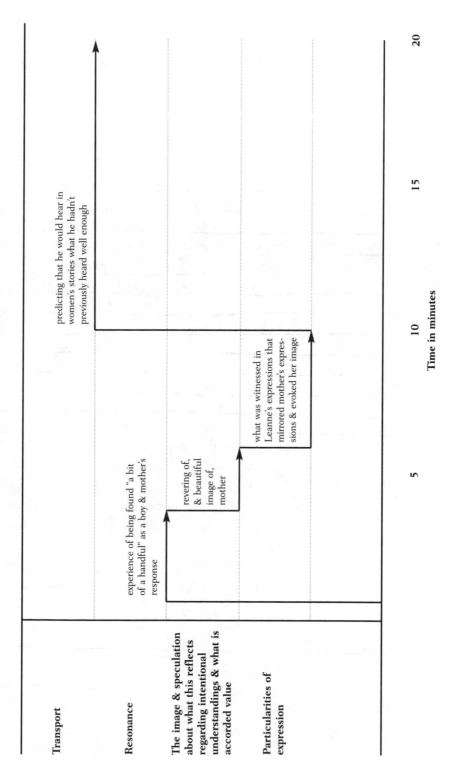

Figure 4.2 Charting Outsider-Witness Retellings (John)

traces of positive subordinate storylines. By the time that these people assume the audience position for the retelling, the outsider witnesses usually have plenty of material with which to ground their responses. At this point, it is common for the outsider witnesses to respond to the expressions of the telling that were specifically associated with the positive subordinate storylines. However, at times the outsider witnesses are drawn to the more anguished expressions, including those relating to frustration and pain. In these circumstances, it is important for therapists to ask questions that draw out the values, hopes, dreams, and so on that are implicit in the anguished expressions. For example, if outsider witnesses have been drawn to expressions of pain, they can be encouraged to speculate about what this might be a testimony to in terms of what the person holds precious. If outsider witnesses have been drawn to expressions of despair, they can be encouraged to speculate about what this might reflect in terms of the person's hopes and dreams about life. If outsider witnesses have been drawn to a lament about the emptiness of a person's life, they can be encouraged to speculate about what this might suggest about what is important to the person in terms of achieving a sense of personal intimacy.

This approach is based on the ideas of Jacques Derrida (1973, 1976, 1978). Although Derrida focused on the deconstruction of texts, I have found his ideas to be very useful in the context of therapeutic conversations. Derrida's basic contention was that the meaning of a word, phrase, or sentence is contingent upon the words, phrases, or sentences surrounding it—that one can only attribute meaning to something by distinguishing the difference between it and everything else in its context. In a therapeutic context, this means that, in order to express an experience of life, people must distinguish that experience from the contrasting experiences surrounding it. For example, to express despair, one must distinguished this despair from another experience that it is not—say, for instance, from an experience in life that is defined as an expression of hope. For one to express pain, the experiences that give rise to this must be distinguished from another experience, such as one that is read as sign of what is given value to in life or is representative of what might be held precious. Thus, pain might be understood to be a testimony to what a person has held precious and has been violated, and ongoing distress might be understood to be a tribute to a person's success in maintaining a relationship with what he or she gives value to despite the forces that discourage this. I have discussed this principle and its implications in more detail elsewhere (White, 2000, 2003).

Therapists can also draw out the implicit during the third stage of outsider witness inquiry (resonance) if the outsider witnesses have provided an account of some of the more painful experiences of their lives. This can be done by asking questions that provide an opportunity for the outsider witnesses to speak of what is precious to them that was touched by the expressions of the people whose lives are at the center of the ceremony. With regard to katharsis, the implicit can be drawn out through questions that help outsider witnesses to go beyond expressions of pain in their effort to identify the ways in which they might have been transported.

The following transcript provides an example of an outsider witness, Roger, recounting of personal resonance that features a theme of pain. The retelling was in response to a story told by a father, Patrick, and his adult son, Kevin, who had been estranged for some years but had, in the context of our meeting, recovered their relationship with each other. This had turned out to be of great importance to both of them. The questions I asked helped Roger to draw out what was implicit in his recounting.

> **Roger:** What really got to me was seeing the joy on Patrick and Kevin's face. And I could see what reconnecting meant to them both. I could see the affection between them. This touched on something really painful for me. (*now tearful*)
>
> **M:** Would you be prepared to say a little about this here?
>
> **Roger:** I never had this sort of connection with my father. He was a really hard man. I really didn't ever get any affection from him. When he wasn't giving me a hard time, I

don't think I really existed for him. So I never had any of this. Even just to talk about it now is painful.

**M:** Were there any other father-type people in your life?

**Roger:** No. And I never got to meet my grandfathers either. I don't know anything about them.

**M:** But you didn't simply just get resigned to what you had?

**Roger:** No, I guess not.

**M:** I don't understand this. There weren't any other father-type figures to give you a different experience. What was it that stopped you from just becoming resigned to what you had? Just accepting what you were accustomed to?

**Roger:** I don't know. Maybe it was just a . . . just this longing that I had for some sort of connection with my father?

**M:** Do you know what kept this longing alive? Are there any stories that you can tell me about your life that might explain how you held onto this longing? Anything at all that might have encouraged and supported this longing or validated it in some way?

**Roger:** Encouraged it? Well . . . you know, this has got me thinking. My mom died when I was quite young, and her stepmother did what she could to care for me. And I remember that things weren't going well for me in high school and I just wanted to drop out. But my nan got a tutor in for a while and this helped to turn things around. This is amazing!

**M:** What's amazing?

**Roger:** I would never have thought about this. But you know, there are some things about Patrick that remind me of this guy who was my tutor. For a start, he was Irish too, and he was kind to me, he really was. Wow!

**M:** My understanding then is that because of what you have witnessed today between Patrick and Kevin that you have openly spoken of this longing for the first time. And that for the first time you are making a connection between this longing and your Irish tutor of many years ago.

**Roger:** Yeah. Yeah.

**M:** What's this been like for you?

**Roger:** Like I've talked about something and discovered something that's been there all along but I couldn't see it.

**M:** Does this make any difference?

**Roger:** Of course. Of course it does. I've got something I didn't know I had that I am going to do more thinking about and more talking about. It sure eases the pain, even now!

It was through this interview that the implicit longing in Roger's expression of pain became visible and was named. His expression of pain was in relation to a longing for recognition from, and connection with, an adult male. This longing had been sustained by this tutor's responses to Roger when he was a boy. The identification of this had a profound effect on Roger's acknowledgment of personal resonance and katharsis. (Figure 4.3 shows my charting of Roger's retelling.) For Patrick and Kevin, witnessing Roger's life being touched in this way by the story of the recovery of their relationship was, in turn, quite profound and contributed significantly to the rich development of the story of their own relationship.

In drawing out the implicit in this way, the therapist is not endeavoring to reduce the intensity of people's expression of frustration or pain, to shy away from these experiences, or to substitute other less vexing experiences for them. Rather, the therapist is being consistent with the assumption that life is multistoried and with the intention of reproducing the tradition of acknowledgment that promotes rich story development.

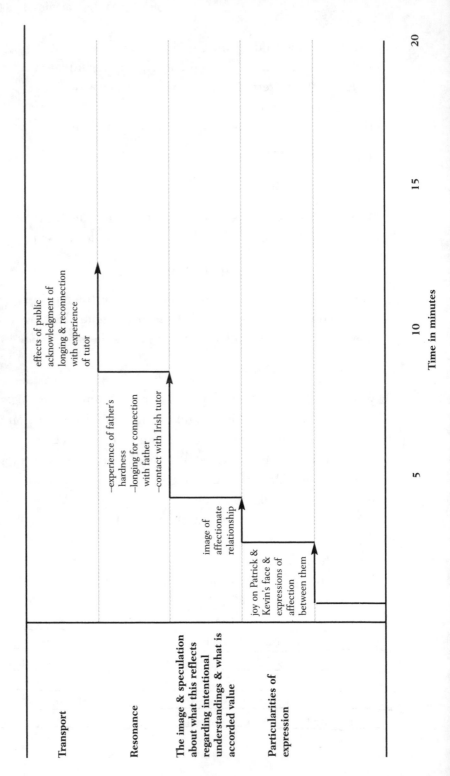

Figure 4.3 Charting Outsider-Witness Retellings (Roger)

## Cautions

In some circumstances therapists may become vulnerable to relinquishing their responsibility for shaping outsider witness responses.
This is particularly likely to occur when the people in the outsider witness position have significant insider knowledge of the experiences
and predicaments of those at the center of the definitional ceremony.
In these circumstances I have on occasion found myself relatively
inactive in the early part of the retellings, and, to my alarm, becoming
a bystander to the development of outsider witness responses that are
very unlikely to contribute to rich story development and personal resonance.

This vulnerability is the outcome of confusing insider knowledge
with know-how. It is one thing to have insider knowledge of specific
experiences and circumstances of life, but it is another to know how
to express this in ways that might contribute to rich story development
and in ways that will be powerfully resonant for and healing of others.
It is possible to assume the responsibility for the shaping of these
retellings while simultaneously acknowledging the significance of the
insider knowledge that is possessed by the outsider witness.

The participation of outsider witnesses drawn from the professional
disciplines is another circumstance in which the therapist can be vulnerable to relinquishing this responsibility in shaping outsider witness
responses. This is particularly the case when these outsider witnesses
have a passing knowledge of definitional ceremony practices, including the categories of inquiry that shape retellings. I have, at times,
relinquished this responsibility in these circumstances, only to find
the outsider witnesses reproducing other traditions of response: theorizing and hypothesizing about people's lives and relationships, evaluating people's expressions and reaching diagnoses according to the
expert knowledges of the professional disciplines, formulating interventions and treatments for the problems of people's lives, and engaging in other practices that are informed by some of the professional
and popular discourses of psychology.

In offering these cautions, I am not trying to be critical of the outsider witnesses who inadvertently reproduce some of these responses

to the stories of people's lives. It can be surprisingly difficult to break from these orthodox responses. Nor do I intend to question the general validity of these discourses. Rather, I am underscoring considerations that I believe are vital in establishing conditions that give rise to rich story development in the context of definitional ceremony practice.

There are, however, circumstances in which it is not necessary for the therapist to take this leading role in the shaping of the outsider witness retelling. When outsider witnesses have more than a passing knowledge of this tradition of retelling, it is possible for the therapist to assume a more backseat role and allow the outsider witnesses to either interview each other according to this tradition or to appoint one member of the group to assume more of this responsibility. I have always found that when outsider witnesses become well acquainted with this tradition of retelling, the requirement for me to actively shape these retellings quickly diminishes.

## Technology, Anonymity, and Ethics

Although I have described definitional ceremony practices as involving the direct participation of outsider witnesses this does not always have to be the case. For example, the technology of conference calls provides an option for outsider witness retellings when it is not possible for the outsider witnesses to be physically present or when anonymity is required by the people who are the focus of these definitional ceremonies.

Technology can also be utilized in the recording of outsider witness retellings in response to the therapist's subsequent accounts of the stories of people's lives. (Of course, the parties involved must agree to this.) In other words, the therapist can meet with someone who has volunteered to participate as a "remote" outsider witness by listening to the therapist recount the stories of the therapeutic conversation. This meeting is audio- or video-recorded, as is the outsider witness retelling in response to the therapist's story. These recordings can then be played at the next meeting with the people who are the subject of the retelling, and the therapist can elicit a retelling of the retelling after these people have watched or listened to the tape. This option is suitable when the appropriate outsider witness cannot be present for a therapeutic conversation or when anonymity is required.

With regard to anonymity generally, this is rarely an issue for those who participate in these contexts. However, the people who are at the center of the definitional ceremony must be fully informed of its processes and structure before decisions about outsider witness participation are made. They should also be provided with the option to speak to others who have first-hand experience in being a the center of definitional ceremony practices. Additionally, therapists must ask if there are any subjects the people do not wish to be interviewed about in the context of the definitional ceremony, and the people should be assured that the therapist will not pass on any personal information to the outsider witness candidates—anything that the outsider witnesses might know about these people's lives will be learned directly from the people during the course of the telling. Further, people should be informed that the usual conventions with regard to confidentiality in group therapy contexts will be explicitly addressed and observed.

It is my experience that people rarely decline the option of directly involving outsider witnesses in their meetings with me. Furthermore, those who have had the opportunity to be the focus of one of these definitional ceremonies almost invariably choose to meet again in the context of a definitional ceremony when they are given the option between it and a solo meeting. With regard to the question of confidentiality and anonymity, it is usually the case that people are enthusiastic about the possibility of sharing the stories of their lives with others.

On a few occasions I have heard members of the professional disciplines voice concerns that engaging in definitional ceremony practices might be in contravention of professional ethics. In reviewing the ethical codes of these professional disciplines, I have not discerned any conflict with the practices that I have described in this chapter. Rather, it has been my conclusion that these practices are in accord with the principles expressed in these ethical codes. However, should readers have concerns about conflict between these practices and the ethical codes of their professional associations, it is important that they resolve this by reviewing the relevant ethical codes and tailoring these practices in a way that honors any concerns they may have.

## Conclusion

In this chapter I have described therapeutic practices associated with definitional ceremonies. These practices contribute to the reproduction of a tradition of acknowledgment that can be strongly resonant for the people at the center of these [definitional] ceremonies. Rich story development and the augmentation of a sense of personal agency is the outcome [of this.] and this provides a foundation for people to proceed to address their predicaments and concerns.

It is relevant to note that a sense of awkwardness and some personal discomfort is often experienced by therapists at the beginning of their explorations of definitional ceremony practices. This awkwardness is probably due to the fact that they are reproducing a tradition of acknowledgment that differs from customary therapeutic responses to the stories of people's lives. This discomfort may also be associated with the structuring of a context that contradicts the direct person-to-person dialogue that shapes most therapeutic conversations today. This sense of awkwardness and this discomfort diminishes as the effects of these practices of acknowledgment become visible and as the importance of disrupting direct person-to-person dialogue becomes apparent.

Of all the therapeutic practices that I have come across in the history of my career, those associated with the definitional ceremony have the potential to be the most powerful. Time and again I have observed outsider witness retellings achieve what is quite beyond my potential to achieve in my role as a therapist. I have also witnessed this on many occasions when observing other therapists' explorations of definitional ceremonies. However, this does not diminish the significance of the therapist's contribution. The retellings of definitional ceremonies achieve resonance for the people who consult therapists when they are shaped by the appropriate outsider witness inquiry and when vital considerations to the success of these practices are closely monitored.

# 5
# Conversations That Highlight Unique Outcomes

lthough life is rich in lived experience, we give meaning to very little of this experience. The aspects of lived experience that are rendered meaningful are those that we take into the known and familiar storylines of our lives; these aspects are highly selected. The myriad experiences of daily life mostly pass like a blip across the screen of our consciousness and into a historical vacuum. Many of these experiences are "out of phase" with the plots or themes of the dominant stories of our lives and thus are not registered or given meaning to. However, these out-of-phase experiences can be potentially significant, and in favourable circumstances they can be constituted as "unique outcomes" or "exceptions." The identification of such out-of-phase aspects of lived experience can provide a point of entry for the development of alternative storylines of people's lives.

In preparation for this storyline development, it is the therapist's task to assist people to render significant some of these neglected aspects of lived experience. Upon engaging in this task, it is not uncommon for therapists to take a leading role in this attribution of meaning. When this is the case, the therapist undertakes efforts to convince people of the worth of these aspects of lived experience and assumes primary authorship. This is hazardous, for it can be imposing and risks alienating people who seek consultation. It also places the therapist at the center of the therapeutic conversation, thus closing the door on possibilities for collaborative inquiry.

Conversations that highlight unique outcomes support a decentered therapist participation, which privileges the authorship of the people seeking consultation. These conversations assist people in rendering specific out-of-phase aspects of their experience significant; they support people in the characterization of, and in reflecting on, these aspects of their experience. This is very often novel for people who consult therapists, as these people often have been simply subject to the meanings given and the position taken by others on the developments of their lives. Among other things, conversations that highlight unique outcomes provide people with the opportunity to give voice to intentions for their own lives and to develop a stronger familiarity with what they accord value to in life. This provides them with a springboard for action in addressing their problems, predicaments and dilemmas.

## Peter and Trudy

I met with Peter, 14, and his single-parent mother, Trudy, along with the referring therapist, Melanie, for a consultation interview. Melanie worked for a medium-security detention center, and at the time of the consultation, Peter was an inmate at this center. This was one of several centers that Peter had spent time in during the course of his young life. Most of these incarcerations had been the outcome of destroying property, but some were for assault and petty theft. Peter had a longstanding habit of going on a rampage when frustrated with life, and he had the capacity to do fearsome damage at these times.

Many efforts had been made to encourage Peter to take responsibility for his actions and to appreciate the seriousness of them, but to no avail. Peter's nonresponsiveness to these efforts had led the people trying to help him to determine that he was generally incapable of reflecting on his life, unable to foresee the consequences of his actions, and relatively inept with regard to taking responsibility. He was judged to be a concrete thinker, lacking a capacity to think in abstract terms.

However, Melanie had recently noticed an interesting development in Peter's life: He had handled an incident at the detention center that he found frustrating by exiting the room and going to the gymnasium instead of lashing out at people and smashing things. As it was more usual for Peter to run amok at these times, Melanie had a strong appreciation of the significance of this response to frustration. However, she also realized that Peter's initiative could easily be lost, and she hoped that in a consultation with me it would be rendered meaningful and that it would open an avenue to the development of an alternative storyline about Peter's life. Melanie also hoped that this consultation would provide a foundation for Peter to take further steps of a similar nature.

A final item on Melanie's agenda for the consultation interview was the improvement of Peter's relationship with his mother, which had been quite disrupted by the circumstances of Peter's and Trudy's lives. As Trudy had recently been awarded a housing unit by a local authority and was now able to provide Peter with a home on the occasions that he was granted leave from the detention center, this seemed a perfect time to explore possibilities for the development of the mother/son alliance.

Melanie's appreciation of Peter's initiative in "walking away" when frustrated, and her understanding that this initiative might provide a point of entry to the development of an alternative storyline of his life, resonated strongly for me. And her agenda for this meeting clearly met with Peter and Trudy's approval. So I asked Peter and Trudy if it would be okay with them for me to ask some further questions about Peter's recent initiative in exiting the scene of frustration. Trudy responded to this proposal:

> **Trudy:** Melanie told me about this, and at the time I thought this was encouraging. So we've already talked about this and I don't know if there is much more to say about it. And just the other day Peter got into more trouble, and things have gone off the rails again.
>
> **M:** Melanie mentioned this recent upset, and I can appre-

ciate that you're concerned about it. From what I understand this sort of upset had been quite common, whereas leaving the scene of frustration isn't so much part of Peter's history.

**Trudy:** Uh! Yeah. That's true. It was different. For sure it was.

**M:** Well, that's why I was interested to learn more about this, because it was different. I would like to ask you and Peter some questions about this so I might get to find out more about it.

**Trudy:** Yeah, I guess that would be interesting.

**M:** What about you, Peter. Do you agree that this is different? That leaving the scene of frustration is different?

**Peter:** Yeah.

**M:** Would you be interested in exploring this a little?

**Peter:** Don't mind.

**M:** Are there other things that you'd prefer to talk about?

**Peter:** Nope.

**M:** Okay. Peter, your mum just said that this was encouraging. These were her words. Would you say the same, or would you have something different to say about leaving the scene of frustration? Maybe different words?

**Peter:** Nope.

**M:** Nope what?

**Peter:** What my mum said is fine.

**M:** So, you'd say the same? That this was an encouraging development?

**Peter:** Yeah, I suppose.

**M:** Why would you say it's encouraging?

**Peter:** Dunno. Suppose because I wasn't in so much trouble this time.

**M:** I understand that you were feeling pretty upset, and you could have done anything. How come you didn't get into so much trouble this time?

**Peter:** Just walked away from it. That's all.

**M:** So that's a name for what you did? It was about "walking away from trouble."

**Peter:** Yeah. I figured, "Who needs it?"

**M:** This time it was different because you figured that you didn't need it. And this made it possible for you to . . .

**Peter:** Step back, I suppose.

**M:** Step back?

**Peter:** Yeah. I stepped back a bit this time.

**M:** So it was about three things. Stepping back, figuring you didn't need it, and walking away from trouble.

**Peter:** Yeah. That's it.

**M:** Say a little more about "figuring you didn't need it."

**Peter:** I just figured things out.

**M:** How were you feeling at the time?

**Peter:** Pretty heated.

**M:** You were feeling pretty heated, but you were still able to step back and to figure things out.

**Peter:** Yeah. I didn't lose it.

**M:** What didn't you lose?

**Peter:** Kept my mind. I didn't lose it.

**M:** Okay, so it was about all these things: stepping back, figuring things out, figuring you didn't need it, keeping your mind, not losing it, and walking away from trouble.

**Peter:** Yeah. That'd be it.

**M:** What did this make possible for you?

**Peter:** What do you mean?

**M:** What happened after this that wouldn't have happened if you'd lost it?

**Peter:** Well, I kept my privileges.

**M:** What privileges?

**Peter:** Weekend leave. My metalwork class. I didn't have to go to counseling.

**M:** Okay. Anything else?

**Peter:** Didn't lose out on television or gym time.

**M:** I am getting to understand what stepping back, figuring things out, figuring you didn't need it, keeping your mind, not losing it, and walking away from trouble made possible for you.

**Peter:** Yeah. And I didn't wreck anything this time. I didn't get wild and bust everything up.

**M:** Sorry?

**Peter:** Instead of getting wild and busting everything up.

**M:** Is there anything that you can tell me that would help me understand how you achieved this? Instead of wrecking things, you kept all of your privileges.

**Peter:** Maybe. Maybe it was . . . I dunno.

*[handwritten margin note:]* Repeats their in a benefit to repeating desired behavior? Is their benefit to repeating desired behavior?

**M:** You said "maybe." What were you thinking when you said "maybe"?

**Peter:** Well . . . maybe I was looking up the road a bit to where I wanted to be.

**M:** That was part of it?

**Peter:** Guess so.

**M:** I don't suppose this all came out of the blue—this stepping back, figuring things out, figuring you didn't need it, keeping your mind, not losing it, walking away from trouble, and looking up the road. Can you think of anything that might have led up to this?

**Peter:** Like what?

**M:** Like anything else that has happened in recent times that might have provided a foundation or a platform for this development, or that might have helped you get ready for this step, or that might have paved the way for you to walk away from trouble?

**Peter:** Um . . . probably there is something. But I can't think of it right now.

**M:** Perhaps I could ask your mum this question?

**Peter:** Go ahead.

**M:** Trudy, we've been talking about what this was all about for Peter. And we've also been talking about what this made possible for him. Can you think of anything that might have led up to this? Any other developments that you have noticed in Peter's life that might have prepared the way for this?

**Trudy:** All I know is that when things go off the rails, like they often do with Peter, there can be some real serious consequences. Breaking the law can get you locked up.

And breaking the law when you are already locked up just makes things worse. Peter's already been locked up enough times, I can tell you that. It just seems that he just isn't capable of running his own life. It just seems like he can't take responsibility.

**M:** I understand that you've had lots of concerns about what's happening to Peter's life, and about what happens when he goes off the rails.

**Trudy:** I sure have.

**M:** How have these concerns affected you? In what way have these concerns affected your life?

**Trudy:** Well, I sure lose sleep over what he does, I can tell you that.

**M:** You lose sleep over this? What is it, the worry, or . . . ?

**Trudy:** For sure it's the worry. It's a constant thing.

**M:** And the worry has the effect of . . . ?

**Trudy:** Stresses me out big time.

**M:** And this makes it hard for you and Peter to . . . ?

**Trudy:** For us to get along. Sure does.

**M:** Getting along is something that's important to . . . ?

**Trudy:** Getting along is what I have always wanted. It is what I keep hoping for. It's what I am holding out for. If only.

**M:** Thanks, Trudy. It's essential that I understand what's important to you, and if it is okay with you we'll come back to this.

**Trudy:** Sure.

**M:** Peter, you've been helping me to understand what this development in walking away from trouble is about, and you have also been catching me up on what this has made possible for you. Later I would like to get back to figuring out what led up to this. But for now, I'd be interested to know what this development is like for you.

**Peter:** Uh! Well, I don't . . . um . . .

**M:** I've got a list here about what this has all been about: walking out on trouble, stepping back, figuring things out, figuring you didn't need it, keeping your mind, not losing it, walking away from trouble, and looking up the road. I've got another list about some of the things that this is making possible for you, like keeping your privileges and avoiding going wild and busting things up. What's this like for you? What is it like for you to see this happening in your life?

**Peter:** It's good to see I suppose.

**M:** There is good and there is good and there is good. There are many different kinds of good. What sort of good is this? And who is it good for? Do you mean that it is good for you, or for your mother, or for the detention center?

**Peter:** It's positive.

**M:** It's positive for whom?

**Peter:** Positive for me.

**M:** It's positive for you. Could you say a bit about the way it's positive for you?

**Peter:** Yeah. It just makes me feel good.

**M:** Do you know why this development makes you feel good?

**Peter:** Like it's a good feeling to be getting somewhere.

**M:** It is about a feeling of getting somewhere. Why is getting somewhere important to you?

**Peter:** Because I'll be able to do something with my life, that's why. I'll be able to say what I want and do something about it.

**M:** You sound quite clear about this.

**Peter:** Yeah. I'll know that I'll be able to make things happen. If things aren't working out, just knowing this means that I'll be able to do something about it.

**M:** Is getting somewhere in your life, and having a say about the direction of your own life, been important to you for very long?

**Peter:** I think it has. Yeah, I think it has been. At least for a year, or maybe more, I think.

**M:** Peter, would it be okay by you for me to ask your mother for some of her ideas about this?

**Peter:** Sure, go ahead.

**M:** Trudy, this is what I understand so far. This recent development was about Peter stepping back, figuring things out, figuring he didn't need it, keeping his mind, not losing it, walking away from trouble, and looking up the road to where he wanted to be. And this made it possible for him avoid going wild and busting things up, and instead to keep privileges, like weekend leave, metalwork class, television, and gym time. When I asked Peter what this was like for him, I learned that it made him feel good because of getting somewhere in life. I also heard that having a say about the direction of his own life has been important to him for a while now. Just standing back and looking at all of this, what name would you give to this overall development?

**Trudy:** I'd have to say it is about him managing his own life. And for a quite a while there I thought we'd never see it.

**M:** Managing his own life. Does this fit for you, Peter?

**Peter:** Yeah. That's what I'm doing.

**M:** Trudy, what's your sense about what this sort of development in managing his own life could make possible for Peter?

**Trudy:** Well, it could make it possible for him to improve his life. It could make it possible for him to stay out of detention centers.

**M:** Improve his life in what way?

**Trudy:** Like I said. It could make it possible for him to stay out of detention centers.

**M:** Anything else?

**Trudy:** It could make it possible for him to improve his life in lots of ways.

**M:** Like?

**Trudy:** Well, even though things went wrong for Peter, I have always known that he's had his talents. He's always been interested in how things work, in pulling things apart, and I can tell you that he has always taken things apart and put them back together again to figure this out. Now that's something that could come in handy if he is managing his own life more. That's something that could help him to get ahead and get a good job that he wouldn't be bored in. And this is something that might give him some space to have his own life. He'd have more space to move.

**M:** What would that be like for you, Peter? If managing your own life made this possible?

**Peter:** That would be real positive.

**M:** I know that you have already answered this question,

but I would like to get more of a sense of what "real positive" means to you. <u>I am asking this again because I think
there might be more to this development in managing your
own life.</u>

**Peter:** I don't know. I'd just be happy to see that I could
make happen what needed to happen. I'd just be happy to
know that I could make happen what I wanted.

**M:** Happy to see that you could make happen what needed
to happen and what you wanted to happen.

**Trudy:** One thing is for sure. He'd be a lot more comfortable with his life.

**M:** Peter?

**Peter:** Yeah. Things would be more comfortable.

**M:** Okay. I understand more about what this development
in managing your own life would be like for you. It would
make things more comfortable, and you'd be happy to see
that you could make happen what you needed and wanted
to happen. I've got a question: Why would you be happy to
see this?

**Peter:** Um . . . I'm not sure.

**M:** Would it be okay for me to ask your mum this question?

**Peter:** Yeah, feel free.

**M:** Trudy, why do you think Peter would judge this development in managing his own future to be real positive?

**Trudy:** He'll be able to figure things out for himself more.
And besides, he's got a right to this.

**M:** He's got a right to what?

**Trudy:** He's got a right to manage his own life. He's got a
right to having his own space. Everyone's got this right, but

it gets taken a lot. I know it was taken from Peter. I know that he hasn't had this chance.

**M:** What do you think of this, Peter? Your mum said that she thought you'd say this was a real positive development because you have a right to manage your own life and a right to your own space. Does this fit for you?

**Peter:** Yeah.

**M:** Why would you say this fits for you?

**Peter:** Because I didn't have that chance when I was a kid.

**M:** What happened?

**Peter:** Oh, my stepdad just gave me a hard time.

**M:** He took this right from you?

**Peter:** Yeah. Totally.

**Trudy:** I have to tell you that I feel very badly about this because I brought this onto Peter's life. I brought this man into our lives, and I let this go on. This was complicity on my part. God it was awful, and forever I'll feel guilty about this. I know that I could have been paralyzed by guilt because of this.

At this point in the therapeutic conversation it was my understanding that we had all traveled a considerable distance in a relatively brief period of time. The point of entry to this conversation was Peter's action in exiting the scene of frustration. When I first began to consult Trudy and Peter about this action, Trudy was of the opinion that because this had already been talked about there was nothing more to discuss about it. However, both Trudy and Peter were willing to respond to my questions about this initiative.

In the context of the therapeutic inquiry that I then instigated, it turned out that there was a lot more to say about Peter's exiting the scene of frustration. This initiative was rendered highly significant. It became saturated with meaning and symbolic of what was important to Peter. It symbolized both his aspiration to affect the course of his future and what he held precious in life; that is, the right to manage his own life and the right to his own space. He'd not previously given voice to this aspiration or emphasized in this way what he accorded value to in his own life.

## Unique Outcomes

In narrative conversations the sort of action that Peter undertook in walking out on trouble is read as a "unique outcome" or "exception." I draw the term *unique outcome* from Erving Goffman (1961) who, in defining it, states that in structuring experience into "any social strand of any person's course through life . . . unique outcomes are neglected in favor of such changes over time as are basic and common to members of a social category, although occurring independently to each of them" (p. 127). Peter's walking out on trouble was of a particular category of unique outcomes that can be classified as an "initiative." Such initiatives, like other unique outcomes, are ever-present in people's lives, but they are mostly neglected and lost. I have a sense that one is likely to have a good life when only 97% of one's initiatives in living are stalled; that is, when 3% of one's initiatives of living survive, one can expect to experience a reasonable quality of life. However, when 98% of one's initiatives in living are lost—when only 2% survive—one can expect to experience a relatively poor quality of life. This leads me to the conclusion that, as therapists, when consulted by people about problems and predicaments, we have a role to play in the un-stalling of, and in supporting the endurance of, 1% of their initiatives in living.

   When developments that might be candidates for unique outcome status become visible to me in my consultations, it is my habit to explore options for these to be rendered weighty, and for this to provide the basis for a conversation in which people have the opportunity to identify and to further develop accounts of what they intend for their lives and of what they accord value to in life. There is a significant gap between the naming of unique outcomes and the process of figuring out what these unique outcomes reflect in terms of what people intend for their lives and what they give value to. The therapist's job is to help people bridge this gap. In my conversation with Trudy and Peter, the navigation of the gap between these two points was shaped by a second version of the statement of position map I discussed in Chapter 1.

## The Statement of Position Map, Version 2

This version of the statement of position map consists of the same basic categories of inquiry included in the first version of the map. However, instead of generating externalizing conversations by focusing on the problems and predicaments of people's lives, this map generates alternative storylines for people's lives by focusing on unique outcomes and exceptions to the dominant and often problem-saturated storylines. Therapeutic inquiry shaped by this version of the statement of position map invariably provides a foundation for the introduction of the sort of re-authoring conversations that are discussed in Chapter 2. For example, in response to the understandings about what people intend for their lives and give value to, the therapist can craft landscape of action questions that encourage people to reengage with their histories and give voice to accounts of the developments that reflect those understandings.

I have received consistent feedback from participants of training events that this version of the statement of position map has assisted them in stepping back from assuming primary authorship in their effort to render the positive but neglected developments of people's lives meaningful. When therapists do assume primary authorship in this way, it is common for them to enter into a "convincing mode" in which their responses are primarily limited to giving affirmations, pointing out positives, and making attempts at reframing. This version of the statement of position map can be of considerable assistance to the therapist in maintaining a decentered but influential participation in these therapeutic conversations. This is a decentered participation in that therapists endeavor to privilege the authorship of the people seeking consultation. And it is an influential participation in the sense that the therapist brings structure to this inquiry about the developments of people's lives that may potentially be unique outcomes. This structure hinges on the following four categories of inquiry.

## Inquiry Category 1. Negotiation of a Particular, Experience-Near Definition of the Unique Outcome

In this first stage, the therapist launches an inquiry into developments that have the potential to be rendered meaningful as unique outcomes. In the context of this inquiry, people are invited to provide an extended description of these developments and to richly characterize them in experience-near and particular terms. I emphasize experience-near and particular terms because no development in life will be perceived or received in identical ways by different people or in identical ways at different times in a person's life, nor is any development a direct replica of any other development in life or in history.

In the first part of my conversation with Peter and Trudy, the initiative of leaving the scene of frustration was defined as 'walking away from trouble." A number of associated developments were also named, including "stepping back" and "figuring, who needs it." I did not make haste in this part of the interview, but rather continued to ask Peter to clarify the meaning of his initiative. Thus the initiative became more richly characterized. For example, when I asked him to say more about figuring he didn't need it, he responded that it was about "figuring things out," about how he "kept his mind" and "didn't lose it," and about "looking up the road." Later this initiative was defined by Trudy as "managing his own life."

This sort of "loitering with intent" allows for an extended description of such developments and promotes a rich characterization of them. This is important in the negotiation of enduring and solid experience-near and particular definitions of unique outcomes.

The development that was rendered meaningful as a unique outcome for Peter and Trudy was of recent history. However, therapists do not need to restrict themselves to events of the past in their effort to identify such developments, as they are also invariably evident in the present. Following is an example of this.

I met with Dillon and his family for a consultation session in the presence of some "guests" who were participants of a training course that I was conducting. The family had been fully briefed on the context of this meeting and had opted to proceed. Dillon was a young man, 15 years old, who was in trouble in virtually every domain of his life. After yet another crisis, he was on the verge of permanent expulsion from his family. Although he had agreed to come to the interview, from the outset he didn't seem at all enthusiastic about participating. I checked again about whether he'd been fully briefed about the circumstances of the interview, and he confirmed that he had. But then he said in a resentful tone: "Who are these people anyway?" This was predominantly expressed as a statement, but there was an element of a question in this.

I took this as an opportunity to ask Dillon about what he wanted to know about these guests. He gruffly responded with: "their hobbies." I then proceeded to interview the guests about their hobbies, and when this was done I asked which of these Dillon found himself relating to. He'd been drawn to what he had heard about horseback riding and humor. I then began to inquire into what sort of step he'd taken in inviting these guests to introduce themselves. Dillon was engaged by this, but he had difficulty naming this initiative. When I asked for the assistance of other family members, his mother described his initiative as "building bridges," stating that she'd been very surprised by this as she had not witnessed Dillon's performing this skill in 5 years. Subsequently, Dillon embraced this definition of his initiative—it was one that was clearly experience-near and particular to his life—and this provided a point of entry for the identification and rich development of a subordinate storyline of his life.

## Inquiry Category 2. Mapping the Effects of the Unique Outcome

This second stage features an inquiry into the effects of the unique outcome that can be traced through the various domains of people's lives, including the domains of home and familial relationships, workplace, school and education, peer contexts and friendships, one's relationship with oneself, and so on. This can also be an inquiry into the "potential" effects of the unique outcome in these domains of life, and on one's future possibilities and life's horizons generally. Additionally, at this stage there is frequently an opportunity to place some focus on the developments that may have led up to the unique outcome.

In my conversation with Peter and Trudy, stages one and two of this "statement of position map" were not as clearly defined in relation to each other as they are in many other conversations. However, with regard to the effects of the unique outcome that was characterized, I learned that, among other things, this had made it possible for Peter to keep his privileges, including weekend leave, metalwork class, television, gym time, and to avoid going wild and busting everything up. Later there was also speculation about how this could make it possible for him to improve his life, to stay out of detention centers, to have space for his own life, and to have space to move.

This inquiry has the effect of bringing the unique outcome into a sequence of developments that unfold through time—of incorporating it into a storyline. This emphasizes and secures the significance of the unique outcome; it is rendered less vulnerable to any conclusions that it was the outcome of luck, an aberration, or entirely of the making of others.

## Inquiry Category 3. Evaluating the Unique Outcome and its Effects

In this stage, the therapist supports people in evaluating the unique outcome and its effects or potential effects. As with the earlier statement of position map, this evaluation can be initiated with questions like: Are these developments okay with you? How do you feel about these developments? How are these developments for you? Where do you stand on these outcomes? What's your position on what is unfolding here? Is this development positive or negative—or both, or neither, or something in between?

These questions invite people to pause and reflect on specific developments of their lives, to identify and speak of their experience of them, and to reach a judgment about them. Many people find this quite a novel experience, for these developments contradict those associated with what is more known and familiar to them about their lives. This can also be a novel experience due to the fact that such developments have often been subject to the judgment of others. The following two excerpts from my conversation with Peter and Trudy illustrate my use of these experience and evaluation questions.

*Excerpt 1*

> **M:** I've got a list here about what this has all been about . . . I've got another list about some of the things that this is making possible for you . . . What's this like for you? What is it like for you to see this happening in your life?
>
> **Peter:** It's good to see I suppose.
>
> **M:** There is good and there is good and there is good. There are many different kinds of good. What sort of good is this? And who is it good for? Do you mean that it is good for you, or for your mother, or for the detention center?
>
> **Peter:** It's positive.
>
> **M:** It's positive for whom?
>
> **Peter:** Positive for me.
>
> **M:** It's positive for you. Could you say a bit about the way it's positive for you?
>
> **Peter:** Yeah. It just makes me feel good.
>
> **M:** Do you know why this development makes you feel good?
>
> **Peter:** Like it's a good feeling to be getting somewhere.

*Excerpt 2*

> **M:** What would that be like for you, Peter? If managing your own life made this possible?
>
> **Peter:** That would be real positive.
>
> **M:** I know that you have already answered this question, but I would like to get more of a sense of what "real positive"

means to you. I am asking this again because I think there might be more to this development in managing your own life.

**Peter:** I don't know. I'd just be happy to see that I could make happen what needed to happen. I'd just be happy to know that I could make happen what I wanted.

**M:** Happy to see that you could make happen what needed to happen and what you wanted to happen.

**Trudy:** One thing is for sure. He'd be a lot more comfortable with his life.

**M:** Peter?

**Peter:** Yeah. Things would be more comfortable.

Because being consulted about this subject can be quite a novel experience, it is usually important for the therapist to preface these evaluation questions with a brief summary of some of the principal effects of the unique outcomes that have already been drawn out in the second stage of the conversation. I refer to these summaries as "editorials," and they provide people with a surface upon which to reflect when responding to the evaluation questions. For example, in my conversation with Peter and Trudy, before asking these evaluation questions, I first gave a brief summary of the meanings attributed to the unique outcome and of what I understood to be the principal consequences of this: "I've got a list here about what this has all been about: walking out on trouble, stepping back, figuring things out, figuring you didn't need it, keeping your mind, not losing it, walking away from trouble, and looking up the road. I've got another list about some of the things that this is making possible for you, like keeping your privileges and avoiding going wild and busting things up. What's this like for you? What is it like for you to see this happening in your life?"

At this time care is also taken to ensure that people have the opportunity to give voice to complexities in their position on the developments that are the subject of inquiry. This is because it is common for therapists to assume that people would evaluate these consequences to be wholly positive (when this might not be the case), to prematurely bring closure to the inquiry, and then to proceed on this assumption.

## Inquiry Category 4. Justifying the Evaluation

This fourth stage features an inquiry into the "why" of the evaluations that people have made in these conversations. As with the earlier statement of position map, this level of inquiry can be initiated with questions like: Why is this okay for you? Why do you feel this way about this development? Why are you taking this stand/position on this development? The inquiry can also be initiated by asking people to share a story that will provide an account of the "why": Would you tell me a story about your life that would help me to understand why you would take this position on this development? What stories about your history would your father/mother/sibling share that might throw some light on why you are so happy about this development? The following excerpts provide an account of this stage of the therapeutic inquiry.

*Excerpt 1*

**M:** Do you know why this development makes you feel good?

**Peter:** Like it's a good feeling to be getting somewhere.

**M:** It is about a feeling of getting somewhere. Why is getting somewhere important to you?

**Peter:** Because I'll be able to do something with my life, that's why. I'll be able to say what I want and do something about it.

**M:** You sound quite clear about this.

**Peter:** Yeah. I'll know that I'll be able to make things happen. If things aren't working out, just knowing this means that I'll be able to do something about it.

**M:** Is getting somewhere in your life, and having a say about the direction of your own life, been important to you for very long?

Peter: I think it has. Yeah, I think it has been. At least for a year, or maybe more, I think.

*Excerpt 2*

**M:** Okay. I understand more about what this development in managing your own life would be like for you. It would make things more comfortable, and you'd be happy to see that you could make happen what you needed and wanted to happen. I've got a question: Why would you be happy to see this?

**Peter:** Um . . . I'm not sure.

**M:** Would it be okay for me to ask your mum this question?

**Peter:** Yeah, feel free.

**M:** Trudy, why do you think Peter would judge this development in managing his own future to be real positive?

**Trudy:** He'll be able to figure things out for himself more. And besides, he's got a right to this.

**M:** He's got a right to what?

**Trudy:** He's got a right to manage his own life. He's got a right to having his own space. Everyone's got this right, but it gets taken a lot. I know it was taken from Peter. I know that he hasn't had this chance.

**M:** What do you think of this, Peter? Your mum said that she thought you'd say this was a real positive development because you have a right to manage your own life and a right to your own space. Does this fit for you?

**Peter:** Yeah.

**M:** Why would you say this fits for you?

**Peter:** Because I didn't have that chance when I was a kid.

**M:** What happened?

**Peter:** Oh, my stepdad just gave me a hard time.

**M:** He took this right from you?

**Peter:** Yeah. Totally.

As with the evaluation questions, these justification questions are usually prefaced by editorials. These editorials provide a "surface" upon which to reflect, and this assists people in the development of responses to these questions. As I discussed in Chapter 1, I strongly believe in the resurrection of "why" questions in therapeutic conversations. For example, it was in response to "why" questions that Peter gave expression to an aspiration to affect the course of his future. These "why" questions open space for people to give voice to and further develop intentional understandings about life and about what they accord value to in life. And it was in response to these "why" questions that Trudy gave value to the concept of one's "right" to manage one's own life, which was then further developed by Peter as the therapeutic conversation proceeded. People are defined by their purposes in life, and the defining of this aspiration and this account of what is accorded value constituted a conclusion about Peter's identity that contradicted the known and familiar negative conclusions that were associated with the dominant storyline of his life.

Intentional understandings of life and about what is accorded value in life can provide the point of entry to re-authoring conversations that contribute to rich story development. For example, in response to the expression of these understandings in this fourth stage of inquiry, people can be invited to reflect on and recount events of their lives that would confirm the relevance and the appropriateness of these understandings. In Chapter 2 I referred to this sort of question as a "landscape of action" question.

I should also note that I never expect an instantaneous response to these justification questions. In fact, people frequently respond with an "I don't know." This is to be expected in a cultural climate in which internal understandings about life and identity have displaced intentional understandings and in which it has become quite rare for people to be consulted about the why of their preferences for particular developments of their lives. Because of this, it is quite common for people to experience this consultation about the why to be quite radical and a significant challenge.

When encountering these "I don't know" responses, it is important that therapists provide more support to people in their effort to answer. This support can be given in many ways. In addition to offering editorials that preface these questions, the therapist can invite people to extend the review of the principal effects of the unique outcomes, as well as their evaluation of these effects. This contributes to the development of a more solid surface upon which to reflect when people are entertaining these "why" questions.

Yet another option for supporting people's efforts to respond to these questions is for the therapist to provide an account of how others have responded to similar questions: "About 6 weeks ago I was meeting with a couple who'd managed a similar feat in their effort to get free of the conflict that had been dominating their relationship. This couple was similarly enthusiastic about the outcome of this initiative, and when I asked why I learned that this was because _____. Does this bear a resemblance to what you would say about why you are enthusiastic about these developments, Or would you put in an entirely different way?" These accounts of the responses of others usually contribute to a foundation for people to be knowledgeable about the "why" of their own position on developments in their lives; having an account of the why in regard to developments in the lives of others makes it possible for people to distinguish their own position on similar developments in their lives.

As I noted in Chapter 1, when therapists are meeting with young children who respond with an "I don't know" to these "why" questions, the inquiry can be facilitated through the introduction of a guessing game. The child's parents and siblings can be invited to make guesses about why the developments are preferred by the child. The therapist can also contribute to this stock of guesses. The child can then be interviewed about whether any of these guesses came close to the mark, and if so, about what words the child would use to develop this "why." If the child determines that these guesses have not come close, he or she can interviewed about how he or she knows this, which usually helps the child puts words to his or her own "why."

The four categories of inquiry that are featured in this version of the statement of position map shape people's orientation to the developments of their lives that might be candidates for a unique outcome status. Of course, they also shape the therapist's orientation to such developments. In the context of this inquiry, the meanings of such developments are negotiated, and these developments are imbued with significance. As these developments become weightier, people become more curious about them, and as the inquiry unfolds, fascination is triggered. This fascination for what would otherwise be neglected or considered trivial contributes to people's engagement in and responsiveness to the inquiry.

In this discussion of this version of the statement of position map, I have presented a linear account of the progress of conversations. However, in actual practice, a strictly linear progression is rarely seen, and clarifications of people's responses at one level of inquiry can bring about revisions in, or the embroidering of, responses at another level of inquiry.

Figures 5.1 and 5.2 show my charting of the conversation with Peter and Trudy onto the statement of position map that I have described in this chapter.

## Midstream Employment of the Statement of Position Map

When people undertake initiatives during the course of the therapeutic conversation, therapists can solidify the initiative as a unique outcome by employing the second version of the statement of position map midstream in the therapeutic conversation.

I did this when Peter clearly articulated that he gave value to the right to have a life that had been taken from him by his stepfather and when Trudy spoke in strong terms about what she regarded to be her

Figure 5.1  Charting Conversations That Highlight Unique Outcomes (Peter)

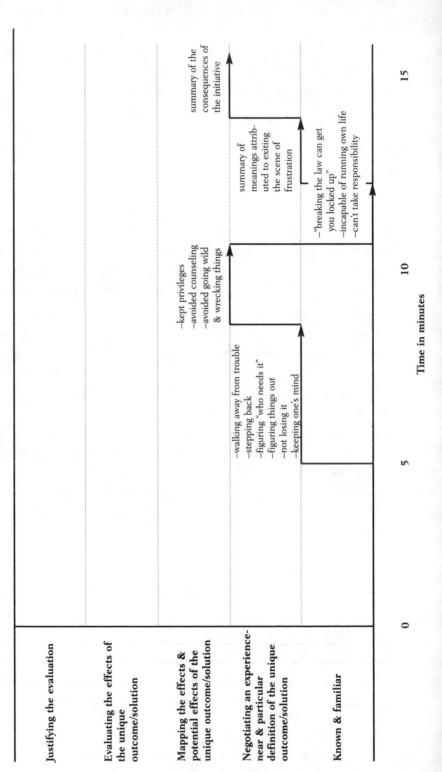

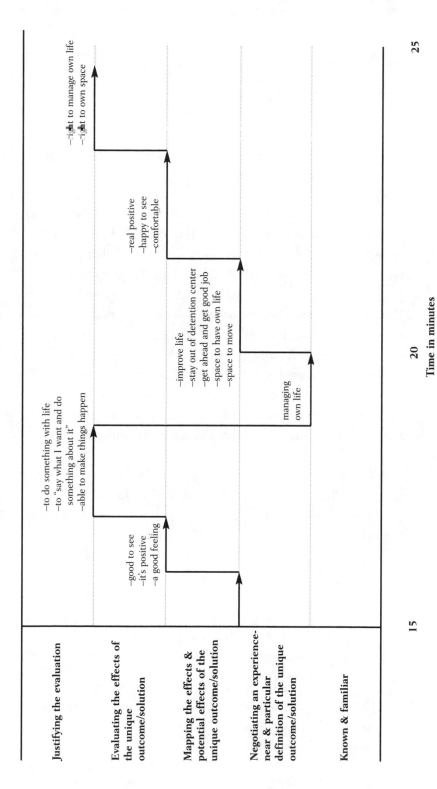

Figure 5.2 Charting Conversations That Highlight Unique Outcomes (Peter)

"complicity" in this tyranny and about the extent to which she could have been paralyzed by guilt on account of this. I detected in these comments two developments that were candidates for unique outcome status. First, Trudy was making an acknowledgment, to Peter, of the part that she believed she had played in what he had been subject to by his stepfather. Second, she had not been paralyzed by guilt in the way that she might have been.

I chose to consult Peter about these initiatives, interviewing him first about the consequences of Trudy's refusal to be paralyzed by guilt and about his evaluation of this refusal (he judged it to be a beneficial contribution to his life), and second about Trudy's initiative in acknowledging what she strongly believed to be her "complicity." My questions were shaped by the four categories of inquiry: Peter characterized her initiative ("owning up" and "being honest"), gave some account of its consequences, evaluated these consequences and, with Trudy's assistance, justified this evaluation (if contributed to the establishment of a sense of security that he highly valued). A significant outcome of this was that in the act of acknowledging some responsibility for what Peter had been subject to, Trudy experienced making a very significant contribution to her son's life.

The following transcript of this part of my conversation with Peter and Trudy illustrates my use of the second version of the statement of position map midstream in the therapeutic conversation. Figure 5.3, following the transcript, shows my charting of their conversation.

> **Trudy:** I have to tell you that I feel very badly about this because I brought this onto Peter's life. I brought this man into our lives, and I let this go on. This was complicity on my part. God it was awful, and forever I'll feel guilty about this. I know that I could have been paralyzed by guilt because of this.
>
> **M:** Peter, what's it like for you to hear your mum talking about how badly she feels about bringing this man into your life? What's it like for you to hear her talk about how

she feels partly responsible for what you went through, and that she is so sorry about this?

**Peter:** It's good I suppose.

**M:** Why is this good?

**Peter:** Because it is the truth.

**M:** What's important to you about this?

**Peter:** It's owning up.

**M:** What is it about the owning up that is important?

**Peter:** It's being honest.

**M:** "Owning up" and "being honest" are good names for the step that your mother is taking here?

**Peter:** Yeah.

**M:** Trudy, do these words "owning up" and "honesty" fit for you?

**Trudy:** Sure. It is past time for this to happen. It's past time to do this. We've both been carrying heavy weights. Mine is guilt.

**M:** How does it affect you to hear your mum's honesty?

**Peter:** Um . . .

**M:** Does this touch how you feel? Does it have some effect on your connection with your mum? For example, does it make you feel closer to her, or more distant, or neither?

**Peter:** Closer.

**M:** Could you say anything else about what this honesty is like for you?

**Peter:** It makes me feel a bit better about what's gone down.

**M:** A bit better about what's gone down. Anything else?

**Peter:** Yeah. I can relax.

**M:** This honesty brings you closer to your mum, and makes you feel a bit better about what happened, and you can relax. And this is happening right now. What's it like for you that this is happening right now?

**Peter:** It makes me a bit happier.

**M:** Anything else?

**Peter:** Can't think of anything right now.

**M:** Do you understand why it makes you a bit happier?

**Peter:** Maybe because it tells me things are different now.

**M:** That . . .

**Peter:** That it won't happen again.

**M:** Perhaps I could ask your mum about why she thinks this makes you feel a bit happier?

**Peter:** Go ahead.

**M:** Trudy?

**Trudy:** Maybe it's because it makes Peter feel more safe. Because it makes him feel, I don't know . . . How would you say it? Maybe more secure in our connection. I think we've always wanted this connection. I certainly have with him. I have always wanted this sort of connection with a child of mine, but everything's got in the way of this, including what I did in bringing this man into our home.

**M:** Peter, does what your mom is saying fit for you? That this makes you a bit happier because you feel safer, and more secure in your connection with her? And that both of you have always wanted this connection?

**Peter:** Sure, it fits.

Figure 5.3 Charting Conversations That Highlight Unique Outcomes (Peter)

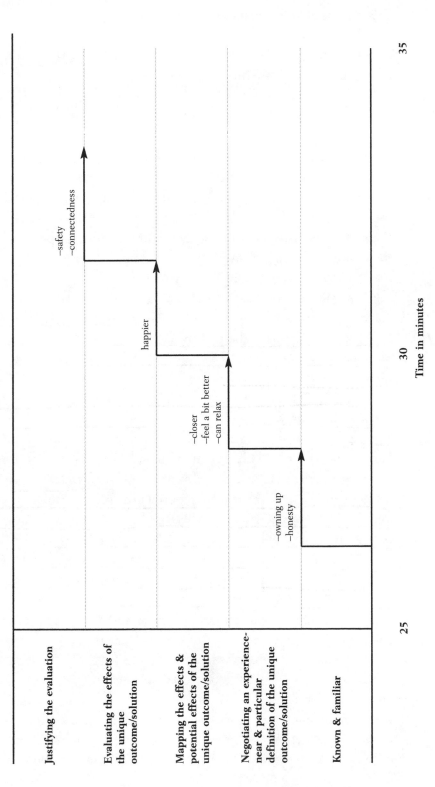

Justifying the evaluation

Evaluating the effects of
the unique
outcome/solution

Mapping the effects &
potential effects of the
unique outcome/solution

Negotiating an experience-
near & particular
definition of the unique
outcome/solution

Known & familiar

–safety
–connectedness

happier

–closer
–feel a bit better
–can relax

–owning up
–honesty

25          30          35

Time in minutes

## The Nature of Narrative Conversations: From Unique Outcomes to Rich Story Development

The distance that can be traveled in one therapeutic conversation from the starting point of a unique outcome to destinations in new territories of life and identity is often truly remarkable. Furthermore, it is entirely impossible to predict this destination at the outset. In my experience with these conversations, the only thing that can safely be predicted is that the outcome will defy any prediction. This is one of the enthralling aspects of engaging with these narrative practices. In the context of these conversations we remain "in suspense" with regard to the outcome, knowing only that at the end of the conversation we will be standing in territories of life and identity that we couldn't have imagined at the outset. The transcript I have included in this section illustrates both of these phenomena: the distance people travel during the course of these conversations and the unpredictability of the destination.

The transcript also illustrates another important point about the maps of narrative practice: that the boundaries between them are often blurred. Throughout this book I have presented these maps as distinct entities so that I could describe them more clearly. However, in practice these maps usually blur into each other. Narrative conversations are not "disciplined." They do not proceed in an orderly cookbook fashion, but are somewhat unruly. The therapist's participation in these conversations is significantly determined by people's responses, and formulating a question before hearing a person's response to a previous question rarely works. It is the opportunities present in people's responses that determine the therapist's participation. In the following excerpt readers will find elements of the re-authoring, re-membering, and definitional ceremony maps of narrative practice.

The focus of the interview again turned to Trudy's declaration that she hadn't allowed herself to be paralyzed by guilt. I was openly curious about what had made this possible for her—about what had provided a foundation for her to resist being captive to guilt. In response to this, Trudy described a crisis in her life some 18 months ago. This crisis had precipitated a number of realizations, and as an outcome of this she found herself "facing a crossroads." She could continue to allow guilt to paralyze her life, or she "could take another road" upon which she would adopt a "more realistic" perspective on some of the forces at play with regard to the predicaments of her history—forces over which she had previously had no control. At this time, she had "made the right call" and was determined that "nothing can get in my way now."

M: So this was a crossroads for you. You suddenly had another option regarding the road that you could travel, and you were determined to make the right call.

Trudy: Yes, that's it exactly.

M: So that attitude "nothing can get in my way now" was a new development?

Trudy: Yeah. I'd have to say that before this I had this attitude like I was defeated. Really defeated. Oh, it was horrible. It was like a shadow over everything.

M: And over the past 18 months you have held onto this different attitude, even through difficult times?

Trudy: Exactly. Although I still get a bit shaky sometimes. But I won't let go of it.

M: You have talked about how you'd always wanted a close connection to a child of yours. Have there been other things that you've always wanted? Are there other longings or hopes that have been important to you that have been frustrated by the circumstances of your life?

Trudy: Yeah. For sure there have been.

M: Would you say a bit about these?

Trudy: Well, to start with, like Peter, I've always wanted something better for my future. I've wanted to have a life where there is more understanding, and at least some consideration. I've wanted a more peaceful life, where there could be some respect.

**M:** Longings and hopes for a better future, for a life where there is more understanding and consideration. And a more peaceful life where there could be some respect.

**Trudy:** Yeah. And like Peter, to have a chance maybe to manage my own life. To have a bit of space to have my own life, too. This is what I always intended to do, but I just couldn't seem to make this happen. It's been very frustrating.

**M:** These intentions for your life go way back?

**Trudy:** Yeah, of course. Of course.

**M:** How far back?

**Trudy:** Well, right back to when I was just a little kid. Yeah, way back. I was always out for something different. I couldn't have said this in the way that I have today. I didn't have the words for it then. But this is what I was out for. I had my hopes. But I just didn't have the opportunity to carry this out like I wanted to. I didn't have the freedom for this. And that's been very frustrating. For a lot of the time I felt that I was banging my head against a brick wall.

**M:** Were these intentions shared by others in the family you grew up in?

**Trudy:** No. No way. There wasn't any understanding. There was no patience. No respect. Everyone just had these strong opinions, and everyone just wrote off anything that anyone else thought. Everyone was always trying to overrule everybody else. It was a tough place to be. I didn't want any part in this. I sure didn't want to continue it on.

**M:** So how did you manage to hold onto these intentions for your life when these weren't supported by anyone else in your family, and when it was such a tough place to be in?

**Trudy:** Oh, I don't know. Resilience I guess. Maybe I had some resilience.

**M:** Resilience. What sustained this resilience? Did anyone ever validate or acknowledge the importance of these intentions and hopes? Was there anyone who might have shared these hopes for your life?

**Trudy:** Actually, there was someone. I had a grandmother who I was close to, who I had a lot of time with when I was young. This was Grandma Lillian—she was my mum's mother.

**M:** How did you know that she supported these intentions and hopes for a different life?

**Trudy:** Some things you just know. She really cared for me. Grandma Lillian gave me a lot of support. She liked that I was thoughtful. She never tried to overrule what I said. It was always okay for me just to say what I felt with her. She was understanding, and she'd never just put her opinion on me.

**M:** Over what period of time did you have this contact with your grandmother?

**Trudy:** Oh, this is a sad story. When I was about 10 years old my father got this new job as a clerk in a mining town up north, and we left. I wanted to go back for holidays with my grandmother, but my father wouldn't let me. He used to say pretty bad things about her. I think he had always been a bit threatened by her. I remember him saying that she was interfering with "his family." He always talked about "his family" as if he owned the rest of us.

**M:** Oh. So you never got to . . .

**Trudy:** I remember feeling really sad about being cut off from her. She used to send cards and letters, but my father stopped this. He kept putting her down, and I found out later that he'd sent most of these back to her unopened without telling me or anybody else. She saved them, and my cousin eventually gave them to me. I realized that she'd never given up. It was really lovely to have those letters and cards, but it also hurt, because I'd missed her a lot.

**M:** You said that you experienced understanding and support from her.

**Trudy:** And lots of love as well.

**M:** Do you why you were such a focus of her understanding and love and support? Do you know what it was that she appreciated about you?

**Trudy:** I think I always knew that she loved me for who I was as a little girl. She didn't have all of these big plans for my life. She liked the way that I wasn't pushy, the way that we could hang out and not have all of this tension around all of the time.

**M:** If your Grandma Lillian could be here now, and I was to ask her about what she appreciated in you, what's your guess about what she would say?

**Trudy:** Let's see . . . I think she'd say that I was a more sensitive person. A more thoughtful person. She saw that I wasn't one of those opinionated people who just crashed their way through things. She liked that I was more gentle. We could be mellowed out together.

**M:** Do you know what it was like for her to have you for a granddaughter who responded to her in the way that you did?

**Trudy:** What it was like for her? How do you mean?

**M:** I understand that there was something special when the two of you were together. I know that this meant a lot to you. And you have put me in touch with what she appreciated about you. I can only guess that for her to be with you also touched her life in ways. What's your guess about this?

**Trudy:** Well, I suppose that she felt that I understood her too. That I had a feeling for what she had a feeling for.

**M:** Do you have any thoughts about how this might have affected her life?

**Trudy:** I know she looked forward to my visits. When I went to her house I would get to the front gate and I could see her looking out of the kitchen window, waiting for me. So I guess that I made her happy in some ways.

**M:** I'd like to ask Peter about what he's been hearing as we've been talking, if this is okay.

**Trudy:** Sure.

**M:** What's it been like for you to be listening to the story about the connection between your mother and her grandmother?

**Peter:** Fine.

**M:** There is fine and there is fine and there is fine. What sort of fine is that?

**Peter:** It's fine because I'm getting a better picture of things.

**M:** What are you getting a better picture of?

**Peter:** Of what happened to my mum and my grandmother.

**M:** What happened to them?

**Peter:** They didn't have the space that they needed, and they wanted something better.

**M:** Do you think that this fits in any way with what you

were saying about walking out on trouble and about your rights to manage your own life and to have your own space? Or is this different?

**Peter:** Yeah. I'd say its something the same. We're a bit connected.

**M:** How do you mean, we're a bit connected?

**Peter:** Well, the three of us have had our troubles, and we all kept going.

**M:** What's it like for you to have this connection?

**Peter:** I didn't know about this. I didn't know about Grandma Lillian.

**M:** You didn't know anything about your great-grand-mother.

**A:** No. Didn't even know that I had a Grandma Lillian.

**M:** Trudy, if your grandmother could be here now, listening to my conversation with Peter about walking out on trouble, and listening to my conversation with you about how you have continued to hold onto what was precious to both of you, what do you think she would be most taken with? What do you think she'd be most drawn to?

**Trudy:** Well, I know that she also had a hard time in the family she grew up in. There was no place for her to have a voice in anything. And yet she didn't give up. She kept trying to find ways to overcome all of this. You know, despite everything she found a way get through all this discouragement with what mattered to her. I'm sure she'd be taken with Peter doing the same thing.

**M:** She'd be taken with Peter doing the same thing. Peter, does what we are hearing about Grandma Lillian fit with what you were saying about having a right to your own life, a right to your own space?

**Peter:** Yeah. I suppose we are a bit the same here too. Yeah, that'd be true.

**M:** Trudy, you said that if Grandma Lillian was here she'd be drawn to Peter's walking away from trouble. What's your guess about how this would affect her sense of Peter? How do you think it would affect her picture of Peter as a person?

**Trudy:** I think she'd see Peter as someone who can steer things in a direction that's more okay for him. Someone who was starting to find his own road and who's moving more toward what's important for him even though the road's still pretty steep and there's lots of work to do. Someone who won't let this turn him back to where he was.

**M:** Why do you think she'd be so drawn to Peter's actions in walking away from trouble?

**Trudy:** Because of her own struggle to get her own life free. She didn't have much of a chance to manage her own life, and she didn't have much power, but she kept up trying. She kept up trying to make a space for her own life. And in the end it's the memories of her and what she did that count.

**M:** Just imagine Lillian being here today as an audience to our conversation about developments in Peter's life and in your life. Where do you think she'd be right now in her thoughts, or in her feelings, or in her understandings, or in her realizations?

**Trudy:** Well, to know that it was what she stood for that won through, that this overcame all of those loud-mouthed efforts to control her life. To know that this is what carried through to her great-grandson would really mean a lot to her.

**M:** So it would mean that all of her struggles against what she was put through were . . .

**Trudy:** Were worthwhile. Yes. That's it. That all of the little things she did to keep these hopes going, to do what she intended for her own life, was totally worth something. I think she would actually feel a huge sense of relief.

**M:** So despite all the . . .

**Trudy:** All the pushing and shoving, and all of the shouting down, she achieved so much more than all of those people who had all the power. You know, she'd feel really proud of Peter.

**M:** She'd feel really proud of Peter?

**Trudy:** Yes. And something else I've thought of as well is that I know that she also struggled with guilt, and this would take the load of guilt off her shoulders too. I know that it would do this.

**M:** Peter, what's it like for you hear this? Does this interest you? Or does it not interest you?

**Peter:** It's sure interesting.

**M:** What parts interest you?

**Peter:** About how hard things were for my grandmother, and about how she didn't let this put her off. And about her being proud of me.

**M:** What does it mean to you that your great-grandmother would be proud of you?

**Peter:** A lot.

**M:** Would you say a little about that?

**Peter:** Because of knowing she would be happy to be with me. And because we're a bit the same. I've had a bit of a hard time too. I haven't had the space that I needed to have, but I've kept going and I'm making some headway. I've got a way to go, but I can see that I'm getting to where I want to be.

As this transcript illustrates, the distance that can be traveled in these conversations is significant. By the end of this conversation, we were a long way from the starting point, which was Peter's act of walking away from trouble at a time of acute frustration. By the end of this interview, this act had become highly symbolic of themes of struggle and of the right to manage one's own life—themes around which Peter was linked to the lives of his mother and great-grandmother. This linking of the stories of people's lives around shared and precious themes contributes to rich story development. In this rich story development the intentional understandings and the understandings about what people give value to are developed and redeveloped, and they become generalized themes about life and identity. This provides a foundation for people to proceed with their lives, as a range of options for actions that would be coherent with these themes becomes more visible and available.

This excerpt also illustrates the unpredictable character of these conversations. At the outset of this conversation I could not have predicted an outcome in which Peter would be experiencing his life linked to the life of his mother and great-grandmother around these themes. I could never have predicted that he would experience profound validation, that witnessing developments in his life would have reinforced his great-grandmother's sense that "her struggles were worthwhile," that his actions would bring her a "huge sense of relief," and that "she would feel really proud of Peter." This recognition of Peter's contribution to such a highly valued legacy constituted a most powerful acknowledgment.

Finally, this conversation also illustrates the blurring of boundaries of the maps of narrative practice. As I noted earlier, elements of re-authoring, re-membering, and definitional ceremony practices are present in this excerpt. For example, with regard to re-membering conversations, Lillian's contribution to Trudy's life was richly described, as was what she appreciated about Trudy's identity. As the conversation evolved, conclusions were derived both about what these developments in Trudy and Peter's life would have contributed to Lillian's life, and about how this would have touched on her sense of what her existence was about. Among other things, it was determined that Trudy and Peter's contribution would have been highly validating of Lillian's struggle to get her own life free and of her determination to make a space for her own life. Aspects of this re-membering conversation were developed in the context of a therapeutic inquiry structured around definitional ceremony practices in which Lillian's presence as an outsider witness was evoked.

Peter did not again run amok, and he won an early release from the detention center. Much of the conflict that had been characteristic of Peter and Trudy's relationship dissipated. Trudy decided to join a group for women who'd been subject to trauma. Peter joined an associated group for young people and, over several months, developed a leadership role in this group. In providing this follow-up information, it is not my intention to make any grand claims about the efficacy of my one narrative conversation with Peter and Trudy. Peter was meeting with, and continued to meet with, a skilled therapist, Melanie, and there were others who also continued to provide him with support and encouragement. However, I do believe that narrative conversations of the sort that I had with Peter and Trudy can play a significant role in such outcomes, even when these conversations are restricted to a single consultation.

## Conclusion

In writing this chapter it was not my intention to include all that might be said about the unique outcome concept or about therapeutic practices that have the potential to render unique outcomes highly significant. There are many other sources of extended discussion on these subjects. My intention was rather to provide an overview of the development of narrative conversations shaped by the second version of the statement of position map. This map guides the shaping of a therapeutic inquiry that has the potential to establish developments in people's lives as candidates for a unique outcome status and as points of entry for rich story development.

It has at times been assumed that this focus on unique outcomes gives rise to the sort of heroic accounts of life that reproduce highly autonomous and independent conceptions of identity that are isolating of people and that obscure the social and relational fabric of their lives. However, this assumption does not fit with what I know about the results of these inquiries. To the contrary, it is my experience that these conversations make it possible for people to redefine their relationships with each other in ways that acknowledge each other's voices in the development of their own sense of identity. This redefinition supports a more relational sense of identity. I believe that this is clearly evident in my conversation with Peter and Trudy.

The map that I have presented in this chapter, like the others in this book, is simply a construction founded upon my explorations of practice and ideas; it is not a requirement for therapeutic conversations that contribute to the foundations of new possibility in people's lives. However, should you, the reader, decide to use this map in the context of your own practice, I hope that it will contribute to pleasure in your work as it does in mine.

# 6
# Scaffolding
# Conversations

P eople consult therapists when they are having difficulty in proceeding with their lives. In these circumstances, they have usually been doing what is known and familiar to them in their
effort to address their predicaments and concerns: They have engaged
in actions that are in keeping with familiar conclusions about their
lives and relationships and with customary knowledges about life. The
gap between what is known and familiar and what might be possible
for people to know about their lives can be considered a "zone of proximal development."

This zone can be traversed through conversational partnerships
that provide the necessary scaffolding to achieve this—that is, the sort
of scaffolding that provides the opportunity for people to proceed
across this zone in manageable steps. In the context of therapeutic
practice, the therapist contributes significantly to the scaffolding of
the proximal zone of development and also recruits others to participate in this. This scaffolding makes it possible for people to incremen-
tally and progressively distance from the known and familiar and more
toward what it might be possible for them to know and to do.

It is in traversing this gap between the known and the familiar and
what is possible that people experience a newfound sense of personal
agency: a sense of being able to regulate one's own life, to intervene in

one's life to affect its course according to one's intentions, and to do this in ways that are shaped by one's knowledge of life and skills of living.

## Petra

Petra, a young adult, sought consultation over the "mess" that her life was in. After she had provided me with an account of the various dilemmas, predicaments, and problems that she was "struggling with," I began to inquire about her experience.

> **M:** And all of this has taken you to a place in which . . .
>
> **Petra:** It's a place of misery. I have come to see you because I have been feeling pretty miserable. As you can see, my life is in such a mess, it really is. And it's been going on like this for too long.
>
> **M:** How long?
>
> **Petra:** Pretty much forever. At least it feels like that.
>
> **M:** Pretty much constant?
>
> **Petra:** Yeah. Every now and then I think that I am starting to get things together, but really it's just an illusion.
>
> **M:** So you have tried lots of things?
>
> **Petra:** Yeah. Well, I sometimes think that I am trying things, that I've got a new idea. But then it all just goes up in smoke.
>
> **M:** How do you mean?
>
> **Petra:** I sometimes have the sense that I am working out a new approach, you know, to sorting things out. But this doesn't work, and then I realize that this wasn't really much different from anything that I've done before. It's like I'm going around and around in circles.

**M:** Going around and around in circles?

**Petra:** Yeah, I wind up just complicating things. You would think I'd learn, wouldn't you? You'd think I'd wise up, wouldn't you? But I just keep falling into the same trap over an over again. It's so frustrating.

**M:** And this leaves you . . .

**Petra:** Feeling totally defeated.

**M:** Have you brought others into the picture about how things are for you?

**Petra:** A bit. But I don't think most people want to know. Anyway, it's my mess, and I'm responsible for it.

**M:** So there have been times when you've talked to others about what you are going through?

**Petra:** A little, but there's no point. It really is my problem, and I just feel embarrassed about the mess that my life is in.

**M:** You have to find a way through this independently?

**Petra:** Well, yeah. It's my problem, and if I can't do myself a simple favor, who can? It is not up to others to pull me out of this. I'm the one who's responsible. If I can't do this for myself then how irresponsible am I? It should be so simple.

**M:** Irresponsible because it should be so simple to do something about . . . ?

**Petra:** Yeah, I tell myself this all of the time. I keep thinking that maybe I'll be able to motivate myself this way.

**M:** But this isn't working?

**Petra:** Well I'm not making any headway, am I? I feel pretty hopeless about the future. I'm not going anywhere in my life, and I reckon that it's not going to be any different. In my future, I mean.

**M:** You have looked to the future, hoping to make a difference?

**Petra:** Yeah. That'd be something. But it shouldn't be so hard, should it?

## Personal Agency and Responsible Action

When people consult therapists about predicaments and concerns that are longstanding, it is not unusual for them to express significant frustration over the fact that their effort to address these predicaments and concerns have come to naught. For some, the frustration is even more intense, for they believe that these very efforts to resolve the problems have actually generated even more complications. Under these conditions, is common for people to berate themselves for lacking the sort of foresight and wisdom that would have enabled them to grasp the inappropriateness of their problem-solving initiatives and to anticipate the development of these complications.

In these circumstances, people usually rebuke themselves for what they discern to be manifest incompetence and inadequacy. Seeking the assistance of a therapist is often taken as verification of this incompetence and inadequacy, for it is a further confirmation of the fact that they are unable to do what anyone else could be reasonably expected to be able to do—that is, to be independently responsible for sorting out matters that intimately affect one's life and to be able to influence the shape of one's life according to what one gives importance to.

For Petra, conclusions of this sort were well-entrenched, and she was mired in a sense of hopelessness and fatalism. She had become certain that her future was simply going to be a reproduction of her very unsatisfactory present life. And yet, despite this, she was still giving expression to the sentiment that doing something about her life "should be so simple."

This begs the question: Is it so simple? Is having this sort of foresight and wisdom that Petra laments the absence of a simple matter? Is achieving a significant level of personal responsibility for one's own life a simple matter? Is undertaking successful autonomous and independent action in addressing the predicaments of one's life a simple matter? And is shaping one's life according to what one gives importance to simple as well?

In the professional culture, the answer that is often given in response to questions like these is a version of: "Yes, given the evolution of normal development, one can expect to have the capacity for insight into one's own circumstances, to become responsible in relation to the intimate matters of one's own life, to be able to initiate successful autonomous and independent action in addressing one's predicaments in living, and to influence the shape of one's own life according to what is important." And the answer that is usually offered in response to questions about why this does not seem obtainable to many people is a version of: "Being unable to achieve this is a sign of dysfunction, which is evident in a person's inability to reflect and to think about her or his life in abstract terms, in an inability to perceive the consequences of her or his own actions, in a dependence on others for resolving her or his problems, and in a failure to influence the shape of her or his own life. And this dysfunction often has psychopathology at its roots."

However, it really does not appear to be that simple. In fact, these ideas about dysfunction and psychopathology obscure the complexities associated with human action, many of which arise from the actual contexts of people's lives. For example, many people find that avenues for the expression of personal agency and responsible action are very limited because they are subject to "traditional power relations" that are institutionalized in local culture. These include the power relations of disadvantage, of race, of gender, of heterosexism, of culture, of ethnicity, and more.

Such power relations are often a significant factor in the frustration that people experience in their effort to influence the shape of their lives according to what is important to them and in the generation of conclusions about their incompetence and inadequacy. When this is the case, it is important that people have the opportunity to fully recognize these power relations as a context of these negative experiences and negative conclusions about identity, and to be supported in addressing these power relations. It is also important that people have the opportunity to question popular definitions of personal agency and responsible action, for, within the context of these traditional power relations, actions that are judged to be a reflection of personal agency and responsible action are those that are founded upon access to privilege.

An understanding of the operations of "modern power,"* in contrast to the operations of traditional power, is also important to any consideration of people's experiences of inadequacy, incompetence, and personal failure. In a system of modern power, social control is established through the construction of norms about life and identity and by inciting people to engage in operations on their own and each others lives to bring their actions and thoughts into harmony with these norms. For this reason, modern power is considered a system of "normalizing judgement." The very concept of "autonomous and independent action"—and for that matter, of what it means to be a "real" or "authentic" person—is founded upon these constructed norms, and failing to reproduce these norms categorizes people as "personal failures" in their own and each other's eyes.

Many of the norms of contemporary Western culture venerate a version of successful personhood that features the "encapsulated self." This concept emphasizes a form of autonomy and independence that is characterized by self-possession, self-containment, self-reliance, self-motivation, and self-actualization. Despite efforts to reproduce these norms of successful personhood, most people experience a secret knowing that they are not quite as "together" as they present themselves to others in everyday life. For many, this discrepancy provides a foundation for conclusions about personal incompetence and inadequacy. When this is the case, it is important that people have the opportunity to place experiences of personal failure

---

* For an account of the rise of modern power and an analysis of the operations of this system of power as a mechanism of social control, see Foucault (1973, 1980).

within the context of this normalizing judgement and to find support in subverting these operations of modern power.

## Personal Agency, Responsible Action, and Concept Development

I have discussed here three perspectives on personal agency and responsible action: personal agency and responsible action as an expression of the outcome of "normal development," and that is an expression of a core self that is given in human nature; personal agency and responsible action as an expression of privilege in the context of traditional power relations; and personal agency and responsible action as a construct of the norms of modern power.

It is not my plan to further discuss these perspectives on personal agency and responsible action here, or the implications of these perspectives for therapeutic practice. This I have done elsewhere. Instead I will present an alternative perspective on personal agency and responsible action. According to this version, the experience of personal agency and the capacity for responsible action are founded upon a special form of social collaboration. This is a social collaboration that assists people to traverse the space between what is known and familiar to them, and what might be possible for them to know about their lives and identities. This is a perspective that is first and foremost informed by my own private research in the context of therapeutic practice. In order to explicate this alternative perspective I will reflect briefly on my conversation with Petra, starting with the relatively straightforward observation that she seemed mired in what was known and familiar to her about life and that, in her effort to address the predicaments of her life, she was apparently reproducing this known and familiar. Petra thus not only felt that she was going nowhere in life, but also that these efforts were further complicating things. She clearly experienced very little in the way of personal agency and responsible action.

This observation provides the basis for some interlinked conclusions about what might be necessary for Petra to successfully address the predicaments of her life and to derive a sense that her life is proceeding. It order to achieve this, it would be necessary for Petra to:

- Separate from aspects of what is known and familiar to her about her life and her identity
- Initiate movement toward what might be possible for her to know about her life and her identity, and toward what might be possible for her to do
- Successfully traverse the space between the known and familiar and what might be possible for her to know and do
- Find the sort of support that might be sustaining of her in any initiatives that she might undertake to navigate her way across this space
- Obtain assistance in the scaffolding of this space so that it might be traversed in manageable steps
- Review her journey across this space in order to adjust its trajectory
- Identify what she is learning about in terms of what is important to her and what she accords value to in life as she is traversing this space
- Begin to speculate about what steps she might take to influence the shape of her life in ways that would be in harmony with what she is learning about what is important to her and with what she accords value to in life

If Petra were to find the sort of social collaboration that would provide support and that would contribute to the scaffolding across the space between what is known and familiar to her and what it might be possible for her to know about her life, she would probably find herself in a position to initiate steps that would be effective in addressing her predicaments and in shaping her own life. This outcome would provide the sense of personal agency and responsible action that Petra has found so elusive.

These terms—*distancing, space, scaffolding, social collaboration, personal agency,* and *responsible action*—invoke the work of Russian psychologist Lev Vygotsky (1986). Vygotsky was a developmental theorist who had special interest in early childhood learning. Although my explorations of narrative practices were not originally informed by Vygotsky's thought, in recent years I have been drawn to many of his ideas. This is principally because I find that these explorations of practice confirm Vygotsky's conclusions about learning and development. I also find that his ideas contribute to new understandings of processes of therapeutic change, lend clarity to what is significant in the conversations of narrative therapy, and reinforce various narrative practices. I am also finding that his ideas are contributing to the further development of some of my narrative practices. I will briefly review some of Vygotsky's ideas in the next section of this chapter.

### The Zone of Proximal Development

Vygotsky was primarily interested in explorations of early childhood development. In these explorations he determined that in a great majority of cases, development is founded upon learning. This was a challenge to much of the prevailing developmental theory of his time, which asserted that development preceded learning and that, on this basis, learning was the outcome of the unfolding of some genetic or neurological imperative.

Vygotsky also emphasized that learning was an achievement not of independent effort, but of social collaboration. In this social collaboration, he observed that adult caretakers and more sophisticated peers structure children's learning in ways that make it possible for them to move from what is known and familiar to them and from routine achievements to what it is possible for them to know and achieve. He described this as a movement across a zone of learning that he termed the "zone of proximal development." This zone is the distance between what the child can know and achieve independently and what is possible for the child to know and achieve in collaboration with others.

Traversing this zone is a significant task in that it requires that the child distance from the immediacy of his or her experience. According to Vygotsky, this is not a task that children can achieve unless it is broken down into manageable portions. It is the caretakers and more sophisticated peers who contribute to the "scaffolding" of this zone of proximal development. This scaffolding encourages the child to "stretch" her or his mind and to "exercise" her or his imagination in the achievement of these learning tasks, but not in ways that require impossible or improbable leaps that would contribute to exhaustion and a sense of failure.

Vygotsky proposed that this progressive and incremental distancing from the known and familiar and from the immediacy of one's experience is what makes it possible for children to develop "chains of association" that establish bonds and relations between what would otherwise simply remain undifferentiated objects and events of their worlds. He referred to this as the development of "complex thinking," and he demonstrated how the development of this complex thinking provides the basis for the development of "concepts" about life and identity. The development of concepts about life is the outcome of the meaning development of words in which they are split off from sepcific concrete experiences and abstracted. For example, in young Amy's life, "friend" means Mary who lives next door, and there is little that Mary might do that will disturb this definition. Over time, with the meaning development of the word "friend," friendship is abstracted as a concept, and Amy may discern actions on Mary's behalf that are a transgression of friendship, and will be able to respond accordingly.

It is this conceptual development that supplies the foundation for people to regulate their lives: to influence their own actions in purposeful ways, to intervene in their own lives to shape the course of events, and to problem-solve. According to this understanding, actions that are considered to be responsible and autonomous have their foundation in social collaboration. The development of this self-regulation is a reflection of what Vygotsky referred to as "self-mastery." He employed this term in a way that is synonymous with what I have referred to as "personal agency."

What follows is a summary of Vygotsky's principal ideas about the zone of proximal development and about learning. In seeking to reveal the genesis of learning, Vygotsky's research brought him to the following conclusions:

- Learning is the outcome of social collaboration, not of independent effort or of the unfolding of any "hard-wired" biogenetic process. In this social collaboration, skilled caretakers and sophisticated peers provide supported learning tasks that are within the reach of the child but that require the investment of significant effort on behalf of the child.

- It is through these learning tasks that children have the opportunity to distance from the immediacy of their experience of the world. This is a movement toward what they might know and do in collaboration with others.

- This is a movement across a zone of learning referred to as the "zone of proximal development." This zone is formed by the distance between what the child can know and achieve independently and what is possible for the child to know and achieve in collaboration with others. To quote Vygotsky (1986, p. 86), the zone of proximal development is "the distance between the actual developmental level as determined by independent problem-solving and the level of potential development as determined through problem-solving under adult guidance or in collaboration with more capable peers."

- In the movement across this zone, there is a shift from gathering the objects and events of the world into "heaps"—from the uniting of diverse objects and events in groups under a common family name—to gathering the objects and events of the world into chains of association or into complexes that establish bonds and relationships between these objects and events.

- There are several levels in the development of these chains of association and complexes, from the preliminary unification of objects and events on the basis of maximum similarity to the grouping of objects and events on the basis of a single attribute (for example, only round objects or flat objects).

- This development of complex thinking provides a foun-

dation for the development of "concepts." To quote
Vygotsky (1986, p. 135), the development of a concept
"presupposes more than unification. To form such a concept it is also necessary to abstract, to single out elements, and to view the abstracted elements apart from
the totality of the concrete experience in which they are
embedded."

- This conceptual development provides a foundation for
  the child to intervene in shaping her or his own actions
  and in the constitution of her or his own life. According
  to Vygotsky, on account of this development, the child is
  now able to operate with these concepts at will and as a
  task demands—and with a consciousness of these operations, understanding them to be processes of a certain
  kind. In his terms, it is this development that leads to
  "self-mastery" in intellectual functions: For example, he
  asserts that this concept development is the foundation
  of "deliberate attention, logical memory, abstraction, the
  ability to compare and to differentiate." In terms that I
  have employed in this chapter, this development of conceptual thought can be considered the foundation of
  "personal agency." It is through the development of conceptual thought that children begin to inhabit their own
  lives.
- Language and word-meaning evolution is crucial to this
  conceptual development, the pathway to concept formation is the development of word meanings. To quote
  Vygotsky (1986, p. 107) again: "When a new word has been
  learned by the child, its development is barely starting; as
  the child's intellect develops, it is replaced by generaliza-
  tions of a higher and higher type—a process that leads in
  the end to the formation of true concepts . . . Real concepts
  are impossible without words, and thinking in concepts
  does not exist beyond verbal thinking. That is why the central movement in concept formation, and its generative
  cause, is a specific use of words as functional tools."

# The Zone of Proximal Development and Therapeutic Practice

Although the focus of Vygotsky's research was on early childhood development, I have found his conclusions about learning and development to be relevant to all stages and ages. And I have also found these conclusions to be relevant to the further understanding and development of effective therapeutic practices.

As I discussed at the beginning of this chapter, the "zone of proximal development" cannot be traversed without the sort of conversational partnership that provides a scaffolding that supports people in proceeding in manageable steps. In the context of therapeutic practice, the therapist (and others recruited by the therapist) contributes significantly to the scaffolding of the proximal zone of development. The incremental and progressive distancing from the known and familiar is not synonymous with a splitting off from one's life. Rather, it is distancing that provides a foundation for people to play a more significant part in influencing the course of their own development and, in so doing, to more fully inhabit their own lives.

Influenced by the ideas of Vygotsky, I have developed a "scaffolding conversations" map that is structured by five categories of inquiry.* This map can be utilized as a guide to the development of therapeutic conversations that facilitate incremental and progressive movements across the proximal zone of learning. The categories of inquiry of this map establish specific learning tasks, which I define as:

- *Low-level distancing tasks,* which support the achievement of a low-level distance from the known and familiar and from the immediacy of one's experience of the events of one's environment. These questions encourage the attribu-

---

* The "scaffolding conversations" map described here was developed at the interface between practice and ideas. Although the categories of distancing tasks represented in this map are shaped by Vygotsky's thought, they were relatively arbitrarily formed. I have developed other versions of this map, some of which are more multilayered; for example, some include "very low-level distancing tasks" that encourage people to discern specific events of their environment that contradict what is known and familiar to them.

tion of meaning to the events of one's world that are either
unfamiliar or have gone unnamed. These questions
encourage the characterization of these events.

- *Medium-level distancing tasks*, which support the achievement of a medium-level distance from the known and
  familiar and from the immediacy of one's experience of the
  events of one's environment. These tasks encourage people to bring into relationship specific events of their world
  in the development of chains of association that establish
  bonds and relationships between these events. These
  tasks also foster the comparison and categorization of the
  events of one's world and the drawing of distinctions with
  regard to difference and similarity.

- *Medium-high-level distancing tasks*, which support the
  achievement of a medium-high-level distance from the
  known and familiar and from the immediacy of one's experience of the events of one's environment. These tasks
  encourage people to reflect on, evaluate, and draw realizations and learnings from these chains of association.

- *High-level distancing tasks*, which support the achievement
  of a high-level distance from the immediacy of one's experience of the events of one's environment. These tasks
  encourage people to formulate concepts about life and
  identity by abstracting these realizations and learnings
  from their concrete and specific circumstances.

- *Very high-level distancing tasks*, which support the achievement of a very high-level distance from the immediacy of
  one's experience of the events of one's environment. These
  tasks encourage the development of proposals for proceeding in life in ways that are in harmony with the newly
  developed concepts about life and identity, the formula-
  tion of predictions about the outcome of these proposed
  actions, and the planning for and initiation of such
  actions.

These categories of inquiry play a significant role in scaffolding the zone between what is known and familiar and what is possible to know and do. For example, what was known and familiar about Peter (see Chapter 5) was that he was a young man who was generally incapable of reflecting on his life, who was unable to foresee the consequences of his actions, and who was relatively incapable of taking responsibility. It was understood that he was a concrete thinker who lacked the capacity to think in abstract terms. Over the course of the first part of our conversation, which was shaped by version two of the statement of position map, Peter and Trudy were provided with an opportunity to distance from this known and familiar and to develop an account of what might be known about Peter's life and identity and of what he might do.

The "negotiating an experience-near and particular definition of the unique outcome" category of inquiry establishes a "low-level distancing task" by encouraging people to characterize events of their world that are unfamiliar or have gone unnamed. The "mapping the effects of the unique outcome" category of inquiry establishes a "medium-level distancing task" by encouraging people to bring into relationship specific events of their world in the development of chains of association that establish bonds and relationships between these events. The "evaluating the effects of the unique outcome" category of inquiry establishes a "medium-high-level distancing task" by encouraging people to reflect on, evaluate, and draw realizations and learnings from these chains of association. And the "justifying the evaluation" category of inquiry establishes a "high-level distancing task" by encouraging people to form concepts about life and identity by abstracting these realizations and learnings from their concrete and specific circumstances.

Figures 6.1 and 6.2 show my charting of the conversation with Peter and Trudy (see Chapter 5) onto the scaffolding conversations map that I have described in this chapter. It was in the context of the scaffolding of this zone between the known and familiar about Peter's life and identity and what might be possible for him to know and do that Peter was able to conceive of a relationship between specific actions and their consequences or potential consequences, to give voice to some very significant reflections on his life, and to form con-

Figure 6.1 Scaffolding Conversations (Peter)

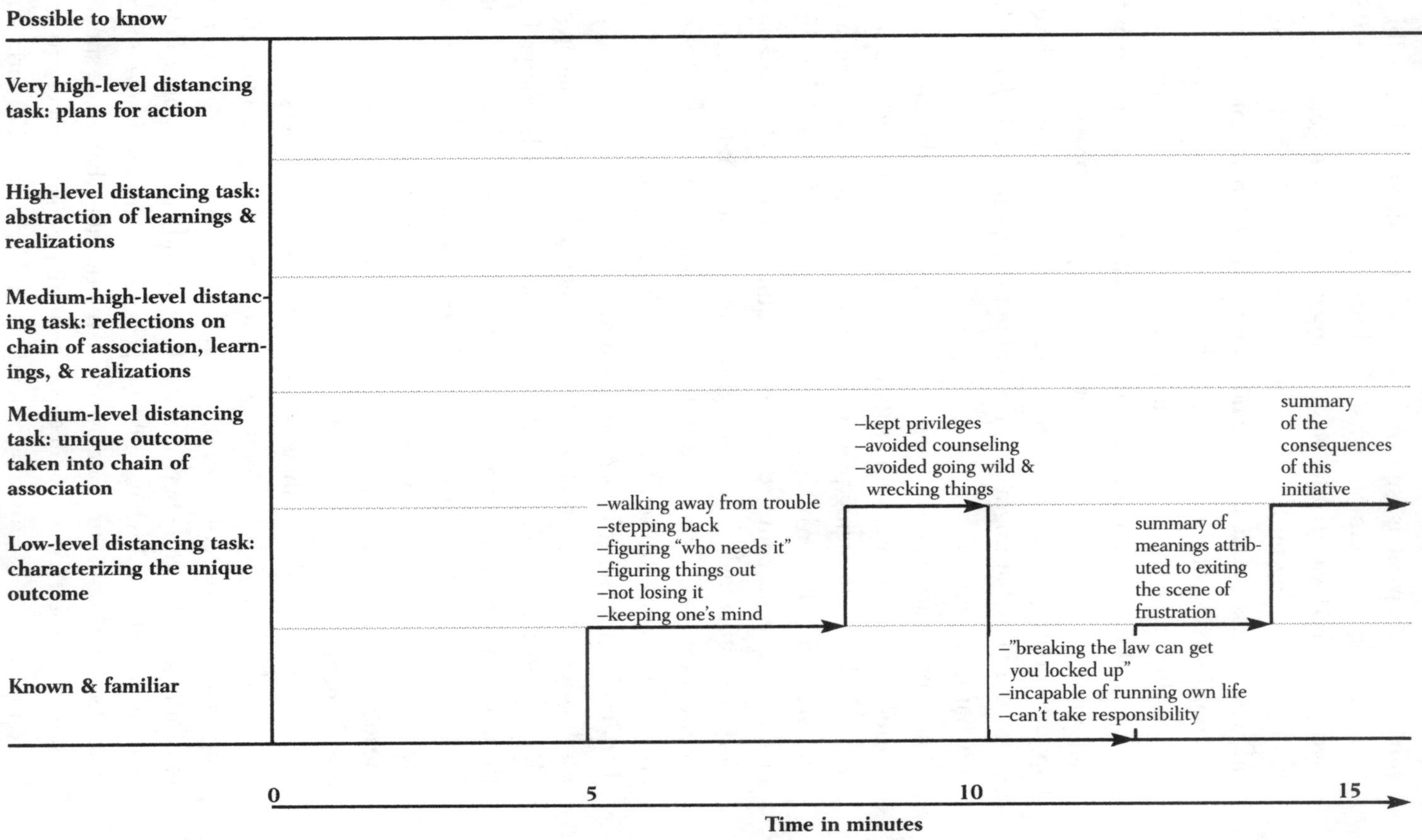

Figure 6.2  Scaffolding Conversations (Peter)

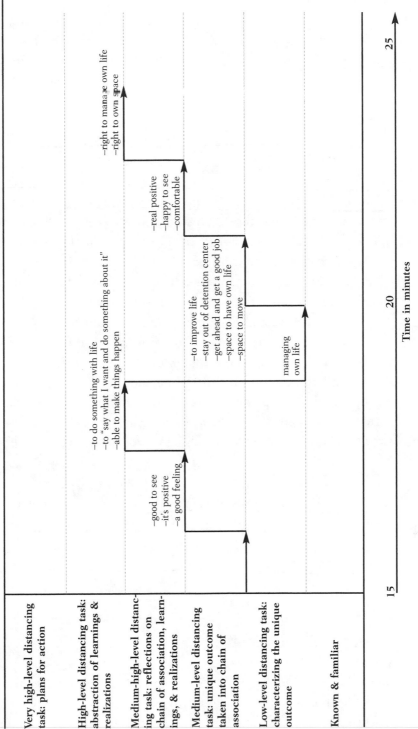

**Possible to know**

**Very high-level distancing task: plans for action**

**High-level distancing task: abstraction of learnings & realizations**

**Medium-high-level distancing task: reflections on chain of association, learnings, & realizations**

**Medium-level distancing task: unique outcome taken into chain of association**

**Low-level distancing task: characterizing the unique outcome**

**Known & familiar**

–right to manage own life
–right to own space

–real positive
–happy to see
–comfortable

–to do something with life
–to "say what I want and do something about it"
–able to make things happen

–to improve life
–stay out of detention center
–get ahead and get a good job
–space to have own life
–space to move

–good to see
–it's positive
–a good feeling

managing
own life

15                    20                    25

**Time in minutes**

cepts about life and identity by abstracting certain realizations and learnings from their concrete, specific circumstances. This powerfully contradicted what was known and familiar about his life and identity: that he was unable to foresee the consequences of his actions, that he was generally incapable of reflecting on his life, and that he was a concrete thinker.

These developments were not independent achievements; they were the outcome of social collaboration between Peter, Trudy, Melanie, and me. This supportive participation created a climate that was conducive to addressing a range of learning tasks. The achievement of a capacity to foresee the consequences of one's actions, to reflect on specific developments of one's life, and to develop concepts about life and identity by abstracting learnings and realizations about one's life are dependent upon such social collaboration. And these achievements are also dependent upon language.

Language is essential in this movement toward concept development. For example, the word freedom was known to Peter, but it had not been developed as a conceptual form. In my meeting with Peter and Trudy, the "word meaning" of freedom was developed and redeveloped, and in this process it was abstracted from concrete and specific circumstances to become a guiding concept of life. It is this concept formation that establishes what Vygotsky referred to as "self-mastery in intellectual functions." It is also the foundation of personal agency and responsible action.

By this account, personal agency is not the simple outcome of human nature and its liberation or the product of some developmental imperative. Rather, it is social collaboration in the development of word meaning that is essential to the attainment of personal agency and responsible action.

## Therapist Responsibilities

I have proposed that Vygotsky's ideas about learning and development have the potential to contribute to understandings of therapeutic change generally, to lend clarity to what is significant in the conversations of narrative therapy, and to assist in the further development of narrative practices. And I have put forward his assertion about the social and relational origins of conceptual development, and about this conceptual development as a foundation of "self-mastery" and "self-regulation." These considerations encourage us, as therapists, to acknowledge and honour the special responsibility that we have to provide the conditions for the development of personal agency for the people who consult us.

Recognizing that it is our task as therapists to scaffold the proximal zone of development is an important aspect of honoring this responsibility. From this perspective, if a person's response to therapeutic inquiry is a not knowing response—"I don't know the answer to that"; "I don't know how to respond to that"—our attention will be drawn to the responsibility we have to further scaffold the conversation. In observing these responsibilities we might drop down a level in the vertical dimension of our inquiry to give people the opportunity to further develop a reflecting surface that will enable them to respond to the next level of inquiry. Or we might provide opportunities for exploration of the horizontal dimension, perhaps by inviting others to speculate about appropriate responses to the questions of this inquiry or by providing accounts of how others in similar predicaments have responded to such questions and inviting reflection on this.

We also have a responsibility to avoid falling prey to conclusions that a person is "simply lacking motivation," is "hopelessly irresponsible," is "resistant," is "incapable of foreseeing the consequences of her or his actions," is "unable to reflect on her or his behavior," is "a concrete thinker," or is "incapable of abstract thought." In fact these conclusions can serve as a wake-up call. They reflect the extent to which this person is mired in the known and familiar and is not experiencing the sort of social collaboration that would support the scaffolding of her or his zone of proximal development. Thus, we alert ourselves to the fact that we have not been fully present with our scaffolding skills or that we have reached the limits of these skills in our consultations with particular people in relation to specific issues. If we recognise that we have reached the limits of our skills, we will take pause to explore ways of extending these limits.

## Externalizing Conversations From the Perspective of the Scaffolding Conversations Map

In the last section of this chapter, I will present an example of an externalising conversation, and give an account of the evolution of this from the perspective of the scaffolding conversations map. I find that this second perspective extends my understanding of the processes associated with externalizing conversations and serves as a guide in the further development of these conversations.

I had agreed to meet with Jack, 13, his mother, Abby, and his father, Neil, at the request of a social service worker. This social service worker was from one of two agencies that had maintained extended involvement with Jack and his family. Jack was in trouble in virtually every domain of his life: with school authorities, with his peers, with the police, with his siblings, and with his parents. One crisis after another had been precipitated by Jack's actions, and now his parents were of the belief that the only viable avenue would be to either find a suitable foster home for him or have him institutionalized.

Many of these crises were triggered by Jack's violence, which was usually directed toward his mother and siblings, although recently he'd also been threatening his father. Jack was widely considered to be a boy who lacked insight into his behavior, who was incapable of taking responsibility for actions, who had limited verbal skills, and who was unmotivated to do anything about his predicament.

From the outset of our meeting, Jack did not appear at all interested in engaging in conversation. During this time Abby and Neil filled me in on their concerns, on the most recent crisis, and on the questions they were now having about Jack's tenure in the family home. Abby reflected on how she felt like a failure as a mother and expressed concern that Jack's younger siblings would not have any good memories of this time in their lives. She also talked about how much she'd been hurt by Jack, both physically and emotionally. Neil expressed strong frustration and spoke of the futility that he experienced in his effort to temper Jack's negative actions. He believed that it was Jack's intention to reject any initiatives in the development of a positive father/son relationship.

Jack was unmoved by Abby and Neil's account of these developments, although he did verify some of the details of this account. In
response to this I decided that I would try to engage Jack in a conversation about how these acts of violence were affecting his own life. To
this end, I began to consult him about how these acts might be characterized. After some exploration of this, he chose to define this violence as "aggro."*

In terms of the statement of position map, this definition of violence was the outcome of "negotiating an experience-near and particular definition of the problem." In the terms of the scaffolding conversations map, this was a "low-level distancing task."

Over the next 20 minutes or so, with my assistance, Jack determined that "agro" was among other things, destroying his education,
excluding him from his family, sapping his strength, dominating his
life in a variety of ways, and giving him a lost feeling in his heart.
According to the statement of position map, the links between "agro"
and these consequences were established by engaging Jack in "mapping the effects of the problem" through various domains of his life.
In terms of the scaffolding conversations map, these links were established in response to the introduction of "medium-level distancing
tasks." It was my understanding that bringing these acts of violence
into relationship with these other events of his life in the development
of a chain of association was, in itself, a significant achievement for
Jack.

I then encouraged Jack to reflect on and evaluate these consequences. In terms of the scaffolding conversations map, this established a series of "medium-high-level distancing tasks." Following this,
Jack was invited to "justify these evaluations." In the terms of the scaffolding conversations map, this established a series of "high-level distancing tasks." It was my hope that this scaffolding would support
Jack in formulating intentional understandings about his life and
about what he accorded value to. Further, it was my hope that these

---

* "Aggro" is an abbreviation of the word *aggression*, and it is widely used in Australian popular culture.

understandings might be further developed as concepts about life and identity. The following brief excerpt of the transcript of my meeting with Jack and his parents illustrates the extent to which I was active in the scaffolding of this conversation and the degree to which I encouraged Abby and Neil to participate. This excerpt gives an account of the scaffolding of medium-high-level distancing and high-level distancing tasks. Figure 6.3 on page 288 shows my mapping of the conversation onto the scaffolding conversations map.

**M:** From what I've heard here, it is my understanding that the agro divides you from your family?

**Jack:** Yeah.

**M:** "Divides" is a word that your mum used. Does this word work for you, or are there other words that would work better?

**Jack:** Like what?

**M:** Like maybe "separates" you from the family. Or "splits you off." Or "destroys your connection." Or . . .

**Jack:** Splits me off.

**M:** Why would you say "splits me off"?

**Jack:** Because things just get ripped up between me and the rest.

**M:** The agro rips things up between you and the rest, and this splits you off?

**Jack:** Yeah.

**M:** What's this like for you?

**Jack:** What?

**M:** Do you mind being split off from the family? Is this okay by you? Are you comfortable about things being ripped up between you and your parents, and between you and your brother and sisters?

**Jack:** It's not so good.

**M:** It's not so good. Are you comfortable about things being not so good?

**Jack:** I do mind.

**M:** How come? Why would you want to be part of the family?

*Jack shrugs.*

**M:** Well, it's my guess that you've got your reasons. I just don't know what they are.

**Jack:** One of my mates is out of his family.

**M:** Is this a problem for him?

**Jack:** Dunno, but I wouldn't want his life.

**M:** Why is that?

**Jack:** Because he's getting into lots of stuff that's going to bring him down in a big way. I don't want that.

**M:** Okay. I understand that you don't want a life like your mate's life. But I still don't understand why you'd want to be part of this family. Is there anything that you would be losing in being split off from your family? Is there something you'd be leaving behind that is important to you? Would something be gone from your life that you want?

*Jack shrugs.*

**M:** Would it be okay by you if I asked your mum and dad for their thoughts about this?

**Jack:** That's okay.

**M:** What's your guess about this? About why Jack minds being split off from the family?

**Abby:** Because there wouldn't be anywhere that he really fitted in. There isn't anywhere else in his life where he'd just be able to feel all right about just being himself.

**M:** Has this been important to you personally?

**Abby:** Sure it has. Feeling needed and wanted is just about the most important thing that I can think of. This is another reason that I get so sad to see what is happening to Jack's life.

**M:** Neil, what's your guess?

**Neil:** Well, I agree with Abby. If Jack wasn't part of the family he just wouldn't belong anywhere. And that'd be pretty miserable I reckon.

**M:** So, your idea is that not belonging could contribute to feeling pretty miserable. What gives you this idea?

**Neil:** There have been some pretty tough times in my life where I didn't feel that I had any place to belong, and it was just about the worst feeling I ever had. Feeling that you belong somewhere has to be something that anybody'd want, in some way or another at least. Belonging somewhere has got be up there with number one.

**M:** Jack, what do you think about your parents' guesses?

**Jack:** What dad said about belonging. That's right.

**M:** Do you know why this word "belonging" fits for you?

**Jack:** Just fits I guess. Like being hooked up to something.

**M:** Belonging fits because . . . ?

**Jack:** I want a decent life.

**M:** You'd say belonging is important to you because it is important to be hooked up and this can give you a decent life.

**Jack:** Yeah.

**M:** What's a decent life?

**Jack:** Where there's some good quality.

Jack's affirmation of "belonging" as a description of what he gave value to signified a step in the meaning development of a word that he had some familiarity with. This word was then revisited and reflected upon over the course of our conversation, and its further meaning development was illustrated late in this interview when I again invited Jack to review the consequences of the "aggro." At that time, his response was that the aggro was "wrecking his belonging." Here "belonging" was clearly abstracted—it had been split off from the concrete and specific circumstances of his life—and it was on the road to achieving conceptual status.

By the end of this interview Jack had given voice to several accounts of what he intended for his life and of what he held precious. Over eight subsequent meetings, some of which were attended by his entire family and a few of which included the participation of outsider witnesses, the meaning development of these words that defined what Jack intended for his life and what he gave value to were further developed as concepts about life and identity. These concepts were in the form of principles of living. This provided Jack with a platform for reinterpreting some of the events of his recent history and for speculating about actions that might be available to him—actions that would be congruent with these concepts and would make it possible for him to address concerns about his violence and the predicaments of his life. Over the course of these meetings Jack became more articulate about matters that concerned his life and his relationships with others, developed a capacity to predict the consequences of his actions, became quite enthusiastic about intervening in the shaping of his life, and developed a capacity

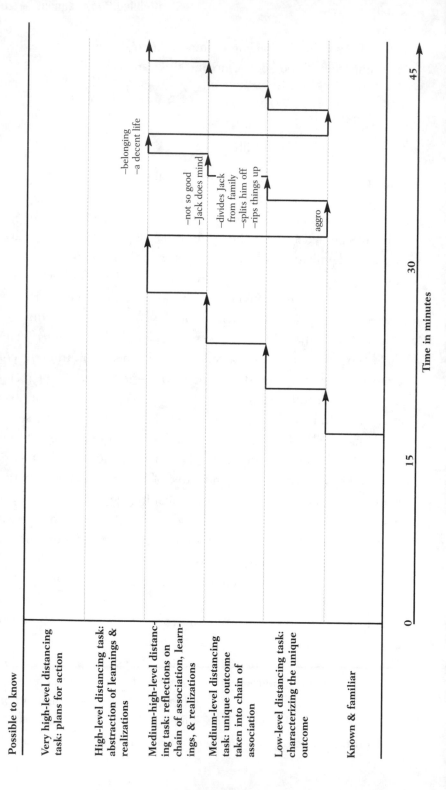

Figure 6.3  Scaffolding Conversations (Jack)

to act on this. Among other things, his violence ceased, and he became keen on making reparations. At the 18-month follow-up I learned that apart from a couple of minor setbacks, these positive developments had been enduring.

The scaffolding of these therapeutic conversations provided a series of "learning tasks" that supported Jack and his parents in crossing the zone between what was known and familiar about Jack's life and identity (that he was a boy who, among other things, lacked insight into his behavior, was incapable of taking responsibility for his actions, had limited verbal skills, and was unmotivated to do anything about his predicament) and what was possible for them to know about his life and identity and possible for him to do.

## Conclusion

Inquiry into the nature of human agency and responsible action has been the focus of this chapter. In this context I provided a brief account of some of Vygotsky's ideas about learning and development. Although the subject of Vygotsky's research was early childhood, I believe that his notion of the "proximal zone of learning," and the importance given to the careful scaffolding of this zone, are relevant to therapeutic conversations, regardless of the age and stage of development of the people who are consulting us.

I discussed some of the implications of these ideas for therapeutic practice, drew out a "scaffolding conversations map," and transposed this map onto both versions of the statement of position map. It is also possible to transpose this scaffolding conversations map onto the other maps of narrative practice that are the subject of this book, but I have not illustrated this here.

At the outset of this chapter I raised a question about the character of personal agency and responsible action and proceeded to explore a version of these ideas that was informed by Vygotsky's ideas about learning and development. According to this version, the experience of personal agency and the capacity for responsible action are founded upon a special form of social collaboration that contributes to the scaffolding of the proximal zone of learning. This understanding of the development of personal agency and responsible action consistently sustains my optimism about the possibilities that can be supported in therapeutic conversations with people who consult me about a range of problems and predicaments for which there appears to be no solution.

# Conclusion

The writing of this book has been a journey in itself. I set out with the aim of bringing together many of my therapeutic explorations of the past two decades or so into a single volume. I hoped to do this in a way that would successfully represent the particularities of these explorations and that would bring them vividly alive in print. I wanted to achieve this in a manner that would give an account of the spirit in which these explorations have been undertaken and in a way that readers would find directly relevant to their own day-to-day therapeutic practice. I also wanted to introduce readers to some of the children, women, and men I've met with in therapeutic consultations and to provide some illustration of the rich conversations we've shared.

The writing of a book is a significant endeavor—one that can be quite daunting at the outset. I began this journey with a blank page, a roughly drawn itinerary in mind, and many hopes and aspirations. I soon found that my head was overcrowded with ideas that wouldn't pour out neatly onto the page, and that took me far past where I could be with the written word. I explored many routes in the expression of what I wanted to say, some of which I subsequently abandoned and others of which I saw through to preferred destinations. There were periods when I found myself in culdesacs, wracking my mind for a way forward. At other times I found myself on thoroughfares, speeding toward my goal with a sense of excitement and exhilaration. There were occasions, along the way, when I teetered on the brink of concluding that my objectives in writing this book were too broad and when I seriously contemplated abandoning elements of the itinerary I'd set and foreshortening the journey. However, I stayed the course, and now, suddenly, and with some surprise, I find that I have arrived at the last pages of this book.

The sense that I have of arriving at the conclusion of this book is akin to the sense that I've had on many occasions when I am on my bicycle and approaching the finish line after a long race through hilly terrain. At this time every contour of the territory I've ridden through is indelibly imprinted on my mind. I am experiencing relief at getting through the more challenging aspects of the course, including the steep ascents and testing weather conditions, and still savoring the exhilaration of the fast descents and of race-lining along the flatter sections in the company of friends. Then, the moment of crossing the finish line is always one of special joy, regardless of my finishing position.

Before I cross the finish line in the writing of this book, there are some further acknowledgments to be made. The first of these is to acknowledge the people who decided to contribute to this book project through the inclusion of their stories and their words. Without this contribution, this text would not constitute a book, but would simply exist as a chronicle of diffuse ideas about therapeutic practice. I can't thank you enough for this contribution. The second is to acknowledge all of the people who have sought my assistance over the years. I view all the therapeutic practices described in these pages as having evolved from our co-research. In the course of therapeutic consultations, I regularly solicit feedback from people about which avenues of conversation are working for them and which are not, and, at the finalé, I initiate a review of what was helpful and what wasn't helpful to our effort to address the predicaments and concerns of their lives. This feedback and these reviews have been instrumental in shaping my practice and fundamental to the development of the ideas and maps presented in this book. In concluding this book I give heartfelt thanks to all of you for these contributions, which I remain ever-conscious of in my work and my life.

# Suggested Reading

## Other Books by Michael White on Narrative Therapy

White, M. (1995). *Re-authoring lives: Interviews and essays*. Adelaide, Australia: Dulwich Centre Publications.

White, M. (1997). *Narratives of therapists' lives*. Adelaide, Australia: Dulwich Centre Publications.

White, M. (2000). *Reflections on narrative practice*. Adelaide, Australia: Dulwich Centre Publications.

White, M. (2004). *Narrative practice and exotic lives: Resurrecting diversity in everyday life*. Adelaide, Australia: Dulwich Centre Publications.

White, M. & Epston, D. (1990). *Narrative means to therapeutic ends*. New York: W. W. Norton.

White, M. & Epston, D. (1992). *Experience, contradiction, narrative, and imagination: Selected papers of David Epston and Michael White, 1989–1991*. Adelaide, Australia: Dulwich Centre Publications.

White, M. & Morgan, A. (2006). *Narrative therapy with children and their families*. Adelaide, Australia: Dulwich Centre Publications.

For further information, articles, and publications about narrative therapy, please consult Dulwich Centre's two Web sites: *www.dulwichcentre.com.au*, *www.narrativetherapylibrary.com*

## Books by Other Authors on Narrative Therapy

Note: There are many books that are readily available on the subject of narrative therapy, and the list below represents just a sample of these.

Denborough, D. (Ed.) (2006). *Trauma: Narrative responses to traumatic experience*. Adelaide, Australia: Dulwich Centre Publications.

Freedman, J. & Combs, G. (1996). *Narrative therapy: The social construction of preferred identities*. New York: W. W. Norton.

Freedman, J. & Combs, G. (2002). *Narrative therapy with couples . . . and a whole lot more!* Adelaide, Australia: Dulwich Centre Publications.

Freedman, J., Epston, D., & Lobovits, D. (1997). *Playful approaches to serious problems: Narrative therapy with children and their families*. New York: W. W. Norton.

Monk, G., Winslade, J., Crocket, K., & Epston, D. (Eds.) (1997). *Narrative therapy in practice: The archaeology of hope*. San Francisco: Jossey Bass.

Morgan, A. (2000). *What is narrative therapy? An easy-to-read introduction*. Adelaide, Australia: Dulwich Centre Publications.

Payne, M. (2000). *Narrative therapy: An introduction for counselors*. London: Sage.

Russell, S. & Carey, M. (2004). *Narrative therapy: Responding to your questions*. Adelaide, Australia: Dulwich Centre Publications.

Smith, C. & Nylund, D. (Eds.) (1997). *Narrative therapies with children and adolescents*. New York: Guilford.

Zimmerman, J. & Dickerson, V. (1996). *If problems talked: Narrative therapy in action*. New York: Guilford.

# References

Andersen, T. (1987). The reflecting team: Dialogue and meta-dialogue in clinical work. *Family Process, 26,* 415–428.

Bachelard, G. (1969). *The poetics of space.* Boston: Beacon.

Bruner, J. (1986). *Actual minds, possible worlds.* Cambridge, MA: Harvard University Press.

Bruner, J. (1990). *Acts of Meaning.* Cambridge, MA: Harvard University Press.

Derrida, J. (1973). *Speech and phenomena, and other essays on Husserl's theory of signs.* Evanston, IL: Northwestern University Press.

Derrida, J. (1976). *Of grammatology.* Baltimore: Johns Hopkins University Press.

Derrida, J. (1978). *Writing and difference.* London: Routledge and Kegan Paul.

Foucault, M. (1965). *Madness and civilization: A history of insanity in the age of reason.* New York: Random House.

Foucault, M. (1973). *The birth of the clinic: An archaeology of medical perception.* London: Tavistock.

Foucault, M. (1980). *Power/knowledge: Selected interviews and other writings.* New York: Pantheon.

Goffman, E. (1961). *Asylums: Essays in the social situation of mental patients and other inmates.* New York: Harper.

Griemas, A. & Courtes, J. (1976, Spring). The cognitive dimension of narrative discourse. *New Literary History, 7,* 433–447.

Iser, W. (1978). *The act of reading.* Baltimore: Johns Hopkins University Press.

Kermode, F. (1980, Fall). Secrets and narrative sequence. *Critical Inquiry*, 7(1), 83–101.

Myerhoff, B. (1982). Life history among the elderly: Performance, visibility, and remembering. In J. Ruby (Ed.), *A crack in the mirror: Reflexive perspective in anthropology* (pp. 99–117). Philadelphia: University of Pennsylvania Press.

Myerhoff, B. (1986). Life not death in Venice: Its second life. In V. Turner & E. Bruner (Eds.), *The anthropology of experience* (pp. 261–286). Chicago: University of Illinois Press.

Todorov, T. (1977). *The poetics of prose*. Ithaca, NY: Cornell University Press.

Vygotsky, L. (1986). *Thought and language*. Cambridge, MA: MIT Press.

White, M. (1984). Pseudo-encopresis: From avalanche to victory, from vicious to virtuous cycles. *Family Systems Medicine*, 2(2), 150–160.

White, M. (1988, Spring). Saying hullo again: The incorporation of the lost relationship in the resolution of grief. *Dulwich Centre Newsletter*, 7–11.

White, M. (1995). Reflecting teamwork as definitional ceremony. In M. White (Ed.), *Re-authoring lives: Interviews and essays* (pp. 172–198). Adelaide, Australia: Dulwich Centre Publications.

White, M. (2000). Re-engaging with history: The absent but implicit. In M. White (Ed.), *Reflections on narrative practice: Essays and interviews* (pp. 35–58). Adelaide, Australia: Dulwich Centre Publications.

White, M. (2003). Narrative practice and community assignments. *The International Journal of Narrative Therapy and Community Work*, (2), 17–55.

White, M. (2004). Narrative practice, couple therapy and conflict dissolution. In M. White (Ed.), *Narrative practice and exotic lives: Resurrecting diversity in everyday life* (pp. 1–41). Adelaide, Australia: Dulwich Centre Publications.

White, M. (2006). Narrative practice with families and children: Externalising conversations revisited. In M. White & A. Morgan (Eds.), *Narrative therapy with children and their families* (pp. 1–56). Adelaide Australia: Dulwich Centre Publications.

# Index

An "m" after a page number indicates a narrative map. An "n" indicates a footnote.